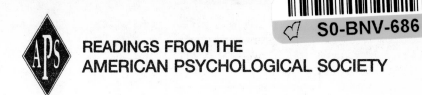

READINGS FROM THE
AMERICAN PSYCHOLOGICAL SOCIETY

S0-BNV-686

Current Directions in
INTRODUCTORY PSYCHOLOGY

EDITED BY

Saul Kassin
Williams College

Kathleen H. Briggs
University of Minnesota

WITH A FOREWORD BY
Carol Tavris

PEARSON
Prentice
Hall

Upper Saddle River, New Jersey 07458

Current Directions © American Psychological Society
1010 Vermont Avenue, NW
Suite 1100
Washington, D.C. 20005-4907

ISBN 0-13-152367-8

Printed in the United States of America

Contents

Readings from
Current Directions in Psychological Science

Foreword by Carol Tavris   *vii*

Introduction   *viii*

Psychology as Science   1

David Klahr and Herbert A. Simon
What Have Psychologists (And Others) Discovered About the
Process of Scientific Discovery? *(Vol. X, No. 3, 2001,
pp. 75–79)*   3

Neuroscience, Brain, and Mind   11

Bryan Kolb, Robbin Gibb, and Terry E. Robinson
Brain Plasticity and Behavior *(Vol. XII, No. 1, 2003,
pp. 1–5)*   13

Matthew Roser and Michael S. Gazzaniga
Automatic Brains—Interpretive Minds *(Vol. XIII, No. 2, 2004,
pp. 56–59)*   19

Marlene Behrmann
The Mind's Eye Mapped Onto the Brain's Matter *(Vol. IX, No. 2,
2000, pp. 50–54)*   26

Gail Martino and Lawrence E. Marks
Synesthesia: Strong and Weak *(Vol. X, No. 2, 2001,
pp. 61–65)*   34

Cognitive Psychology   41

Arien Mack
Inattentional Blindness: Looking Without Seeing *(Vol. XII, No. 5,
2003, pp. 180–184)*   42

Peter A. Frensch and Dennis Rünger
Implicit Learning *(Vol. XII, No. 1, 2003, pp. 13–18)*   50

Emre Özgen
Language, Learning, and Color Perception *(Vol. XIII, No. 3, 2004, pp. 95–98)* 58

Henry L. Roediger, III, and Kathleen B. McDermott
Tricks of Memory *(Vol. IX, No. 4, 2000, pp. 123–124)* 65

Gary L. Wells, Elizabeth A. Olson, and Steve D. Charman
The Confidence of Eyewitnesses in Their Identifications From Lineups *(Vol. XI, No. 5, 2002, pp. 151–154)* 73

Human Motivation and Emotion 79

Arne Öhman and Susan Mineka
The Malicious Serpent: Snakes as a Prototypical Stimulus for an Evolved Module of Fear *(Vol. XII, No. 1, 2003, pp. 5–9)* 80

Martin V. Covington
Intrinsic Versus Extrinsic Motivation in Schools: A Reconciliation *(Vol. IX, No. 1, 2000, pp. 22–25)* 87

Letitia Anne Peplau
Human Sexuality: How Do Men and Women Differ? *(Vol. XII, No. 2, 2003, pp. 37–40)* 93

Christina Maslach
Job Burnout: New Directions in Research and Intervention *(Vol. XII, No. 5, 2003, pp. 189–192)* 100

Piotr Winkielman and Kent C. Berridge
Unconscious Emotion *(Vol. XIII, No. 3, 2004, pp. 120–123)* 106

Nature, Nurture, and Human Development 115

Janet A. DiPietro
The Role of Prenatal Maternal Stress in Child Development *(Vol. XIII, No. 2, 2004, pp. 71–74)* 106

Renée Baillargeon
Infants' Physical World *(Vol. XIII, No. 3, 2004, pp. 89–94)* 123

Eleanor E. Maccoby
Gender and Group Process: A Developmental Perspective *(Vol. XI, No. 2, 2002, pp. 54–58)* 132

Wyndol Furman
The Emerging Field of Adolescent Romantic Relationships *(Vol. XI, No. 5, 2002, pp. 177–180)* 138

Arthur F. Kramer and Sherry L. Willis
Enhancing the Cognitive Vitality of Older Adults
(Vol. XI, No. 5, 2002, pp. 173–177)   144

Social and Cultural Psychology   *151*

Hilary Anger Elfenbein and Nalini Ambady
Universals and Cultural Differences in Recognizing Emotions
(Vol. XII, No. 5, 2003, pp. 159–164)   152

Michael Ross and Anne E. Wilson
Autobiographical Memory and Conceptions of Self: Getting Better
All the Time *(Vol. XII, No. 2, 2003, pp. 66–69)*   160

John M. Darley
Citizens' Sense of Justice and the Legal System *(Vol. X, No. 1,
2001, pp. 10–13)*   167

Robert B. Cialdini
Crafting Normative Messages to Protect the Environment
(Vol. XII, No. 4, 2003, pp. 105–109)   173

John F. Dovidio and Samuel L. Gaertner
Reducing Prejudice: Combating Intergroup Biases
(Vol. VIII, No. 4, 1999, pp. 101–105)   181

Personality, Disorder, and Health   *1*

Robert R. McCrae and Paul T. Costa, Jr.
The Stability of Personality: Observations and Evaluations
(Vol. III, No. 6, 1994, pp. 173–175)   190

Richard J. McNally
Recovering Memories of Trauma: A View From the Laboratory
(Vol. XII, No. 1, 2003, pp. 32–35)   196

Susan Nolen-Hoeksema
Gender Differences in Depression *(Vol. X, No. 5, 2001,
pp. 173–176)*   203

Robert Ader
Psychoneuroimmunology *(Vol. X, No. 3, 2001, pp. 94–98)*   210

Bert N. Uchino, Darcy Uno, and Julianne Holt-Lunstad
Social Support, Physiological Processes, and Health *(Vol.VIII,
No. 5, 1999, pp. 145–148)*   217

Foreword

When the American Psychological Society decided to publish *Current Directions in Psychological Science*, I cheered their intentions but gloomily resigned myself to the likely results. The original mission of the new journal was "to inform psychologists and other interested parties about the frontiers and major issues in scientific and applied psychology." Nice, but vague. But the first editors, translating this mission statement into reality, snuck in some requirements that were heretical in a new academic journal: Articles were to be readable! Short! No list of citations as long as the Philadelphia phone book! For years I had heard psychological scientists speak wistfully of their longing to convey their work to what they so charmingly call "the real world" (which, presumably, includes students). At last, *Current Directions* has gotten them to do it. The editors, flinging tradition to the winds, have somehow managed to cudgel their contributors into writing succinct, useful essays—little "states of the art" on topics of enormous interest and relevance not only to scientists but also the public (which, presumably, includes students).

Every professional writer knows how hard it is to write briefly. Over the years I've watched colleagues cheerfully sign on to write 50-page talks and 100-page chapters as if they were agreeing to go to the movies. But ask them to write a brief essay or an op-ed piece, and they say, "Oh, I'm so sorry, but I don't have the time." The art of the brief essay is especially elusive for academics, who seem to feel embarrassed, as if they had been caught naked in the cafeteria, when they are forced to write a short, unadorned sentence—"He shouted obscenities," say, instead of "He engaged in aggressive verbal behavior." Naturally, therefore, I am curious about how *Current Directions* manages to get all these psychologists to make their case succinctly. Fear? Flattery? Vast sums of money? Vodka?

Never mind; somehow, they have succeeded. These articles will give students a sense of having a direct connection with the psychological scientists whose work they would otherwise only read about. Each essay provides a concise overview of the problem at hand, and an insider's glimpse into the issues and controversies involved in investigating it. These articles also stimulate critical and scientific thinking—they illustrate why psychological science matters.

Many instructors like the *idea* of a reader more than they like the actual collection that lands on their desks. They like knowing it's there in case of emergencies, rather like a fire extinguisher, even if they never break it open. I hope you will not be like them, and instead read and enjoy this assortment of intellectual candies, and dispense them to your students, too.

Carol Tavris

Introduction

As a student preparing for the future, you will find certain tools necessary for success. Being educated in the basics of reading, writing, and math, is certainly essential. Knowing something about history and science, having a sense of geography, knowing how to use a computer, and perhaps even speaking a second language, are useful too. Regardless of what you do, however, you'll need to understand yourself and others you will encounter. For that reason, psychology—the scientific study of mind and behavior—is an invaluable part of a college education.

Culled from the riches of the journal *Current Directions in Psychological Science*, this reader presents recent articles that summarize hot issues and important findings written by some of psychology's leading researchers. This reader is divided into seven sections. The first consists of a single article that addresses psychology as a science and the process of discovery. The second section focuses on the biological aspects of human nature, with articles on the neuroscience of the brain and nervous system and their influences on our thoughts, feelings, and behavior. The third section focuses on cognitive processes that occur "inside the head"—such as attention, perception, learning, thinking, language, and memory. The fourth section considers some of the ways in which we warm-blooded humans are driven by motivations and emotions, making us responsive to reward and punishment, fear, sexual stimulation, and burnout on the job. Section Five considers topics in human development across the lifespan, from the effects of maternal stress on the growing fetus to the ways in which older people can stay intellectually vital. Section Six focuses on social and cultural influences on our perceptions of and behavior toward others, as when we form stereotypes and prejudices. The last section shifts the focus onto personality, psychological disorders such as depression, and the effects of stress and other psychological states on the immune system and on our health.

This reader is intended to supplement an introductory psychology class. If you are like most students taking psychology for the first time, you are not a major, well, at least not yet. You may or may not take another psychology course. And you may or may not embark on a career that is directly related. Either way, this collection of articles will help broaden your horizons, give you a firsthand glimpse of the way psychologists engage a scientific process of discovery, and help you to understand the people, events, problems, and opportunities of your life.

Psychology as Science

Psychologists approach the subject matter of mind and behavior from a scientific standpoint. The scientific method is a process of creating knowledge through systematic, carefully controlled observations. Is it similarly possible to study the scientists and the process itself?

In the opening article of this Reader, David Klahr and Herbert Simon (2001) provide a model and four different methods for studying this process of discovery. Three of the methods will be familiar to students from introductory psychology class: historical or case studies, laboratory experiments, and naturalistic observation. The fourth method is more specialized, computational modeling.

What Have Psychologists (And Others) Discovered About the Process of Scientific Discovery?

David Klahr[1] and Herbert A. Simon

Department of Psychology, Carnegie Mellon University, Pittsburgh, Pennsylvania

Abstract

We describe four major approaches to the study of science—historical accounts of scientific discoveries, psychological experiments with nonscientists working on tasks related to scientific discoveries, direct observation of ongoing scientific laboratories, and computational modeling of scientific discovery processes—by viewing them through the lens of the theory of problem solving. We compare and contrast the different approaches, indicate their complementarities, and provide examples from each approach that converge on a set of principles of scientific discovery.

Keywords

scientific discovery; problem solving

Early in the 20th century, Einstein, in reflecting on his own mental processes leading to the theory of relativity, said, "I am not sure whether there can be a way of really understanding the miracle of thinking" (Wertheimer, 1945, p. 227). However, in the past 25 years, several disciplines, including psychology, history, and artificial intelligence,[2] have produced a substantial body of knowledge about the process of scientific discovery that allows us to say a great deal about it.[3] Although the strengths of one approach are often the weaknesses of another, the work has collectively yielded consistent insights into the scientific discovery process.

ASSESSING THE FOUR MAJOR APPROACHES

Historical accounts of the great scientific discoveries—typically based on diaries, scientific publications, autobiographies, lab notebooks, correspondence, interviews, grant proposals, and memos of famous scientists—have high face validity. That is, it is clear that they are based on what they purport to study: real science. However, such studies have some weaknesses. For one thing, their sources are often subjective and unverifiable. Moreover, the temporal resolution of historical analysis is often coarse, but it can become much finer when laboratory notebooks and correspondence are available. Historical investigations often generate novel results about the discovery process, by focusing on a particular scientist and state of scientific knowledge, as well as by highlighting social and motivational factors not addressed by other approaches.

Although historical studies of discovery focus much more on successes than on failures, laboratory studies are designed to manipulate the discovery context in order to examine differences in processes associated with success and failure. Face validity of lab studies varies widely: from studies only distantly related to real scientific tasks to those that model essential aspects of specific scientific discoveries (e.g., Dunbar's, 1993, simulated molecular genetics laboratory; Schunn & Anderson's, 1999, comparison of experts' and novices' ability to design and interpret memory experiments; Qin & Simon's, 1990, study in which college sophomores rediscovered Kepler's third law of planetary motion). Laboratory studies tend to generate fine-grained data over relatively brief periods and typically ignore or minimize social and motivational factors.

The most direct way to study science is to study scientists in their day-to-day work, but this is extraordinarily difficult and time-consuming. A recent example is Dunbar's (1994) analysis of discovery processes in several world-class molecular genetics research labs. Such studies have high face validity and potential for detecting new phenomena. Moreover, they may achieve much finer-grained temporal resolution of ongoing processes than historical research, and they provide rigor, precision, and objectivity that is lacking in retrospective accounts.

A theory of discovery processes can sometimes be incorporated in a computational model that simulates and reenacts discoveries. Modeling draws upon the same kinds of information as do historical accounts, but goes beyond history to hypothesize cognitive mechanisms that can make the same discoveries, following the same path. Modeling generates theories and tests them against data obtained by the other methods. It tests the sufficiency of the proposed mechanisms to produce a given discovery and allows comparison between case studies, interpreting data in a common language to reveal both similarity and differences of processes. Modeling enables us to express a theory rigorously and to simulate phenomena at whatever temporal resolution and for whatever durations are relevant.

SCIENTIFIC DISCOVERY AS PROBLEM SOLVING

Crick argued that discoveries are major when they produce important knowledge, whether or not they employ unusual thought processes: "The path [to the double helix]. . . was fairly commonplace. What was important was *not the way it was discovered*, but the object discovered—the structure of DNA itself" (Crick, 1988, p. 67; italics added). Psychologists have been making the case for the "nothing special" view of scientific thinking for many years. This does not mean that anyone can walk into a scientist's lab and make discoveries. Practitioners must acquire an extensive portfolio of methods and techniques, and must apply their skills aided by an immense base of shared knowledge about the domain and the profession. These components of expertise constitute the *strong methods*. The equally important *weak methods* scientists use underlie all human problem-solving processes.

A problem consists of an initial state, a goal state, and a set of operators for transforming the initial state into the goal state by a series of intermediate steps. Operators have constraints that must be satisfied before they can be applied. The set of states, operators, and constraints is called a *problem space*, and the problem-solving process can be characterized as a search for a path that links initial state to goal state.

Initial state, goal state, operators, and constraints can each be more or less well-defined. For example, one could have a well-defined initial state and an ill-defined goal state and set of operators (e.g., make "something pretty" with these materials and tools), or an ill-defined initial state and a well-defined final state (e.g., find a vaccine against HIV). But well-definedness depends on the familiarity of the problem-space elements, and this, in turn, depends on an interaction between the problem and the problem solver.

Although scientific problems are much less well-defined than the puzzles commonly studied in the psychology laboratory, they can be characterized in these terms. In both cases, well-definedness and familiarity depend not only on the problem, but also on the knowledge that is available to the scientist. For that reason, much of the training of scientists is aimed at increasing the degree of well-definedness of problems in their domain. The size of a problem space grows exponentially with the number of alternatives at each new step in the problem (e.g., the number of possible paths one must consider at each possible move when planning ahead in chess). Effective problem solving must constrain search to only a few such paths. Strong methods, when available, find solutions with little or no search. For example, in chess, there are many standard openings that allow experts to make their initial moves with little search. Similarly, someone who knows algebra can use simple linear equations to choose between two sets of fixed and variable costs when deciding which car to rent instead of painstakingly considering the implications of driving each car a different distance. But the problem solver must first recognize the fit between the given problem (renting a car) and the strong method (high school algebra).

Weak methods, requiring little knowledge of a problem's structure, do not constrain search as much. One particularly important weak method is analogy, which attempts to map a new problem onto one previously encountered, so that the new problem can be solved by a known procedure. However, the mapping may be quite complex, and it may fail to produce a solution.

Analogy enables the problem solver to shift the search from the given problem space to one in which the search may be more efficient, sometimes making available strong methods that greatly abridge search. Prior knowledge can then be used to plan the next steps of problem solving, replace whole segments of step-by-step search, or even suggest an immediate solution. The recognition mechanism uses this store of knowledge to interpret new situations as instances of previously encountered situations. This is a key weapon in the arsenal of experts and a principal factor in distinguishing expert from novice performance.

In the past 25 years, analogy has assumed prominence in theories of problem solving and scientific discovery. Nersessian (1984) documented its role in several major 19th-century scientific discoveries. Recent studies of contemporary scientists working in their labs have revealed the central role played by analogy in scientific discovery (Dunbar, 1994; Thagard, 1998).

Although many strong methods are applied in scientific practice, weak methods are of special interest for scientific discovery because they are applicable in a wide variety of contexts, and strong methods become less available as the scientist approaches the boundaries of knowledge.

COMPLEMENTARITY OF APPROACHES

Viewing scientific discovery as problem solving provides a common language for describing it and facilitates studying the same discovery using more than one approach.

In the late 1950s, Monod and Jacob discovered how control genes regulate the synthesis of lactose (a sugar found in milk) in bacteria (Jacob & Monod, 1961). The literature explaining this discovery (e.g., Judson, 1996) tends to use terms such as "a gleam of perception," but to characterize a discovery as a gleam of perception is to not describe it at all. One must identify specific and well-understood cognitive processes and then determine their role in the discovery. Among the most important steps for Jacob and Monod in discovering the mechanisms of genetic control were representational changes that enabled them to replace their entrenched idea—that genetic control must involve some kind of activation—with the idea that it employed inhibition instead.

Dunbar (1993) created a laboratory task that captured important elements of Monod and Jacob's problem, while simplifying to eliminate many others. His participants—asked to design and run (simulated) experiments to discover the lactose control mechanism—faced a real scientific task with high face validity. Although the task was simplified, the problem, the "givens," the permissible research methods, and the structure of the solution were all preserved. Dunbar's study cast light on the problem spaces that Monod and Jacob searched, and on some of the conditions of search that were necessary or sufficient for success (e.g., knowing that there was such a thing as a control gene, but not exactly how it worked).

In this example, a historically important scientific discovery provided face validity for the laboratory study, and the laboratory provided information about the discovery processes with fine-grained temporal resolution.

CONVERGENT EVIDENCE OF DISCOVERY PRINCIPLES

In this section, we give a few additional examples of convergent evidence obtained by using two or more approaches to study the same discovery.

Surprise

Recently, reigning theories of the scientific method have generally taken hypotheses as unexplained causes that motivate experiments designed to test them. In this view, the hypotheses derive from scientists' "intuitions," which are beyond explanation. Historians of science have taken a less rigid position with respect to hypotheses, and include their origins within the scope of historical inquiry.

For example, the discovery of radium by the Curies started with their attempt to obtain pure radioactive uranium from pitchblende. As they proceeded, they were surprised to find in pitchblende levels of radioactivity higher than in pure uranium. As a surprise calls for an explanation, they conjectured that the pitchblende contained a second substance (which they named radium) more radioactive than uranium. They succeeded in extracting the radium and determined its key properties. In this case, a phenomenon led to a hypothesis, rather than a hypothesis leading to an experimental phenomenon. This occurs frequently in science. A surprise violates prior expectations. In the face of surprise, scientists frequently divert their path to ascertain the scope and import of the surprising phenomenon and its mechanism.

Response to surprise was investigated in a laboratory study (Klahr, Fay, & Dunbar, 1993) in which participants had to discover the function of an unknown key on a simulated rocket ship. They were given an initial hypothesis about how the key worked. Some participants were given a plausible hypothesis, and others were given an implausible hypothesis. In all cases, the suggested hypothesis was wrong, and the rocket ship produced some unexpected, and sometimes surprising, behavior. Adults reacted to an implausible hypothesis by proposing a competing hypothesis and then generating experiments that could distinguish between them. In contrast, children (third graders) tended to dismiss an implausible hypothesis and ignore evidence that supported it. Instead, they attempted to demonstrate that their favored hypothesis was correct. It seems that an important step in acquiring scientific habits of thinking is coming to accept, rather than deny, surprising results, and to explore further the phenomenon that gave rise to them.

Krebs's biochemical research leading to the discovery of the chain of reactions (the reaction path) by which urea (the end product of protein metabolism) is synthesized in the body has been the topic of convergent studies focusing on response to unexpected results. The discovery has been studied historically by Holmes (1991) and through the formulation of two computational models (Grasshoff & May, 1995; Kulkarni & Simon, 1988), both of which have modeled the discovery. After the models proposed an experiment and were given its outcome, they then proposed another experiment, using the previous outcomes to guide their decision about what sort of experiment would be useful. Using no more knowledge of biochemistry than Krebs possessed at the outset, both programs discovered the reaction path by following the same general lines of experimentation as Krebs followed. One of these models (Kulkarni & Simon, 1988) addressed the surprise issue directly (in this case, surprise in finding a special catalytic role for the amino acid ornithine). The simulated scientist formed expectations (as did Krebs) about experimental outcomes. When the expectations were violated, steps were taken to explain the surprise. Thus, historical studies, simulation models, and laboratory experiments all provide evidence that the scientist's reaction to phenomena—either observational or experimental—that are surprising can lead to generating and testing new theories.

Multiple Search Spaces

This reciprocal relation between hypotheses and phenomena arises in laboratory studies, historical studies, and computational models of discovery, enabling us to characterize scientists' thinking processes as problem-solving search in multiple spaces.

Dual Search

The discovery process can be characterized as a search in two spaces: a hypothesis space and an experiment space. When attempting to discover how a particular control button worked on a programmable device, participants in the "rocket ship" study described earlier (Klahr & Dunbar, 1988) had to negotiate this dual search by (a) designing experiments to disclose the button's functions (searching the experiment space) and (b) proposing rules that explained the device's behavior (searching the hypothesis space). Thus, participants were required to coordinate two kinds of problems, and they approached this dual search with different emphases. Some ("experimenters") focused on the space of possible manipulations, whereas others ("theorists") focused on the space of possible explanations of the responses.

Historical studies usually reveal both hypothesis-space search and experiment-space search. For example, most histories of Faraday's discovery of induction of electricity by magnets place much emphasis on the influence of Ampère's theory of magnetism on Faraday's thought. However, a strong case can be made that Faraday's primary search strategy was in the space of experiments, his discovery path being shaped by phenomena observed through experimentation more than by theory.

The number of search spaces depends on the nature of the scientific problem. For example, in describing the discovery of the bacterial origins of stomach ulcers, Thagard (1998) demonstrated search in three major spaces: hypothesis space, experiment space, and a space of instrumentation.

Analogy in Search for Representations

Bohr used the solar system analogy to arrive at his quantum model of the hydrogen atom. He viewed the electrons in the hydrogen atom as planets orbiting the nucleus, although, according to classical understanding of the solar system, this would mean that the charged electrons would dissipate energy until they fell into the nucleus. Instead of abandoning the analogy, Bohr borrowed Planck's theory that energy could be dissipated only in quantum leaps, then showed that these leaps would produce precisely the spectrum of light frequencies that scientists 30 years previously had demonstrated hydrogen produces when its electrons move from a higher-energy stationary state to a lower-energy one.

Search in the Strategy Space

Finally, changes in strategy, even while the representation of a problem is fixed, may enable discovery. Often the change in strategy results from, or leads to, the invention of new scientific instruments or procedures. Breeding experiments go back to Mendel (and experiments for stock breeding go much further back), but the productivity of such experiments depended on mutation rates. Müller, with the "simple" idea that x-rays could induce higher rates of mutation, substantially raised that productivity.

CREATIVITY AND PROBLEM SOLVING IN SCIENCE AND BEYOND

Scientific discovery is a type of problem solving using both weak methods that are applicable in all disciplines and strong methods that are mainly domain-specific. Scientific discovery is based on heuristic search in problem spaces: spaces of instances, of hypotheses, of representations, of strategies, of instruments, and perhaps others. This heuristic search is controlled by general mechanisms such as trial-and-error, hill-climbing, means-ends analysis, analogy, and response to surprise. Recognition processes, evoked by familiar patterns in phenomena, access knowledge and strong methods in memory, linking the weak methods to the domain-specific mechanisms.

All of these constructs and processes are encountered in problem solving wherever it has been studied. A painter is not a scientist; nor is a scientist a lawyer or a cook. But they all use the same weak methods to help solve their respective problems. When their activity is described as search in a problem space, each can understand the rationale of the other's activity, however abstruse and arcane the content of any special expertise may appear.

At the outer boundaries of creativity, problems become less well structured, recognition becomes less able to evoke prelearned solutions or domain-specific search heuristics, and more reliance has to be placed on weak methods. The more creative the problem solving, the more primitive the tools. Perhaps this is why "childlike" characteristics, such as the propensity to wonder, are so often attributed to creative scientists and artists.

Recommended Reading

Klahr, D. (2000). *Exploring science: The cognition and development of discovery processes.* Cambridge, MA: MIT Press.
Klahr, D., & Simon, H.A. (1999). Studies of scientific discovery: Complementary approaches and convergent findings. *Psychological Bulletin, 125,* 524–543.
Zimmerman, C. (2000). The development of scientific reasoning skills. *Developmental Review, 20,* 99–149.

Acknowledgments—Preparation of this article and some of the work described herein were supported in part by a grant from the National Institute of Child Health and Human Development (HD 25211) to the first author. We thank Jennifer Schnakenberg for a careful reading of the penultimate draft.

Notes

1. Address correspondence to David Klahr, Department of Psychology, Carnegie Mellon University, Pittsburgh, PA 15213.

2. In addition, the sociology of science explains scientific discovery in terms of political, anthropological, or social forces. The mechanisms linking such forces to scientific practice are usually motivational, social-psychological, or psychodynamic, rather than cognitive. Although this literature has provided important insights on how social and professional constraints influence scientific practices, we do not have much to say about it in this brief article.

3. This article summarizes an extensive review listed as the second recommended reading. Full references to historical sources alluded to in the present article can be found there, as well as in the first recommended reading. The third recommended reading focuses on developmental aspects of the discovery process.

References

Crick, F. (1988). *What mad pursuit: A personal view of scientific discovery.* New York: Basic Books.
Dunbar, K. (1993). Concept discovery in a scientific domain. *Cognitive Science, 17,* 397–434.
Dunbar, K. (1994). How scientists really reason: Scientific reasoning in real-world laboratories. In R.J. Sternberg & J. Davidson (Eds.), *The nature of insight* (pp. 365–395). Cambridge, MA: MIT Press.

Grasshoff, G., & May, M. (1995). From historical case studies to systematic methods of discovery: Working notes. In *American Association for Artificial Intelligence Spring Symposium on Systematic Methods of Scientific Discovery* (pp. 45–56). Stanford, CA: AAAI.

Holmes, F.L. (1991). *Hans Krebs: The formation of a scientific life, 1900–1933, Volume 1.* New York: Oxford University Press.

Jacob, F., & Monod, J. (1961). Genetic regulatory mechanisms in the synthesis of proteins. *Journal of Molecular Biology, 3,* 318–356.

Judson, H.F. (1996). *The eighth day of creation: Makers of the revolution in biology* (expanded ed.). Plainview, NY: Cold Spring Harbour Laboratory Press.

Klahr, D., & Dunbar, K. (1988). Dual space search during scientific reasoning. *Cognitive Science, 12,* 1–55.

Klahr, D., Fay, A.L., & Dunbar, K. (1993). Heuristics for scientific experimentation: A developmental study. *Cognitive Psychology, 24,* 111–146.

Kulkarni, D., & Simon, H.A. (1988). The process of scientific discovery: The strategy of experimentation. *Cognitive Science, 12,* 139–176.

Nersessian, N.J. (1984). *Faraday to Einstein: Constructing meaning in scientific theories.* Dordrecht, The Netherlands: Martinus Nijhoff.

Qin, Y., & Simon, H.A. (1990). Laboratory replication of scientific discovery processes. *Cognitive Science, 14,* 281–312.

Schunn, C.D., & Anderson, J.R. (1999). The generality/specificity of expertise in scientific reasoning. *Cognitive Science, 23,* 337–370.

Thagard, P. (1998). Ulcers and bacteria: I. Discovery and acceptance. *Studies in the History and Philosophy of Biology and Biomedical Science, 9,* 107–136.

Wertheimer, M. (1945). *Productive thinking.* New York: Harper & Row.

Critical Thinking Questions

1. What are the four approaches used to study the process of scientific discovery?

2. How does the process of scientific discovery exemplify problem solving?

3. Describe the role of surprise in scientific discovery—and the difference in the way adults and children react to an implausible hypothesis.

Neuroscience, Brain, and Mind

All aspects of our existence—every sight, sound, taste, and smell, every twitch, every movement, every feeling of pleasure or pain, all of our habits, memories, thoughts, and emotions, and even our personalities and social interactions—are biological events. The subfield of psychology that focuses on these links is behavioral neuroscience.

The human brain is an extraordinary organ and is the centerpiece of the nervous system. It weighs only about three pounds, it feels like a lump of jelly, and it looks like an oversized walnut. Yet it is more complex than any computer. Today's neuroscientists study the links between brain, mind, and behavior. Enabled by recent breakthroughs in biomedical technology, which allow researchers to observe the living brain in action, this area is generating a great deal of excitement.

In the first article of this section, Bryan Kolb and others (2003) describe some of the exciting new research showing that the brain has "plasticity" and a capacity to change through usage, practice, and other types of experience. Matthew Roser and Michael Gazzaniga (2004) then discuss how certain areas of the brain are involved in specific functions. They argue that conscious awareness emerges from a complex integration of neural impulses and a "left-hemisphere interpreter." Marlene Behrmann (2000) reviews research on the neural and psychological processes involved in mental imagery and its link to visual perception. Gail Martino and Lawrence Marks (2001) describe strong and weak forms of synesthesia, a rare condition in which a person experiences vivid sensory "crossovers"—such as hearing lights, feeling colors, or tasting sounds.

Brain Plasticity and Behavior

Bryan Kolb,[1] Robbin Gibb, and Terry E. Robinson

Canadian Centre for Behavioural Neuroscience, University of Lethbridge, Lethbridge, Alberta, Canada (B.K., RG.), and Department of Psychology, University of Michigan, Ann Arbor, Michigan (T.E.R.)

Abstract

Although the brain was once seen as a rather static organ it is now clear that the organization of brain circuitry is constantly changing as a function of experience. These changes are referred to as brain plasticity, and they are associated with functional changes that include phenomena such as memory, addiction, and recovery of function. Recent research has shown that brain plasticity and behavior can be influenced by a myriad of factors, including both pre- and postnatal experience, drugs, hormones maturation, aging, diet, disease, and stress. Understanding how these factors influence brain organization and function is important not only for understanding both normal and abnormal behavior, but also for designing treatments for behavioral and psychological disorders ranging from addiction to stroke.

Keywords

addiction; recovery; experience; brain plasticity

One of the most intriguing questions in behavioral neuroscience concerns the manner in which the nervous system can modify its organization and ultimately its function throughout an individual's lifetime, a property that is often referred to as plasticity. The capacity to change is a fundamental characteristic of nervous systems and can be seen in even the simplest of organisms, such as the tiny worm *C. elegans*, whose nervous system has only 302 cells. When the nervous system changes, there is often a correlated change in behavior or psychological function. This behavioral change is known by names such as learning, memory, addiction, maturation, and recovery. Thus, for example, when people learn new motor skills, such as in playing a musical instrument, there are plastic changes in the structure of cells in the nervous system that underlie the motor skills. If the plastic changes are somehow prevented from occurring, the motor learning does not occur. Although psychologists have assumed that the nervous system is especially sensitive to experience during development, it is only recently that they have begun to appreciate the potential for plastic changes in the adult brain. Understanding brain plasticity is obviously of considerable interest both because it provides a window to understanding the development of the brain and behavior and because it allows insight into the causes of normal and abnormal behavior.

THE NATURE OF BRAIN PLASTICITY

The underlying assumption of studies of brain and behavioral plasticity is that if behavior changes, there must be some change in organization or properties of the neural circuitry that produces the behavior. Conversely, if neural networks are changed by experience, there must be some corresponding change in the functions mediated by those networks. For the investigator interested in understanding the factors that can change brain circuits, and ultimately behavior, a major challenge is to find and to quantify the changes. In principle, plastic changes in neuronal circuits are likely to reflect either modifications of existing circuits or the generation of new circuits. But how can researchers measure changes in neural circuitry? Because neural networks are composed of individual neurons, each of which connects with a subset of other neurons to form interconnected networks, the logical place to look for plastic changes is at the junctions between neurons, that is, at synapses. However, it is a daunting task to determine if synapses have been added or lost in a particular region, given that the human brain has something like 100 billion neurons and each neuron makes on average several thousand synapses. It is clearly impractical to scan the brain looking for altered synapses, so a small subset must be identified and examined in detail. But which synapses should be studied? Given that neuroscientists have a pretty good idea of what regions of the brain are involved in particular behaviors, they can narrow their search to the likely areas, but are still left with an extraordinarily complex system to examine. There is, however, a procedure that makes the job easier.

In the late 1800s, Camillo Golgi invented a technique for staining a random subset of neurons (1–5%) so that the cell bodies and the dendritic trees of individual cells can be visualized (Fig. 1). The dendrites of a cell function as the

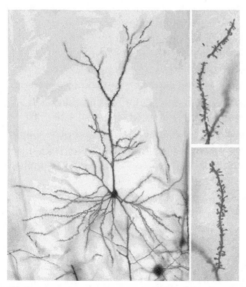

Fig. 1. Photograph of a neuron. In the view on the left, the dendritic field with the extensive dendritic network is visible. On the right are higher-power views of dendritic branches showing the spines, where most synapses are located. If there is an increase in dendritic length, spine density, or both, there are presumed to be more synapses in the neuron.

scaffolding for synapses, much as tree branches provide a location for leaves to grow and be exposed to sunlight. The usefulness of Golgi's technique can be understood by pursuing this arboreal metaphor. There are a number of ways one could estimate how many leaves are on a tree without counting every leaf. Thus, one could measure the total length of the tree's branches as well as the density of the leaves on a representative branch. Then, by simply multiplying branch length by leaf density, one could estimate total leafage. A similar procedure is used to estimate synapse number. About 95% of a cell's synapses are on its dendrites (the neuron's branches). Furthermore, there is a roughly linear relationship between the space available for synapses (dendritic surface) and the number of synapses, so researchers can presume that increases or decreases in dendritic surface reflect changes in synaptic organization.

FACTORS AFFECTING BRAIN PLASTICITY

By using Golgi-staining procedures, various investigators have shown that housing animals in complex versus simple environments produces widespread differences in the number of synapses in specific brain regions. In general, such experiments show that particular experiences embellish circuitry, whereas the absence of those experiences fails to do so (e.g., Greenough & Chang, 1989). Until recently, the impact of these neuropsychological experiments was surprisingly limited, in part because the environmental treatments were perceived as extreme and thus not characteristic of events experienced by the normal brain. It has become clear, however, not only that synaptic organization is changed by experience, but also that the scope of factors that can do this is much more extensive than anyone had anticipated. Factors that are now known to affect neuronal structure and behavior include the following:

- experience (both leading pre- and post-natal)
- psychoactive drugs (e.g., amphetamine, morphine)
- gonadal hormones (e.g., estrogen, testosterone)
- anti-inflammatory agents (e.g., COX-2 inhibitors)
- growth factors (e.g., nerve growth factor)
- dietary factors (e.g., vitamin and mineral supplements)
- genetic factors (e.g., strain differences, genetically modified mice)
- disease (e.g., Parkinson's disease, schizophrenia, epilepsy, stroke)
- stress
- brain injury and leading disease

We discuss two examples to illustrate.

Early Experience

It is generally assumed that experiences early in life have different effects on behavior than similar experiences later in life. The reason for this difference is not understood, however. To investigate this question, we placed animals in complex environments either as juveniles, in adulthood, or in senescence (Kolb, Gibb, & Gorny, 2003). It was our expectation that there would be quantitative differences in the effects of experience on synaptic organization, but to our surprise, we also found *qualitative* differences. Thus, like many investigators before us, we found that the length of dendrites and the density of synapses were increased in neurons in the motor and sensory cortical regions in adult and aged animals housed in a complex environment (relative to a standard lab cage). In contrast, animals placed in the same environment as juveniles showed an increase in dendritic length but a decrease in spine density. In other words the same environmental manipulation had qualitatively different effects on the organization of neuronal circuitry in juveniles than in adults.

To pursue this finding, we later gave infant animals 45 min of daily tactile stimulation with a little paintbrush (15 min three times per day) for the first 3 weeks of life. Our behavioral studies showed that this seemingly benign early experience enhanced motor and cognitive skills in adulthood. The anatomical studies showed, in addition, that in these animals there was a decrease in spine density but no change in dendritic length in cortical neurons—yet another pattern of experience-dependent neuronal change. (Parallel studies have shown other changes, too, including neurochemical changes, but these are beyond the current discussion.) Armed with these findings, we then asked whether prenatal experience might also change the structure of the brain months later in adulthood. Indeed, it does. For example, the offspring of a rat housed in a complex environment during the term of her pregnancy have increased synaptic space on neurons in the cerebral cortex in adulthood. Although we do not know how prenatal experiences alter the brain, it seems likely that some chemical response by the mother, be it hormonal or otherwise, can cross the placental barrier and alter the genetic signals in the developing brain.

Our studies showing that experience can uniquely affect the developing brain led us to wonder if the injured infant brain might be repaired by environmental treatments. We were not surprised to find that postinjury experience, such as tactile stroking, could modify both brain plasticity and behavior because we had come to believe that such experiences were powerful modulators of brain development (Kolb, Gibb, & Gorny, 2000). What was surprising, however, was that prenatal experience, such as housing the pregnant mother in a complex environment, could affect how the brain responded to an injury that it would not receive until after birth. In other words, prenatal experience altered the brain's response to injury later in life. This type of study has profound implications for preemptive treatments of children at risk for a variety of neurological disorders.

Psychoactive Drugs

Many people who take stimulant drugs like nicotine, amphetamine, or cocaine do so for their potent psychoactive effects. The long-term behavioral consequences of abusing such psychoactive drugs are now well documented, but much less is known about how repeated exposure to these drugs alters the nervous system. One experimental demonstration of a very persistent form of drug experience-dependent plasticity is known as behavioral sensitization. For example, if a rat is given a small dose of amphetamine, it initially will show a small increase in motor activity (e.g., locomotion, rearing). When the rat is given the same dose on subsequent occasions, however, the increase in motor activity increases, or sensitizes, and the animal may remain sensitized for weeks, months, or even years, even if drug treatment is discontinued.

Changes in behavior that occur as a consequence of past experience, and can persist for months or years, like memories, are thought to be due to changes in patterns of synaptic organization. The parallels between drug-induced sensitization and memory led us to ask whether the neurons of animals sensitized to drugs of abuse exhibit long-lasting changes similar to those associated with memory (e.g., Robinson & Kolb, 1999). A comparison of the effects of amphetamine and saline treatments on the structure of neurons showed that neurons in amphetamine-treated brains had greater dendritic material, as well as more densely organized spines. These plastic changes were not found throughout the brain, however, but rather were localized to regions such as the prefrontal cortex and nucleus accumbens, both of which are thought to play a role in the rewarding properties of these drugs. Later studies have shown that these drug-induced changes are found not only when animals are given injections by an experimenter, but also when animals are trained to self-administer drugs, leading us to speculate that similar changes in synaptic organization will be found in human drug addicts.

Other Factors

All of the factors we listed earlier have effects that are conceptually similar to the two examples that we just discussed. For instance, brain injury disrupts the synaptic organization of the brain, and when there is functional improvement after the injury, there is a correlated reorganization of neural circuits (e.g., Kolb, 1995). But not all factors act the same way across the brain. For instance, estrogen stimulates synapse formation in some structures but reduces synapse number in other structures (e.g., Kolb, Forgie, Gibb, Gorny, & Rowntree, 1998), a pattern of change that can also be seen with some psychoactive drugs, such as morphine. In sum, it now appears that virtually any manipulation that produces an enduring change in behavior leaves an anatomical footprint in the brain.

CONCLUSIONS AND ISSUES

There are several conclusions to draw from our studies. First, experience alters the brain, and it does so in an age-related manner. Second, both pre- and postnatal experience have such effects, and these effects are long-lasting and can influence not only brain structure but also adult behavior. Third, seemingly similar experiences can alter neuronal circuits in different ways, although each of the alterations is manifest in behavioral change. Fourth, a variety of behavioral conditions, ranging from addiction to neurological and psychiatric disorders, are correlated with localized changes in neural circuits. Finally, therapies that are intended to alter behavior, such as treatment for addiction, stroke, or schizophrenia, are likely to be most effective if they are able to further reorganize relevant brain circuitry. Furthermore, studies of neuronal structure provide a simple method of screening for treatments that are likely to be effective in treating disorders such as dementia. Indeed, our studies show that the new generation of antiarthritic drugs (known as COX-2 inhibitors), which act to reduce inflammation, can reverse age-related synaptic loss and thus ought to be considered as useful treatments for age-related cognitive loss.

Although much is now known about brain plasticity and behavior, many theoretical issues remain. Knowing that a wide variety of experiences and agents can alter synaptic organization and behavior is important, but leads to a new question: How does this happen? This is not an easy question to answer, and it is certain that there is more than one answer. We provide a single example to illustrate.

Neurotrophic factors are a class of chemicals that are known to affect synaptic organization. An example is fibroblast growth factor-2 (FGF-2). The production of FGF-2 is increased by various experiences, such as complex housing and tactile stroking, as well as by drugs such as amphetamine. Thus, it is possible that experience stimulates the production of FGF-2 and this, in turn, increases synapse production. But again, the question is how. One hypothesis is that FGF-2 somehow alters the way different genes are expressed by specific neurons and this, in turn, affects the way synapses are generated or lost. In other words, factors that alter behavior, including experience, can do so by altering gene expression, a result that renders the traditional gene-versus-environment discussions meaningless.

Other issues revolve around the limits and permanence of plastic changes. After all, people encounter and learn new information daily. Is there some limit to how much cells can change? It seems unlikely that cells could continue to enlarge and add synapses indefinitely, but what controls this? We saw in our studies of experience-dependent changes in infants, juveniles, and adults that experience both adds and prunes synapses, but what are the rules governing when one or the other might occur? This question leads to another, which is whether plastic changes in response to different experiences might interact. For example, does exposure to a drug like nicotine affect how the brain changes in learning a motor skill like playing the piano? Consider, too, the issue of the permanence of plastic changes. If a person stops smoking, how long do the nicotine-induced plastic changes persist, and do they affect later changes?

One additional issue surrounds the role of plastic changes in disordered behavior. Thus, although most studies of plasticity imply that remodeling neural circuitry is a good thing, it is reasonable to wonder if plastic changes might also be the basis of pathological behavior. Less is known about this possibility, but it does seem likely. For example, drug addicts often show cognitive deficits, and it seems reasonable to propose that at least some of these deficits could arise from abnormal circuitry, especially in the frontal lobe.

In sum, the structure of the brain is constantly changing in response to an unexpectedly wide range of experiential factors. Understanding how the brain changes and the rules governing these changes is important not only for understanding both normal and abnormal behavior, but also for designing treatments for behavioral and psychological disorders ranging from addiction to stroke.

Recommended Reading

Kolb, B., & Whishaw, I.Q. (1998). Brain plasticity and behavior. *Annual Review of Psychology, 49*, 43–64.

Robinson, T.E., & Berridge, K.C. (in press). Addiction. *Annual Review of Psychology.*
Shaw, C.A., & McEachern, J.C. (2001). *Toward a theory of neuroplasticity.* New York: Taylor and Francis.

Acknowledgments—This research was supported by a Natural Sciences and Engineering Research Council grant to B.K. and a National Institute on Drug Abuse grant to T.E.R.

Note

1. Address correspondence to Bryan Kolb, CCBN, University of Lethbridge, Lethbridge, AB, Canada T1K 3M4.

References

Greenough, W.T., & Chang, F.F. (1989). Plasticity of synapse structure and pattern in the cerebral cortex. In A. Peters & E.G. Jones (Eds.), *Cerebral cortex: Vol. 7* (pp. 391–440). New York: Plenum Press.

Kolb, B. (1995). *Brain plasticity and behavior.* Mahwah, NJ: Erlbaum.

Kolb, B., Forgie, M., Gibb, R., Gorny, G., & Rowntree, S. (1998). Age, experience, and the changing brain. *Neuroscience and Biobehavioral Reviews, 22,* 143–159.

Kolb, B., Gibb, R., & Gorny, G. (2000). Cortical plasticity and the development of behavior after early frontal cortical injury. *Developmental Neuropsychology, 18,* 423–444.

Kolb, B., Gibb, R., & Gorny, G. (2003). Experience-dependent changes in dendritic arbor and spine density in neocortex vary with age and sex. *Neurobiology of Learning and Memory, 79,* 1–10.

Robinson, T.E., & Kolb, B. (1999). Alterations in the morphology of dendrites and dendritic spines in the nucleus accumbens and prefrontal cortex following repeated treatment with amphetamine or cocaine. *European Journal of Neuroscience, 11,* 1598–1604.

Critical Thinking Questions

1. What does it mean to say that the brain has "plasticity" and that one must "use it or lose it?"

2. Describe the Golgi-staining procedure and factors that affect neuronal structure.

3. Discuss the interaction between early experience, age, and neuronal circuitry.

4. How might the authors' conclusions about brain plasticity be applied to social policy?

Automatic Brains—Interpretive Minds

Matthew Roser and Michael S. Gazzaniga

Dartmouth College

Abstract

The involvement of specific brain areas in carrying out specific tasks has been increasingly well documented over the past decade. Many of these processes are highly automatic and take place outside of conscious awareness. Conscious experience, however, seems unitary and must involve integration between distributed processes. This article presents the argument that this integration occurs in a constructive and interpretive manner and that increasingly complex representations emerge from the integration of modular processes. At the highest levels of consciousness, a personal narrative is constructed. This narrative makes sense of the brain's own behavior and may underlie the sense of a unitary self. The challenge for the future is to identify the relationships between patterns of brain activity and conscious awareness and to delineate the neural mechanisms whereby the underlying distributed processes interact.

Keywords

neural correlates of consciousness; interpreter; integration

Although it has been known for more than a century that particular parts of the brain are important for particular functions, the past decade of functional magnetic resonance imaging (fMRI) research has lead to a huge upsurge in evidence for functional specialization. This work has identified areas of the cortex, the convoluted outer layer of the brain, that are involved in processing particular stimulus attributes, or performing certain tasks. For example, cortical areas especially responsive to faces, movement, and places have been found, and these experimental results have been replicated by many independent observers. Although some of the initial claims for functional specialization have been tempered somewhat in the light of new findings, it is becoming ever more clear that the cortex is not a homogeneous, general-purpose computing device, but rather is a complex of circumscribed, modular processes occupying distinct locations.

Most of the work undertaken by these specialist systems occurs automatically and outside of conscious control. For instance, if certain stimuli trick your visual system into constructing an illusion, knowing that you have been tricked does not mean that the illusion disappears. The part of the visual system that produces the illusion is impervious to correction based on such knowledge. Additionally, a convincing illusion can leave behavior unaffected, as when observers are asked to scale the distance between their fingers to the size of a line presented with an arrowhead attached to each end. Although the arrowheads can alter the perceived size of a line (the Müller-Lyer illusion), observers do not

Address correspondence to Matthew Roser, Department of Psychological and Brain Sciences, Moore Hall, Dartmouth College, Hanover, NH 03755; e-mail: matthew.rosser@dartmouth.edu.

make a corresponding adjustment in the distance between their fingers, suggesting that the processes determining the overt behavior are isolated from those underlying the perception. Thus, a visuo-motor process in response to a stimulus can proceed independently of the simultaneous perception of that stimulus (Aglioti, DeSouza, & Goodale, 1995).

Stimuli that are not consciously perceived by subjects can, nonetheless, affect behavior. For example, stimuli that are presented very briefly and followed by a masking stimulus go unperceived by subjects, but still activate response mechanisms and speed the recognition of following stimuli that share their semantic properties (Dehaene et al., 1998). When you add to this the observation that robust perceptual aftereffects can be induced by stimuli that are not consciously perceived (Rees, Kreiman, & Koch, 2002), it becomes evident that a great deal of the brain's work occurs outside of conscious awareness and control. Thus, the systems built into our brains carry out their jobs automatically when presented with stimuli within their domain, often without our knowledge.

The most striking evidence for the isolation of function from consciousness comes from studies of patients showing either neglect or blindsight. Neglect is a condition in which the patient ignores a part of space, usually the left; it is typically found in people with damage to the right parietal area of the brain and is thought to be due to the disruption of the brain's mechanisms for allocating attention. Astonishingly, patients with neglect often deny that they have any such condition. It is as if their consciousness of the deficit is destroyed by the lesion just as their actual awareness of a part of space is, even though early visual areas of the brain (i.e., areas that receive and process incoming visual information) are intact and functioning.

The even more bizarre condition known as blindsight describes the residual visual function shown by some patients following a lesion in early visual areas. Although these patients claim to be completely blind in the side of visual space contralateral to the lesion, they are nonetheless able to discriminate, locate, and guide motion toward a stimulus in that area, all without a conscious percept (Rees et al., 2002).

Together, these syndromes and studies in normal subjects suggest that the activity of the brain is not strictly continuous with our conscious experience. Instead, we are sometimes oblivious to complex processing that occurs in the brain. The question then becomes, what determines whether a process is conscious or not?

BRAIN ACTIVITY AND CONSCIOUSNESS

The neural correlates of consciousness in the human brain have been investigated using fMRI and a technique known as binocular rivalry. In this kind of study, a different stimulus is presented to each eye, and the conscious percept typically switches back and forth between the two stimuli, each percept lasting for a few seconds. Subjects indicate when their perception changes from one stimulus to the other, and because the stimuli themselves are static, any changes in neural activity that correlate with a change in the reported percept can be ascribed to changes in the contents of awareness (Tong, Nakayama, Vaughan,

& Kanwisher, 1998). Brain activations elicited by rivalrous stimuli are very similar in magnitude and location to activations seen in response to separate stimuli that are presented alternately, suggesting that areas involved in processing a type of stimulus are also involved in the conscious perception of that type of stimulus (Zeki, 2003).

fMRI studies have also revealed substantial brain activations in response to stimuli that are not consciously perceived by subjects (Moutoussis & Zeki, 2002). For example, when color-reversed faces (e.g., an outlined red face on a green background and an outlined green face on a red background) are displayed separately to the two eyes, binocular fusion occurs, and subjects report seeing only the color that results from the combination of the two stimulus color (in this case, yellow). The color inputs to the brain are "mixed," like paint on an artist's palette, and the face stimuli become invisible. Despite not being consciously seen, these stimuli typically activate those areas of the brain that are activated by perceived faces. Why then are some seen and some not?

Brain activations correlated with perceived stimuli and those correlated with unseen stimuli show differences in both their intensity and their spatial extent (Dehaene et al., 2001). Dehaene and his colleagues found that although unperceived stimuli and perceived stimuli activated similar locations in the brain, the activations associated with perceived stimuli were many times more intense than those seen with unperceived stimuli and were accompanied by activity at additional sites. Thus, consciousness may have a graded relationship to brain activity, or a threshold may exist, above which activation reaches consciousness (Rees et al., 2002). At present this issue is unresolved, but the development of increasingly sophisticated designs in fMRI may yield progress by allowing the degree of activation to be determined as the availability of a stimulus to awareness is manipulated.

The increased spatial extent of activations elicited by perceived stimuli in the experiment by Dehaene and his colleagues suggests another possible mechanism for determining whether a stimulus reaches consciousness. Processing of a stimulus may reach consciousness if it is integrated into a large-scale system of cortical activity.

CONSCIOUSNESS SEEMS UNITARY

Despite the evidence that processing is distributed around the brain in functionally localized units, and that much processing proceeds outside of awareness, we personally experience consciousness as a unitary whole. How can these observations be resolved?

One possibility is that processes occurring within localized areas and circumscribed domains become available to consciousness only when they are integrated with other domains. Dehaene and Naccache (2001) have hypothesized that there is a *global neuronal work space* in which unconscious modular processes can be integrated in a common network of activation if they receive amplification by an attentional gating system. Attentional amplification leads to increased and prolonged activation and allows processing at one site to affect processing at another. In this way, brain areas involved in perception, action, and emotion can interact with each other and with circuits that can reinstate past states of this work space.

According to this hypothesis, consciousness is the collection of modular processes that are mobilized into a common neuronal work space and integrated in a dynamic fashion. It is a global pattern of activity across the brain, allowing information to be maintained and influence other processes. For instance, consider the task in which subjects are asked to match the distance between their fingers to the size of a Müller-Lyer figure. If a small delay is introduced between the observation of the figure and the reaching response, subjects must rely on their memory of the perceived size when scaling their grip to the size of the figure. Memory involves a consciously maintained representation. In this situation, the illusion does, in fact, affect the subject's motor response (Aglioti et al., 1995).

This model can explain some of the bizarre deficits of consciousness that occur as the result of brain lesions. As processing that does not achieve amplification remains entirely outside of consciousness, a neglect patient may not be aware of his or her deficit because the mechanism linking local processing to global patterns of activation has been disrupted. Thus, a lesion in a specific location may wipe out not merely processing of an attribute, but also the consciousness of the attribute.

Patients with severe cognitive deficits often confabulate wildly in order to produce an explanation of the world that is consistent with their conscious experience. These confabulations include completely denying the existence of a deficit and probably result from interpretations of incomplete information, or a reduced range of conscious experience (Cooney & Gazzaniga, 2003). Wild confabulations that seem untenable to most people, because of conscious access to information that contradicts them, probably seem completely normal to patients to whom only a subset of the elements of consciousness are available for integration.

MIND IS INTERPRETIVE AND CONSTRUCTIVE

The corpus callosum, which connects the two hemispheres, is the largest single fiber tract in the brain. What happens, then, when you cut this pathway for hemispheric communication and isolate the modular systems of the right hemisphere from those in the left? In the so-called split brain, only processes within a hemisphere can be integrated via cortical routes, and only a limited number of processes that can propagate via subcortical routes can be integrated between the hemispheres. Upon introspection, split-brain patients will tell you that they feel pretty normal. And yet, splitting the brain can reveal some of the most striking disconnections between brain processes and awareness. Each hemisphere can be presented with information that remains unknown to the opposite hemisphere.

Experimental designs that exploit this lack of communication have revealed that the left hemisphere tends to interpret what it sees, including the actions of the right hemisphere (Gazzaniga, 2000). For example, suppose two different scenes are presented simultaneously, one to each hemisphere, and the patient is asked to use his or her left hand to choose an appropriate item from an array of pictures of objects that may or may not be typically found within the presented scenes. The left hand is controlled by the right hemisphere, so the patient's left hemisphere, which has no knowledge of what was presented to the right hemisphere, can observe the subsequent actions of the right hemisphere. If the patient is asked why he or she chose a particular item, the patient's verbal reply will be largely controlled by the left hemisphere, where the brain's primary language centers are located. Studies using this procedure have shown that patients often reply with an interpretation of the action that is congruent with the scene presented to the left hemisphere. Thus, patients resolve one hemisphere's actions with the other hemisphere's perceptions, by producing an explanation that eliminates conflict between the two. Patients' responses in such studies are very similar to the confabulations produced by brain-damaged patients who deny that they have a serious deficit by rationalizing their bizarre behavior (Cooney & Gazzaniga, 2003).

The hypothesis-generating nature of the left hemisphere has also been demonstrated in a nonlinguistic manner. When each hemisphere of a split brain is asked to predict whether a light will appear on the top or the bottom of a computer screen on a series of trials, and to indicate its prediction by pushing one of two buttons with the contralateral hand, the two hemispheres employ radically different strategies. The right hemisphere takes the simple approach and consistently chooses the more probable alternative, thereby maximizing performance. By contrast, the left hemisphere does what neurologically normal subjects do and distributes its responses between the two alternatives according to the probability that each will occur, despite the fact that this is a suboptimal strategy (Wolford, Miller, & Gazzaniga, 2000). It seems that the left hemisphere is driven to hypothesize about the structure of the world even when this is detrimental to performance.

The left-hemisphere interpreter may be responsible for our feeling that our conscious experience is unified. Generation of explanations about our perceptions, memories, and actions, and the relationships among them, leads to the construction of a personal narrative that ties together elements of our conscious experience into a coherent whole. The constructive nature of our consciousness is not apparent to us. The action of an interpretive system becomes observable only when the system can be tricked into making obvious errors by forcing it to work with an impoverished set of inputs, such as in the split brain or in lesion patients. But even in the damaged brain, this system still lets us feel like "us."

CONCLUSIONS AND FUTURE DIRECTIONS

It is becoming increasingly clear that consciousness involves disunited processes that are integrated in a dynamic manner. It is assembled on the fly, as our brains respond to constantly changing inputs, calculate potential courses of action, and execute responses. But it is also constrained by the nature of modular processes that occur without conscious control, and large parts of it can be destroyed, leaving a rump that operates only within its reduced sphere. Progress toward an overarching theory of consciousness will involve putting our picture of the brain back together. Although carving cognition and brain function up at the joints has been a hugely productive approach, future progress must depend on a variety of approaches that integrate disparate and circumscribed processes.

To this end, developing techniques in brain mapping hold much promise. Statistical analysis of fMRI data allows the correlations between activations in different areas to be assessed, yielding maps of cerebral interactivity. The application of these techniques to investigation of the neural correlates of consciousness is extremely relevant, as the activation of large networks is thought to be a necessary condition for consciousness.

A further step involves integrating maps of cerebral interactivity with data about neuroanatomical connections. This technique allows a subset of brain processes to be explicitly modeled as a functional network and yields a map of the strengths of anatomical connections that best fits the imaging data (Horwitz, Tagamets, & McIntosh, 1999). At present, much of the data on neuroanatomical connections comes from postmortem studies in monkeys, but a developing noninvasive MRI technique known as diffusion-tensor imaging (DTI) allows the paths of neurons to be tracked and should provide more accurate data about the human brain. DTI is set to have a huge future impact on this field (Le Bihan et al., 2001).

The brain sciences of the coming years promise to yield great progress in our understanding of integrative processes in the brain. The ultimate aim is to come to a theory of consciousness that, while acknowledging that our brains are elaborate assemblies of myriad processes, explains how it is that we feel so unified.

Recommended Reading

Driver, J., & Mattingley, J.B. (1998). Parietal neglect and visual awareness. *Nature Neuroscience, 1*, 17–22.
Gazzaniga, M.S. (2000). (See References)
Savoy, R.L. (2001). History and future directions of human brain mapping and functional neuroimaging. *Acta Psychologica, 107*, 9–42.

Acknowledgments—Preparation of this article was supported by Grant NS31443 from the National Institutes of Health. We are grateful to Margaret Funnell, Paul Corballis, and Michael Corballis for interesting discussions on the topics covered here.

References

Aglioti, S., DeSouza, J.F., & Goodale, M.A. (1995). Size-contrast illusions deceive the eye but not the hand. *Current Biology, 5*, 679–685.
Cooney, J.W., & Gazzaniga, M. (2003). Neurological disorders and the structure of human consciousness. *Trends in Cognitive Sciences, 7*, 161–165.
Dehaene, S., & Naccache, L. (2001). Towards a cognitive neuroscience of consciousness: Basic evidence and a workspace framework. *Cognition, 79*, 1–37.
Dehaene, S., Naccache, L., Cohen, L., Bihan, D.L., Mangin, J.F., Poline, J.B., & Riviere, D. (2001). Cerebral mechanisms of word masking and unconscious repetition priming. *Nature Neuroscience, 4*, 752–758.
Dehaene, S., Naccache, L., Le Clec, H.G., Koechlin, E., Mueller, M., Dehaene-Lambertz, G., van de Moortele, P.F., & Le Bihan, D. (1998). Imaging unconscious semantic priming. *Nature, 395*, 597–600.
Gazzaniga, M.S. (2000). Cerebral specialization and interhemispheric communication: Does the corpus callosum enable the human condition? *Brain, 123*, 1293–1326.
Horwitz, B., Tagamets, M.-A., & McIntosh, A.R. (1999). Neural modeling, functional brain imaging, and cognition. *Trends in Cognitive Sciences, 3*, 91–98.
Le Bihan, D., Mangin, J.F., Poupon, C., Clark, C.A., Pappata, S., Molko, N., & Chabriat, H. (2001). Diffusion tensor imaging: Concepts and applications. *Journal of Magnetic Resonance Imaging, 13*, 534–546.

Moutoussis, K., & Zeki, S. (2002). The relationship between cortical activation and perception investigated with invisible stimuli. *Proceedings of the National Academy of Sciences, USA, 99,* 9527–9532.

Rees, G., Kreiman, G., & Koch, C. (2002). Neural correlates of consciousness in humans. *Nature Reviews Neuroscience, 3,* 261–270.

Tong, F., Nakayama, K., Vaughan, J.T., & Kanwisher, N. (1998). Binocular rivalry and visual awareness in human extrastriate cortex. *Neuron, 21,* 753–759.

Wolford, G., Miller, M.B., & Gazzaniga, M. (2000). The left hemisphere's role in hypothesis formation. *Journal of Neuroscience, 20,* RC64.

Zeki, S. (2003). The disunity of consciousness. *Trends in Cognitive Sciences, 7,* 214–218.

Critical Thinking Questions

1. What evidence supports the idea that the brain is a "complex of circumscribed, modular processes occupying distinct locations"?

2. What do the authors mean when they say, "consciousness may have a graded relationship to brain activity?"

3. What evidence is there to suggest that the left hemisphere but not the right is an "interpreter," providing for a unified conscious experience?

The Mind's Eye Mapped Onto the Brain's Matter

Marlene Behrmann[1]

Department of Psychology, Carnegie Mellon University, Pittsburgh, Pennsylvania

Abstract

Research on visual mental imagery has been fueled recently by the development of new behavioral and neuroscientific techniques. This review focuses on two major topics in light of these developments. The first concerns the extent to which visual mental imagery and visual perception share common psychological and neural mechanisms; although the research findings largely support convergence between these two processes, there are data that qualify the degree of overlap between them. The second issue involves the neural substrate mediating the process of imagery generation. The data suggest a slight left-hemisphere advantage for this process, although there is considerable variability across and within subjects. There also remain many unanswered questions in this field, including what the relationship is between imagery and working memory and what representational differences, if any, exist between imagery and perception.

Keywords

mental imagery; visual perception; cognitive neuroscience

Consider sitting in your office and answering the question "How many windows do you have in your living room?" To decide how to answer, you might construct an internal visual representation of your living room from the stored information you possess about your home, inspect this image so as to locate the windows, and then count them. This type of internal visual representation (or "seeing with the mind's eye"), derived in the absence of retinal stimulation, is known as visual mental imagery, and is thought to be engaged in a range of cognitive tasks including learning, reasoning, problem solving, and language. Although much of the research on mental imagery has been concerned specifically with visual mental imagery, and hence the scope of this review is restricted to this topic, similar internal mental representations exist in the auditory and tactile modalities and in the motor domain.

The past decade has witnessed considerable progress in our understanding of the psychological and neural mechanisms underlying mental imagery. This is particularly dramatic because, in the not-too-distant past, during the heyday of behaviorism, discussions of mental imagery were almost banished from scientific discourse: Given that there was no obvious way of measuring so private an event as a mental image and there was no homunculus available for viewing the pictures in the head even if they did exist, the study of mental imagery fell into disrepute. Indeed, through the 1940s and 1950s, Psychological Abstracts recorded only five references to imagery. The study of mental imagery was revived in the 1970s, through advances such as the experiments of Shepard and colleagues (Shepard & Cooper, 1982) and of Kosslyn and colleagues (see Kosslyn, 1994), and the dual coding theory of Paivio (1979).

Although a general consensus endorsing the existence of mental imagery began to emerge, it was still not fully accepted as a legitimate cognitive process. Some researchers queried whether subjects were simply carrying out simulations of their internal representations in symbolic, nonvisual ways rather than using a visual, spatially organized code. Other researchers suggested that subjects were simply conforming to the experimenters' expectations and that the data that appeared to support a visual-array format for mental imagery merely reflected the experimenters' belief in this format rather than the true outcome of a mental imagery process (Pylyshyn, 1981). In recent years, powerful behavioral and neuroscientific techniques have largely put these controversies to rest. This review presents some of this recent work.

RELATIONSHIP BETWEEN VISUAL IMAGERY AND VISUAL PERCEPTION

Perhaps the most hotly debated issue is whether mental imagery exploits the same underlying mechanisms as visual perception. If so, generating a visual mental image might be roughly conceived of as running perception backward. In perception, an external stimulus delivered to the eye activates visual areas of the brain, and is mapped onto a long-term representation that captures some of the critical and invariant properties of the stimulus. During mental imagery, the same long-term representations of the visual appearance of an object are used to activate earlier representations in a top-down fashion through the influence of preexisting knowledge. This bidirectional flow of information is mediated by direct connections between higher-level visual areas (more anterior areas dealing with more abstract information) and lower-level visual areas (more posterior areas with representations closer to the input).

Mental Imagery and Perception Involve Spatially Organized Representations

Rather than being based on propositional or symbolic representations, mental images appear to embody spatial layout and topography, as does visual perception. For example, many experiments have shown that the distance that a subject travels in mental imagery is equivalent to that traveled in perceptual performance (e.g., imagining the distance between New York and Los Angeles vs. looking at a real map to judge the distance). Recent neuroimaging studies have also provided support for the involvement of spatially organized representations in visual imagery (see Kosslyn et al., 1999); for example, when subjects form a high-resolution, depictive mental image, primary and secondary visual areas of the occipital lobe (areas 17 and 18, also known as V1 and V2), which are spatially organized, are activated.[2] Additionally, when subjects perform imagery, larger images activate relatively more anterior parts of the visual areas of the brain than smaller images, a finding consistent with the known mapping of how visual information from the world is mediated by different areas of primary visual cortex. Moreover, when repetitive transcranial magnetic stimulation[3] is applied and disrupts the normal function of area 17, response times in both perceptual and imagery tasks increase, further supporting the involvement of primary visual areas in mental imagery (Kosslyn et al., 1999).

Shared Visual and Imagery Areas Revealed Through Functional Imaging

Not only early visual areas but also more anterior cortical areas can be activated by imagined stimuli; for example, when subjects imagine previously seen motion stimuli (such as moving dots or rotating gratings), area MT/MST, which is motion sensitive during perception, is activated (Goebel, Khorram-Sefat, Muckli, Hacker, & Singer, 1998). Color perception and imagery also appear to involve some (but not all) overlapping cortical regions (Howard et al., 1998), and areas of the brain that are selectively activated during the perception of faces or places are also activated during imagery of the same stimuli (O'Craven & Kanwisher, in press). Higher-level areas involved in spatial perception, including a bilateral parieto-occipital network, are activated during spatial mental imagery, and areas involved in navigation are activated during mental simulation of previously learned routes (Ghaem et al., 1997). As is evident, there is considerable overlap in neural mechanisms implicated in imagery and in perception both at lower and at higher levels of the visual processing pathways.

Neuropsychological Data for Common Systems

There is also neuropsychological evidence supporting the shared-systems view. For example, many patients with cortical blindness (i.e., blindness due to damage to primary visual areas of the brain) or with scotomas (blind spots) due to destruction of the occipital lobe have an associated loss of imagery, and many patients with visual agnosia (a deficit in recognizing objects) have parallel imagery deficits. Interestingly, in some of these latter cases, the imagery and perception deficits are both restricted to a particular domain; for example, there are patients who are unable both to perceive and to image only faces and colors, only facial emotions, only spatial relations, only object shapes and colors, or only living things. The equivalence between imagery and perception is also noted in patients who, for example, fail both to report and to image information on the left side of space following damage to the right parietal lobe.

There are, however, also reports of patients who have a selective deficit in either imagery or perception. This segregation of function is consistent with the functional imaging studies showing that roughly two thirds of visual areas of the brain are activated during both imagery and perception (Kosslyn, Thompson, & Alpert, 1997). That is, selective deficits in imagery or perception may be explained as arising from damage to the nonoverlapping regions. Selective deficits are particularly informative and might suggest what constitutes the nonoverlapping regions. Unfortunately, because the lesions in the neuropsychological patients are rather large, one cannot determine precise anatomical areas for these nonoverlapping regions, but insights into the behaviors selectively associated with imagery or perception have been obtained, as discussed next.

Patients with impaired imagery but intact perception are unable to draw or describe objects from memory, to dream, or to verify propositions based on memory ("does the letter W have three strokes?"). It has been suggested that in these cases, the process of imagery generation (which does not overlap with perception) may be selectively affected without any adverse consequences for recognition. I review this generation process in further detail in a later section. It has also been suggested that low- or intermediate-level processes may play a greater (but not exclusive) role in perception than they do in imagery. For example, when asked to image a "kangaroo," one accesses the intact long-term representation of a kangaroo, and this is then instantiated and available for inspection. When one is perceiving a kangaroo, however, featural analysis, as well as perceptual organization such as figure-ground segregation and feature grouping or integration, is required. If a patient has a perceptual deficit because of damage to these low- or intermediate-level processes, the patient will be unable to perceive the display, but imagery might well be spared because it relies less on these very processes (Behrmann, Moscovitch, & Winocur, 1994).

Summary and Challenges

There is substantial evidence that imagery and perception share many (although not all) psychological and neural mechanisms. However, some results suggest that the early visual regions in the occipital lobe are not part of the shared network. For example, it has been shown that reliable occipital activation is not always observed in neuroimaging studies when subjects carry out mental imagery tasks. A possible explanation for these null results concerns the task demands: When the task does not require that the subjects form a highly depictive image, no occipital activation is obtained. A second explanation might have to do with subject sampling: There are considerable individual differences in mental imagery ability, and subjects who score poorly on a mental imagery vividness questionnaire show less blood flow in area 17 than those who score higher. If a study includes only low-imagery individuals, no occipital lobe activation might be obtained. A final explanation concerns the nature of the baseline, or control, condition used in neuroimaging experiments: If subjects are instructed to rest but instead continue to activate internal representations, when the activation obtained in the baseline is subtracted from that obtained in the imagery condition, no primary visual cortex activation will be observed.

Another challenge to the conclusion that primary visual areas are involved in imagery comes from studies of patients who have bilateral occipital lesions and complete cortical blindness but preserved imagery. Indeed, some of these patients are capable of generating such vivid images that they believe these to be veridical perceptions. For example, when a set of keys was held up before one such subject, she correctly identified the stimulus based on the auditory signal but then went on to provide an elaborate visual description of the keys, convinced that she could actually see them (Goldenberg, Müllbacher, & Nowak, 1995). Another subject with bilateral occipital lesions whose perception was so impaired that he could not even differentiate light from dark was still able to draw well from memory and performed exceptionally well on standard imagery tasks (Chatterjee & Southwood, 1995).

In sum, although the data supporting a strong association between imagery and perception are compelling, some findings are not entirely consistent with this conclusion.

GENERATION OF MENTAL IMAGES

A second major debate in the imagery literature concerns the mechanisms involved in generating a mental image. This is often assumed to be a process specific to imagery (or perhaps more involved in imagery than in perception) and involves the active construction of a long-term mental representation. Although there has been debate concerning whether there is such a process at all, several lines of evidence appear to support its existence and role in imagery. There are, for example, reports of neuropsychological patients who have preserved perception but impaired imagery and whose deficit is attributed to image generation. Patient R.M., for example, could copy well and make good shape discriminations of visually presented objects but could not draw even simple shapes nor complete from memory visually presented shapes that were partially complete (Farah, Levine, & Calvanio, 1988).

One controversial and unanswered issue concerns the neural substrate of the generation process. The growing neuropsychological literature has confirmed the preponderance of imagery generation deficits in patients with lesions affecting the left temporo-occipital lobe regions. There is not, however, a perfect relationship between this brain region and imagery generation, as many patients with such lesions do not have an impairment in imagery generation.

In many studies, normal subjects show a left-hemisphere advantage for imagery generation; when asked to image half of an object, subjects are more likely to image the right half, reflecting greater left-hemisphere than right-hemisphere participation in imagery generation. Additionally, right-handed subjects show a greater decrement in tapping with their right than left hand while performing a concurrent imagery task, reflecting the interference encountered by the left hemisphere while tapping and imaging simultaneously. (The left hemisphere controls movement on the right side of the body.) Studies in which information is presented selectively to one visual field (and thereby one hemisphere) have, however, yielded more variable results with normal subjects. Some studies support a left-hemisphere superiority, some support a right-hemisphere superiority, and some find no hemispheric differences at all. Studies with split-brain patients[4] also reveal a trend toward left-hemisphere involvement, but also some variability. Across a set of these rather rare patients, imagery performance is better when the stimulus is presented to the left than to the right hemisphere, although this finding does not hold for every experiment and the results are somewhat variable even within a single subject.

Neuroimaging studies in normal subjects have also provided some support for a left-hemisphere basis for imagery generation. For example, functional magnetic resonance imaging showed more activation of the left inferior occipital-temporal region when subjects generated images of heard words compared with when they were simply listening to these words (D'Esposito et al., 1997). This result had also been observed previously using ERPs[5]; an asymmetry in the waveforms of the two hemispheres implicated the left temporo-occipital regions in imagery generation (see Farah, 1999).

In sum, there is a slight but not overwhelming preponderance of evidence favoring the left hemisphere as mediating the imagery generation process. A conservative conclusion from these studies suggests that there may well be some degree of left-hemisphere specialization, but that many individuals have some capability for imagery generation by the right-hemisphere. Another suggestion is that both hemispheres are capable of imagery generation, albeit in different ways; for example, subjects showed a left-hemisphere advantage in a generation task when they memorized how the parts of a stimulus were arranged but showed a right-hemisphere advantage when they memorized the metric positions of the parts and how they could be "mentally glued" together (see Kosslyn, 1994).

CONCLUSION

Although considerable progress has been made in analyzing the convergence between imagery and perception, there are several outstanding issues. One of these is the relationship between imagery and the activation of internal representations in other cognitive tasks. For example, during visual working memory tasks, a mental representation of an object or spatial location is maintained over a delay period, in the absence of retinal stimulation. In these tasks, areas in the very front of the brain, rather than occipital cortex, are activated despite the similarities between this task and mental imagery. Similarly, in tasks that involve top-down forms of attention, subjects are verbally instructed to search for a target (such as a red triangle) in an upcoming display. Although subjects likely generate an image of a red triangle, this is generally not conceived of as an instance of mental imagery, and in neuroimaging studies the location of activation is not usually sought in occipital cortex.

Another perplexing and unresolved issue concerns the reasons that vivid imagery and hallucinations are not confused with reality, especially given that functional imaging studies show identical activations during hallucinations and perception (ffytche et al., 1998). Several solutions to this dilemma have been proposed, among them the idea that hallucinations derive from a failure to self-monitor an inner voice, with the result that the source of the stimulus is located in the external world. A second explanation suggests that perceptions are deeper and contain more detail than images. As Hume (1739/1963) stated, "The difference betwixt these [imagery-ideas and perception] consists in the degree of force and liveliness, with which they strike upon the mind . . . . Perceptions enter with most force and violence . . . . By ideas I mean the faint images of these in thinking and reasoning" (p. 311). How to verify these claims empirically is not obvious, yet this issue clearly demands resolution.

Recommended Reading

Behrmann, M., Moscovitch, M., & Winocur, G. (1999). Visual mental imagery. In G.W. Humphreys (Ed.), *Case studies in vision* (pp. 81–110). London: Psychology Press.
Farah, M.J. (1999). (See References)
Kosslyn, S.M. (1994). (See References)
Richardson, J.T.E. (1999). *Imagery.* Philadelphia: Psychology Press.

Acknowledgments—This work was supported by grants from the National Institute of Mental Health (MH54246 and MH54766). I thank Martha Farah and Steven Kosslyn for helpful discussions about mental imagery and Nancy Kanwisher for her insightful comments on this manuscript.

Notes

1. Address correspondence to Marlene Behrmann, Department of Psychology, Carnegie Mellon University, Pittsburgh, PA 15213-3890; e-mail: behrmann+@cmu.edu.

2. Visual information is received initially via the retina of the eye and is then transmitted through various visual pathways to the brain. This information is sent initially to the primary visual area of the brain, housed posteriorly in the occipital cortex, and is then sent more anteriorly through secondary visual areas to the temporal lobe of the brain for the purposes of recognition. The primary visual area is also known as area 17 or V1, and the secondary area is known as area 18 or V2. The visual input is also sent from the occipital cortex up to the parietal areas of the brain, which represent and code spatial information.

3. Repetitive transcranial magnetic stimulation is a new method in which magnetic pulses are delivered to the brain from a magnet placed externally on the scalp. The electrical pulses disrupt the function of the underlying brain area temporarily and are thus analogous to a reversible lesion. This method allows investigators to determine the involvement of certain brain areas in particular cognitive processes.

4. Split-brain patients are individuals who have undergone a separation of the two sides of the brain (cerebral hemispheres). This is done in individuals who have intractable and uncontrolled epilepsy in order to prevent the seizure activity from spreading across the entire brain. Unfortunately, it also prevents the transfer of all other forms of information from one hemisphere to the other.

5. ERPs, or evoked response potentials, are recordings of the brain's electrical activity in response to stimuli that are presented to the subject. The potentials are measured over time as waveforms obtained from electrodes placed at specific sites on the scalp, and different waveforms roughly reflect differential participation of some brain sites in the task under examination.

References

Behrmann, M., Moscovitch, M., & Winocur, G. (1994). Intact visual imagery and impaired visual perception in a patient with visual agnosia. *Journal of Experimental Psychology: Human Perception and Performance, 20*, 1068–1087.

Chatterjee, A., & Southwood, M.H. (1995). Cortical blindness and visual imagery. *Neurology, 45*, 2189–2195.

D'Esposito, M., Detre, J.A., Aguirre, G.K., Stallcup, M., Alsop, D.C., Tippett, L.J., & Farah, M.J. (1997). Functional MRI study of mental image generation. *Neuropsychologia, 35*, 725–730.

Farah, M.J. (1999). Mental imagery. In M. Gazzaniga (Ed.), *The cognitive neurosciences* (Vol. 2, pp. 965–974). Cambridge, MA: MIT Press.

Farah, M.J., Levine, D.N., & Calvanio, R. (1988). A case study of a mental imagery deficit. *Brain and Cognition, 8*, 147–164.

ffytche, D.H., Howard, R.J., Brammer, M.J., David, A., Woodruff, P., & Williams, S. (1998). The anatomy of conscious vision: An fMRI study of visual hallucinations. *Nature Neuroscience, 1*, 738–742.

Ghaem, O., Mellet, E., Crivello, F., Tzourio, N., Mazoyer, B., Berthoz, A., & Denis, M. (1997). Mental navigation along memorized routes activates the hippocampus, precuneus and insula. *NeuroReport, 8*, 739–744.

Goebel, R., Khorram-Sefat, D., Muckli, L., Hacker, H., & Singer, W. (1998). The constructive nature of vision: Direct evidence from functional magnetic resonance imaging studies of apparent motion and motion imagery. *European Journal of Neuroscience, 10*, 1563–1573.

Goldenberg, G., Müllbacher, W., & Nowak, A. (1995). Imagery without perception—A case study of anosognosia for cortical blindness. *Neuropsychologia, 33*, 39–48.

Howard, R.J., ffytche, D.H., Barnes, J., McKeefry, D., Ha, Y., Woodruff, P.W., Bullmore, E.T., Simmons, A., Williams, S.C.R., David, A.S., & Brammer, M. (1998). The functional anatomy of imagining and perceiving colour. *NeuroReport, 9*, 1019–1023.

Hume, D. (1963). A treatise of human nature. In V.C. Chappel (Ed.), *The philosophy of David Hume* (pp. 11–311). New York: Modern Library. (Original work published 1739)

Kosslyn, S.M. (1994). *Image and brain.* Cambridge, MA: MIT Press.

Kosslyn, S.M., Pascual-Leone, A., Felician, O., Camposano, S., Keenan, J.P., Thompson, W.L., Ganis, G., Sukel, K.E., & Alpert, N.M. (1999). The role of Area 17 in visual imagery: Convergent evidence from PET and TMS. *Science, 284*, 167–170.

Kosslyn, S.M., Thompson, W.L., & Alpert, N.M. (1997). Neural systems shared by visual imagery and visual perception: A positron emission tomography study. *Neuroimage, 6*, 320–334.

O'Craven, K., & Kanwisher, N. (in press). Mental imagery of faces and places activates corresponding stimulus-specific brain regions. *Journal of Cognitive Neuroscience.*

Paivio, A. (1979). *Imagery and verbal processes.* Hillsdale, NJ: Erlbaum.

Pylyshyn, Z.W. (1981). The imagery debate: Analogue media versus tacit knowledge. *Psychological Review, 88*, 16–45.

Shepard, R.N., & Cooper, L.A. (1982). *Mental images and their transformations.* Cambridge, MA: MIT Press.

Critical Thinking Questions

1. Why does the author see generating a mental image as "running perception backward?"

2. Why do researchers think that mental images, like visual perceptions, are spatially represented?

3. What neuropsychological evidence is there for the belief that mental imagery and vision share a common system?

Synesthesia: Strong and Weak

Gail Martino[1] and Lawrence E. Marks

The John B. Pierce Laboratory, New Haven, Connecticut (G.M., L.E.M.), and Department of Diagnostic Radiology (G.M.) and Department of Epidemiology and Public Health (L.E.M.), Yale Medical School, Yale University, New Haven, Connecticut

Abstract

In this review, we distinguish strong and weak forms of synesthesia. Strong synesthesia is characterized by a vivid image in one sensory modality in response to stimulation in another one. Weak synesthesia is characterized by cross-sensory correspondences expressed through language, perceptual similarity, and perceptual interactions during information processing. Despite important phenomenological dissimilarities between strong and weak synesthesia, we maintain that the two forms draw on similar underlying mechanisms. The study of strong and weak synesthetic phenomena provides an opportunity to enrich scientists' understanding of basic mechanisms involved in perceptual coding and cross-modal information processing.

Keywords

synesthesia; cross-modal perception; selective attention

Color is central to Carol's life. As a professional artist, she uses color to create visual impressions in her paintings. Yet unlike most people, Carol also uses color to diagnose her health. She is able to accomplish this by consulting the colored images she sees in connection with pain. For example, a couple of years ago, Carol fell and damaged her leg badly while climbing on rocks at the beach. She diagnosed the severity of her accident not only by the intensity of her pain, but also by the intensity of the orange color that spread across her mind's eye. She said, "When I saw that everything was orange, I knew I should be rushed to the hospital."

Carol's tendency to see colors in response to pain is an example of strong synesthesia. Synesthesia means "to perceive together," and strong synesthesia occurs when a stimulus produces not only the sensory quality typically associated with that modality, but also a quality typically associated with another modality. Strong synesthesia typically arises on its own, although it also can follow the ingestion of drugs such as mescaline and LSD. In this article, we confine our discussion to synesthesia unrelated to drug use.

Over the two centuries since strong synesthesia was first identified in the scientific literature, several heterogeneous phenomena have been labeled as synesthetic. These phenomena range from strong experiences like Carol's, on the one hand, to weaker cross-modal literary expressions, on the other. We believe it is a mistake to label all of these phenomena simply as synesthesia because the underlying mechanisms cannot be identical, although they may overlap. In this review, we distinguish between *strong synesthesia*, which describes the unusual experiences of individuals such as Carol, and *weak synesthesia*, which describes milder forms of cross-sensory connections revealed through language and perception. In both types of synesthesia, cross-modal correspondences are evident, suggesting that the neural processes underlying strong and weak synesthesia, although not wholly identical, nonetheless may have a common core.

STRONG SYNESTHESIA

The Synesthete

Strong synesthesia is an uncommon condition with an unusual demographic profile. Although estimates vary, one recent estimate places the incidence at 1 in 2,000, with females outnumbering males 6 to 1 (Baron-Cohen, Burt, Laittan-Smith, Harrison, & Bolton, 1996). Strong synesthesia clusters in families, leading some researchers to suggest that it has a genetic basis (Baron-Cohen et al., 1996). Empirical evidence for this notion remains sparse.

Except for the finding that there are more female than male synesthetes, few other generalizations characterize strong synesthetes as a group. Attempts have been made to link synesthesia with artistic creativity: Several strong synesthetes described in case studies have worked in the visual arts or music (Cytowic, 1989). Furthermore, several artists who have produced highly creative work—Kandinsky, Rimbaud, and Scriabin—have drawn inspiration from synesthesia. It is unlikely, however, that these artists were themselves strong synesthetes (Dann, 1998). Thus, there are no empirical data to support the idea that strong synesthetes show high artistic creativity.

Strong Synesthetic Correspondence

Case studies offer several characteristics of strong synesthesia (see Cytowic, 1989). In all cases, an association or correspondence exists between an *inducer* in one modality (e.g., pain in Carol's case) and an *induced* percept or image in another (e.g., color). These correspondences have several salient characteristics. For example, they can be idiosyncratic and systematic at the same time. Correspondences are idiosyncratic in that each synesthete has a unique scheme of associations. Middle C on the piano may be blue to one color-music synesthete and green to another. Yet both synesthetes will reveal a systematic relationship between color brightness or lightness and auditory pitch: The higher the pitch of the sound, the lighter or brighter the color of the image (Marks, 1978). Thus C', an octave above middle C, will evoke a correspondingly brighter blue or a lighter green synesthetic color. Besides pitch-brightness and pitch-lightness, auditory-visual synesthesia reveals several other systematic associations. Notable is the association of pitch to shape and size: The higher the pitch of the sound, the sharper, more angular, and smaller the visual image (Marks, 1978).

Synesthetic images are typically simple (e.g., consist of a color or shape), but dynamic (e.g., as the inducer waxes and wanes, so does the image). In some cases, the induced image is so vivid as to be distracting. S, a mnemonist (professional memorizer) and synesthete described by Luria (1968), explained that "crumbly and yellow" images coming from a speaker's mouth were so intense that S had difficulty attending to the intended message. This observation exemplifies another general principle—induced images tend to be visual, whereas inducing stimuli tend to be auditory, tactile, or gustatory (Cytowic, 1989). The reason for this asymmetry is unknown.

Because strong synesthesias are noticed in early childhood, it is possible they are inborn. Many strong synesthetes claim that their cross-modal experiences "have always been there" (e.g., Cytowic, 1989). Harrison and Baron-Cohen (1997) argued that the higher incidence of synesthesia in females speaks against synesthesia being learned. If synesthesia is learned, why should more synesthetes be female than male?

The connection between the inducer and induced is so entrenched that the image is considered part of the percept's literal identity. For S to refer to a voice as "crumbly and yellow" is to offer a literal rather than a metaphorical description. Given the close connection between the inducer and the induced, one would expect correspondences to be highly memorable and durable. In a study of color-word synesthesia (Baron-Cohen et al., 1996), strong synesthetes and control subjects were asked to report the color induced by many words (the control subjects named the first color that came to mind). One hour later, the strong synesthetes were 97% accurate in recalling pairs, whereas the control subjects were 13% accurate. Baron-Cohen et al. argued that this result means that synesthetic perception is highly memorable and genuine. It is not clear to us, however, whether to attribute the synesthetes' superior performance to their synesthesia or perhaps to better memory for word-color pairings in general.

Processing

Reports of strong synesthetes offer clues about how strong synesthesia is produced and where it arises. With regard to production, the relation between the inducer and the induced is typically unidirectional. That is, although a voice induces a yellow image, a yellow percept need not induce an image of a voice.

Some investigators postulate that strong synesthesia arises from a disorder within low-level sensory mechanisms. The sensory leakage hypothesis claims that information leaks from one sensory channel into another, producing strong synesthesia (Harrison & Baron-Cohen, 1997). Leakage might occur, for example, if nerve cells fail to form or migrate properly during neonatal development.

Another hypothesis places the mechanism within specific regions of the brain. Measurement of cerebral blood flow in a single strong synesthete, M.W., suggests that increased activation of areas involved in memory and emotion (i.e., limbic areas) and simultaneous suppression of areas involved in higher reasoning (i.e., cortical areas) produce synesthetic perceptions (Cytowic, 1989). This "limbic-cortex disconnection" has not yet been replicated (see Frith & Paulesu, 1997). Failures to replicate may be related to the unique nature of strong synesthesia in each individual or due to methodological differences across studies.

Besides knowing where strong synesthesia occurs, it is important to know how and why it takes on its phenomenological form (meaning known through the senses, rather than through thought or intuition). In this regard, case studies of strong synesthetes have provided some insights. Yet case studies are not sufficient to explain how and why strong synesthetes' perceptions differ from the norm. Toward this end, future research should be guided by a perceptual or cognitive framework. Table 1 offers a summary of characteristics such a framework must address.

Table 1 Summary of claims about strong and weak synesthesia

| Characteristic | Synesthesia | |
	Strong	Weak
Prevalance	Uncommon, gender bias favoring females	Common
Experience of pairings	One stimulus is perceived, the other is experienced as an image	Both stimuli are perceived
Organization of correspondences	Idiosyncratic and systematic	Systematic
Definition of correspondences	Aboslute	Contextual
Role of learning	Some may be unlearned	Some learned, some unlearned
Semantic association	Literal	Metaphorical
Memory	Easily identified and remembered	Easily identified and remembered
Processing	Unidirectional at a low-level sensory locus	Bidirectional at a high-level semantic locus

WEAK SYNESTHESIA

The phenomenology of strong synesthesia led us to ask whether individuals who lack strong synesthesia nevertheless show analogous cross-modal associations. There is considerable evidence that one can create, identify, and appreciate cross-modal connections or associations even if one is not strongly synesthetic. These abilities constitute weak synesthesia. One form of association is the cross-modal metaphor found in common language (e.g., *warm* color and *sweet* smell) and in literature (e.g., Baudelaire's poem "Correspondences"). Other evidence for weak synesthesia comes from the domain of music. Some people believe that music, like language, contains cross-modal connections. For example, the idea that pitches and colors are associated motivated the invention of the color organ by Castel and inspired the composition *Prometheus* by Scriabin.

Laboratory experiments square with the idea that most people can appreciate cross-modal associations. In such studies, participants are asked to pair a stimulus from one sensory modality to a stimulus from another. These studies show that pairings are systematic. For example, given a set of notes varying in pitch and a set of colors varying in lightness, the higher the pitch, the lighter the color paired with it (see Marks, 1978). This pitch-lightness relation resembles the one observed in strong synesthesia, with one notable difference. In weak synesthesia, the correspondences are defined by context, so that the highest pitch is always associated with the lightest color. Here lies a distinction between strong and weak synesthesia: Although cross-modal correspondences in weak synesthesia are systematic and contextual, those in strong synesthesia are systematic and absolute (display a one-to-one mapping). Despite this difference, it appears that strong and weak synesthetes share an understanding of how visual and auditory dimensions are related (Marks, 1978).

Role of Learning

Are cross-modal correspondences inborn or learned? The answer appears to be, a bit of both. Infants who have not yet learned language show a kind of cross-modal "matching" of loudness-brightness (Lewkowicz & Turkewitz, 1980) and pitch-position (Wagner, Winner, Cicchetti, & Gardner, 1981). Other correspondences develop over time. For example, 4-year-old children can match pitch and brightness systematically, but not pitch and visual size. By age 12, children perform these matches as well as do adults (Marks, Hammeal, & Bornstein, 1987).

Processing

What mental processes underlie the ability to form cross-modal associations? The self-reports of strong synesthetes indicate cross-modal interactions are unidirectional and may involve sensory processes. We wondered whether these characteristics of strong synesthesia apply to cross-modal processing more generally. To address this issue, we developed a cross-modal selective attention task. This task measures a person's ability to respond to a stimulus in one modality while receiving concurrent input from a different, "unattended" modality. If an unattended stimulus affects your ability to respond to an attended one, then the two stimuli are said to interact during information processing.

In a typical task, participants may be asked to classify a sound (high or low tone) in the presence of a color (black or white square), so there are four possible combinations of sounds and colors. Participants are faster at classifying high-pitched tones when these are accompanied by white (vs. black) colors, and are faster at identifying low-pitched tones when they are accompanied by black (vs. white) colors. Analogous results are obtained when participants classify the lightness of a square and color is the unattended stimulus (Melara, 1989). This pattern of findings is termed a congruence effect. Congruence effects entail superior performance when attended and unattended stimuli "match" cross-modally (e.g., high pitch + white square; low pitch + black square) rather than "mismatch" (e.g., high pitch + black square; low pitch + white square). Congruence effects suggest that (a) there is cross-modal interaction (unattended signals can affect one's ability to make decisions about attended ones), (b) the cross-modal correspondence between stimuli is important in determining when interactions occur, and (c) interactions are bidirectional (congruence effects can occur when either sounds or colors are attended). (See Martino & Marks, 1999, for converging evidence.)

Why do congruence effects occur? Two accounts predominate. According to *a sensory hypothesis*, congruence effects involve absolute correspondences processed within low-level sensory mechanisms. These correspondences may arise from common properties in underlying neural codes (e.g., temporal properties of neural impulses may link visual brightness to auditory pitch). This account is consistent with the sensory leakage theory of strong synesthesia and with reports that infants show cross-modal correspondences. Alternatively, we propose that congruence effects involve high-level mechanisms, which develop over childhood from experience with percepts and language—an idea we term the *semantic-coding hypothesis* (SCH; e.g., Martino & Marks, 1999).

The SCH makes four claims. First, although cross-modal correspondence may arise from sensory mechanisms in infants, these correspondences reflect postsensory (meaning-based) mechanisms in adults. Second, experience with percepts from various modalities and the language a person uses to describe these percepts produces an abstract semantic network that captures synesthetic correspondence. Third, when synesthetically corresponding stimuli are perceived, they are recoded from sensory representations into abstract ones based on this semantic network. Fourth, the coding of stimuli from different modalities as matching or mismatching depends on the context within which the stimuli are presented. As mentioned previously, cross-modal matches are defined contextually, so the stimuli are perceived as matching or mismatching only when two or more values are presented in each modality.

Critical support for the SCH comes from selective attention studies like the one described earlier. For example, congruence effects occur when tones and colors both vary from trial to trial, but not when either the tone or the color remains constant (Melara, 1989). The sensory account incorrectly predicts that matches should be processed more efficiently than mismatches in both conditions because correspondences are absolute. The SCH explains the result as a context effect: Trial-by-trial variation provides a context in which to define stimulus values relative to one another, thus highlighting a synesthetic association.

Even stronger evidence for the SCH is that linguistic stimuli are sufficient to drive congruence effects. That is, like the colors black and white, the words *black* and *white* produce congruence effects when paired with low- and high-pitched tones (see Martino & Marks, 1999). The sensory hypothesis cannot account for these findings because interaction is claimed to occur at a sensory level. The SCH accounts for them by proposing that all stimuli (sensory and linguistic) are recoded postperceptually into a single abstract representation that captures the synesthetic correspondence between them.

CONCLUSIONS

Synesthesia is not a unitary phenomenon, but instead takes on strong and weak forms. Strong and weak synesthesia differ in phenomenology, prevalence, and perhaps even some mechanisms underlying their expression. Whereas strong synesthesia expresses itself in perceptual experience proper, weak synesthesia is most clearly evident in cross-modal metaphorical language and in cross-modal matching and selective attention.

Several questions about the nature of strong and weak synesthesia await further investigation. Some concern cognitive and neurological underpinnings: Is strong synesthesia mediated by semantic codes, as weak synesthesia appears to be? Are the brain regions involved in the two kinds of synesthesia similar? For example, do both recruit sensory and semantic areas of the brain? Other issues concern development: To what extent may strong synesthesia be learned or embellished over time? The opportunity to tackle such fundamental questions makes synesthesia an exciting topic for future research.

Recommended Reading

Dann, K.T. (1998). (See References) Harrison, J.E., & Baron-Cohen, S. (1997). (See References)
Marks, L. (1978). (See References)

Acknowledgments—Support was provided by National Institutes of Health (NIH) Training Grant T32 DC00025-13 to the first author and by NIH Grant R01 DC02752 to the second author.

Note

1. Address correspondence to Gail Martino, The John B. Pierce Laboratory, 290 Congress Ave., New Haven, CT 06519; e-mail: gmartino@jbpierce.org.

References

Baron-Cohen, S., Burt, L., Laittan-Smith, F., Harrison, J.E., & Bolton, P. (1996). Synaesthesia: Prevalence and familiarity. *Perception, 25,* 1073–1080.

Cytowic, R.E. (1989). *Synaesthesia: A union of the senses.* Berlin: Springer.

Dann, K.T. (1998). *Bright colors falsely seen.* New Haven, CT: Yale University Press.

Frith, C.D., & Paulesu, E. (1997). The physiological basis of synaesthesia. In S. Baron-Cohen & J.E. Harrison (Eds.), *Synaesthesia: Classic and contemporary readings* (pp. 123–147). Cambridge, MA: Blackwell.

Harrison, J.E., & Baron-Cohen, S. (1997). Synaesthesia: A review of psychological theories. In S. Baron-Cohen & J.E. Harrison (Eds.), *Synaesthesia: Classic and contemporary readings* (pp. 109–122). Cambridge, MA: Blackwell.

Lewkowicz, D.J., & Turkewitz, G. (1980). Cross-modal equivalence in early infancy: Auditory-visual intensity matching. *Developmental Psychology, 16,* 597–601.

Luria, A.R. (1968). *The mind of a mnemonist.* New York: Basic Books.

Marks, L. (1978). *The unity of the senses: Interrelations among the modalities.* New York: Academic Press.

Marks, L.E., Hammeal, R.J., & Bornstein, M.H. (1987). Perceiving similarity and comprehending metaphor. *Monographs of the Society for Research in Child Development, 52*(1, Serial No. 215).

Martino, G., & Marks, L.E. (1999). Perceptual and linguistic interactions in speeded classification: Tests of the semantic coding hypothesis. *Perception, 28,* 903–923.

Melara, R.D. (1989). Dimensional interactions between color and pitch. *Journal of Experimental Psychology: Human Perception and Performance, 15,* 69–79.

Wagner, S., Winner, E., Cicchetti, D., & Gardner, H. (1981). "Metaphorical" mapping in human infants. *Child Development, 52,* 728–731.

Critical Thinking Questions

1. What is synesthesia, and what is the difference between the strong and weak forms of it?

2. How prevalent is strong synesthesia, and are some people more likely than others to have it?

3. What evidence is there that many people can appreciate the cross-modal associations that characterize the weak form of synesthesia?

4. Are cross-modal associations inborn or learned? What's the research evidence?

Cognitive Psychology

One of the most dramatic changes to sweep through psychology, starting in the second half of the twentieth century, was (and still is) the "cognitive revolution." Using the computer as a model of the human mind, and interested in what goes on "inside the head," cognitive psychologists study such topics as attention and perception, learning, intelligence, memory and forgetting, thought, and language. Many researchers in this area raise questions about the extent to which people are competent, rational, and objective in the way they process information about the world.

As reflected in the articles in this section, cognitive psychologists are intensely interested in consciousness and the extent to which people are "aware" of who they are, what they know, and how they know it. Recent studies suggest that much of what we see, learn, think about, and remember, occurs outside of our awareness. Arien Mack (2003) review the current status of research on inattentional blindness, the odd but common phenomenon by which people might "look" but not "see." Peter Frensch and Dennis Runger (2003) describe the cognitive processes of implicit learning, the ubiquitous tendency for people to learn complex skills such as speaking a language or catching a fly ball without conscious effort or explicit instruction. Demonstrating the interplay between thought and language, Emre Ozgen (2004) reviews a long tradition of studies suggesting that people's perceptions of color are shaped by the language they speak and the extent of its vocabulary of color words. Noting that memory is a constructive process that involves a blend of fact and fiction, Henry Roediger and Kathleen McDermott (2000) describe a laboratory procedure that they and others have used to implant vivid but false memories in their subjects. Applying the study of human memory to eyewitness identifications, a disturbing source of error in criminal justice, Gary Wells and others (2002) review recent studies showing that eyewitness confidence can be inflated by social factors unrelated to the accuracy of a memory.

Inattentional Blindness: Looking Without Seeing

Arien Mack[1]

Psychology Department, New School University, New York, New York

Abstract

Surprising as it may seem, research shows that we rarely see what we are looking at unless our attention is directed to it. This phenomenon can have serious life-and-death consequences. Although the inextricable link between perceiving and attending was noted long ago by Aristotle, this phenomenon, now called inattentional blindness (IB), only recently has been named and carefully studied. Among the many questions that have been raised about IB are questions about the fate of the clearly visible, yet unseen stimuli, whether any stimuli reliably capture attention, and, if so, what they have in common. Finally, is IB an instance of rapid forgetting, or is it a failure to perceive?

Keywords

inattention; perception; awareness

Imagine an experienced pilot attempting to land an airplane on a busy runway. He pays close attention to his display console, carefully watching the airspeed indicator on his windshield to make sure he does not stall, yet he never sees that another airplane is blocking his runway!

Intuitively, one might think (and hope) that an attentive pilot would notice the airplane in time. However, in a study by Haines (1991), a few experienced pilots training in flight simulators proceeded with their landing when a clearly visible airplane was blocking the runway, unaware of the second airplane until it was too late to avoid a collision.

As it turns out, such events are not uncommon and even may account for many car accidents resulting from distraction and inattention. This is why talking on cell telephones while driving is a distinctly bad idea. However, the pervasive assumption that the eye functions like a camera and our subjective impression of a coherent and richly detailed world lead most of us to assume that we see what there is to be seen by merely opening our eyes and looking. Perhaps this is why we are so astonished by events like the airplane scenario, although less potentially damaging instances occur every day, such as when we pass by a friend without seeing her.

These scenarios are examples of what psychologists call inattentional blindness (IB; Mack & Rock, 1998). IB denotes the failure to see highly visible objects we may be looking at directly when our attention is elsewhere. Although IB is a visual phenomenon, it has auditory and tactile counterparts as well; for example, we often do not hear something said to us if we are "not listening."

INATTENTIONAL BLINDNESS

The idea that we miss a substantial amount of the visual world at any given time is startling even though evidence for such selective seeing was first reported in the 1970s by Neisser (1979). In one of several experiments, he asked participants to view a video of two superimposed ball-passing games in which one group of players wore white uniforms and another group wore black uniforms. Participants counted the number of passes between members of one of the groups. When the participants were subsequently asked to report what they had seen, only 21% reported the presence of a woman who had unexpectedly strolled though the basketball court carrying an open umbrella, even though she was clearly in view some of the time. Researchers recently replicated this finding with a study in which a man dressed in a gorilla costume stopped to thump his chest while walking through the court and remained visible for between 5 and 9 s (Simons & Chabris, 1999).

Although it is possible that some failures to see the gorilla or the umbrella-carrying woman might have resulted from not looking directly at them, another body of work supports the alternative explanation that the observers were so intent on counting ball passes that they missed the unexpected object that appeared in plain view. Research I have conducted with my colleagues (Mack & Rock, 1998) conclusively demonstrates that, with rare exceptions, observers generally do not see what they are looking directly at when they are attending to something else. In many of these experiments, observers fixated on specified locations while simultaneously attending to a demanding perceptual task, the object of which might be elsewhere. Under these conditions, observers often failed to perceive a clearly visible stimulus that was located exactly where they were looking.

INATTENTIONAL BLINDNESS OR INATTENTIONAL AMNESIA?

Not surprisingly, there is a controversy over whether the types of failures documented in such experiments are really evidence that the observers did not see the stimulus, or whether they in fact saw the stimulus but then quickly forgot it. In other words, is IB more correctly described as *inattentional amnesia* (Wolfe, 1999)? Although this controversy may not lend itself to an empirical resolution, many researchers find it difficult to believe that a thumping gorilla appearing in the midst of a ball game is noticed and then immediately forgotten. What makes the argument for inattentional amnesia even more difficult to sustain is evidence that unseen stimuli are capable of priming, that is, of affecting some subsequent act. (For example, if a subject is shown some object too quickly to identify it and is then shown it again so that it is clearly visible, the subject is likely to identify it more quickly than if it had not been previously flashed. This is evidence of priming: The first exposure speeded the response to the second.) Priming can occur only if there is some memory of the stimulus, even if that memory is inaccessible.

UNCONSCIOUS PERCEPTION

A considerable amount of research has investigated unconscious, or *implicit*, perception and those perceptual processes that occur outside of awareness. This work has led many researchers to conclude that events in the environment, even if not consciously perceived, may direct later behavior. If stimuli not seen because of IB are in fact processed but encoded outside of awareness, then it should be possible to demonstrate that they prime subsequent behavior.

The typical method for documenting implicit perception entails measuring reaction time over multiple trials. Such studies are based on the assumption that an implicitly perceived stimulus will either speed up or retard subsequent responses to relevant stimuli depending on whether the priming produces facilitation or inhibition.[2] However, because subjects in IB experiments cannot be made aware of the critical stimulus, unlike in many kinds of priming studies, only one trial with that stimulus is possible. This requirement rules out reaction time procedures, which demand hundreds of trials because reaction time differences tend to be small and therefore require stable response rates that can be achieved only with many trials. Fortunately, an alternate procedure, stem completion, can be used when the critical stimuli are words. In this method, some observers (experimental group) are exposed to a word in an IB procedure, and other observers (control group) are not. Then, the initial few letters of the unseen word are presented to all the observers, who are asked to complete the string of letters with one or two English words. If the members of the experimental group complete the string with the unseen word more frequently than do the members of the control group, this is taken as evidence that the experimental group implicitly perceived and encoded the word.

IB experiments using this method have demonstrated significant priming (Mack & Rock, 1998), as well as other kinds of evidence that visual information undergoes substantial processing prior to the engagement of attention. For example, evidence that aspects of visual processing take place before attention is allocated has been provided by a series of ingenious IB experiments by Moore and her collaborators (e.g., Moore & Egeth, 1997). This work has shown that under conditions of inattention, basic perceptual processes, such as those responsible for the grouping of elements in the visual field into objects, are carried out and influence task responses even though observers are unable to report seeing the percepts that result from those processes. For example, in one study using a modification of the IB procedure, Moore and Egeth investigated the Müller-Lyer illusion, in which two lines of equal length look unequal because one has outgoing fins, which make it look longer, and the other has ingoing fins, which make it look shorter. In this case, the fins were formed by the grouping of background dots: Dots forming the fins were closer together than the other dots in the background. Moore and Egeth demonstrated that subjects saw the illusion even when, because of inattention, the fins were not consciously perceived. Whatever processes priming entails, the fact that it occurs is evidence of implicit perception and the encoding of a stimulus in memory. Thus, the fact that the critical stimulus in the IB paradigm can prime subsequent responses is evidence that this stimulus is implicitly perceived and encoded.

When Do Stimuli Capture Attention and Why?

That unconsciously perceived stimuli in IB experiments undergo substantial processing in the brain is also supported by evidence that the select few stimuli able to capture attention when attention is elsewhere are complex and meaningful (e.g., the observer's name, an iconic image of a happy face) rather than simple features like color or motion. This fact suggests that attention is captured only after the meaning of a stimulus has been analyzed. There are psychologists who believe that attention operates much earlier in the processing of sensory input, before meaning has been analyzed (e.g., Treisman, 1969). These accounts, however, do not easily explain why modest changes, such as inverting a happy face and changing one internal letter in the observer's name, which alter the apparent meaning of the stimuli but not their overall shape, cause a very large increase in IB (Mack & Rock, 1998).

Meaning and the Capture of Attention

If meaning is what captures attention, then it follows axiomatically that meaning must be analyzed before attention is captured, which is thought to occur at the end stage of the processing of sensory input. This therefore implies that even those stimuli that we are not intending to see and that do not capture our attention must be fully processed by the brain, for otherwise their meanings would be lost before they had a chance of capturing our attention and being perceived. If this is the case, then we are left with some yet-unanswered, very difficult questions. Are all the innumerable stimuli imaged on our retinas really processed for meaning and encoded into memory, and if not, which stimuli are and which are not?

Although we do not yet have answers to these questions, an unpublished doctoral dissertation by Silverman, at New School University, has demonstrated that there can be priming by more than one element in a multielement display, even when these elements cannot be reported by the subject. This finding is relevant to the question whether all elements in the visual field are processed and stored because up to now there has been scarcely any evidence of priming by more than one unreportable element in the field. The fact of multielement priming begins to suggest that unattended or unseen elements are processed and stored, although it says nothing about how many elements are processed and whether the meaning of all the elements is analyzed.

One answer to the question of how much of what is not seen is encoded into memory comes from an account of perceptual processing based on the assumption that perception is a limited-capacity process and that processing is mandatory up to the point that this capacity is exhausted (Lavie, 1995). According to this analysis, the extent to which unattended objects are processed is a function of the difficulty of the perceptual task (i.e., the perceptual load). When the perceptual load is high, only attended stimuli are encoded. When it is low, unattended stimuli are also processed. This account faces some difficulty because it is not clear how perceptual load should be estimated. Beyond this, however, it is difficult to reconcile this account with evidence suggesting that observers are likely to see their own names even when they occur among the stimuli that must be ignored in order to perform a demanding perceptual task (Mack, Pappas, Silverman, & Gay, 2002). It should be noted, however, that these latter results are at odds with a published report (Rees, Russell, Firth, & Driver, 1999) I describe in the next section.

EVIDENCE FROM NEURAL IMAGING

Researchers have used magnetic imaging techniques to try to determine what happens in the brain when observers fail to detect a visual stimulus because their attention is elsewhere. Neural recording techniques may be able to show whether visual stimuli that are unconsciously perceived arouse the same areas of the brain to the same extent as visual stimuli that are seen. This is an important question because it bears directly on the nature of the processing that occurs outside of awareness prior to the engagement of attention and on the difference between the processing of attended and unattended stimuli.

In one study, Scholte, Spekreijse, and Lamme (2001) found similar neural activity related to the segregation of unattended target stimuli from their backgrounds (i.e., the grouping of the unattended stimuli so they stood out from the background on which they appeared), an operation that is thought to occur early in the processing of visual input. This activation was found regardless of whether the stimuli were attended and seen or unattended and not seen, although there was increased activation for targets that were attended and seen. This finding is consistent with the behavioral findings of Moore and Egeth (1997), cited earlier, showing that unattended, unseen stimuli undergo lower-level processing such as grouping, although the additional neural activity associated with awareness suggests that there may be important differences in processing of attended versus unattended stimuli.

In another study, Rees and his colleagues (Rees et al., 1999) used functional magnetic resonance imaging (fMRI) to picture brain activity while observers were engaged in a perceptual task. They found no evidence of any difference between the neural processing of meaningful and meaningless lexical stimuli when they were ignored, although when the same stimuli were attended to and seen, the neural processing of meaningful and meaningless stimuli did differ. These results suggest that unattended stimuli are not processed for meaning. However, in another study that repeated the procedure used by Rees et al. (without fMRI recordings) but included the subject's own name among the ignored stimuli, many subjects saw their names, suggesting that meaning was in fact analyzed (Mack et al., 2002). Thus, one study shows that ignored stimuli are not semantically processed, and the other suggests that they are. This conflict remains unresolved. Are unattended, unseen words deeply processed outside of awareness, despite these fMRI results, which show no evidence of semantic neural activation by ignored words? How can one reconcile behavioral evidence of priming by lexical stimuli under conditions of inattention (Mack & Rock, 1998) with evidence that these stimuli are not semantically processed?

NEUROLOGICAL DISORDER RELATED TO INATTENTIONAL BLINDNESS

People who have experienced brain injuries that cause lesions in the parietal cortex (an area of the brain associated with attention) often exhibit what is called unilateral visual neglect, meaning that they fail to see objects located in the visual field opposite the site of the lesion. That is, for example, if the lesion is on the right, they fail to eat food on the left side of their plates or to shave the left half of their faces. Because these lesions do not cause any sensory deficits, the apparent blindness cannot be attributed to sensory causes and has been explained in terms of the role of the parietal cortex in attentional processing

(Rafal, 1998). Visual neglect therefore seems to share important similarities with IB. Both phenomena are attributed to inattention, and there is evidence that in both visual neglect (Rafal, 1998) and IB, unseen stimuli are capable of priming. In IB and visual neglect, the failure to see objects shares a common cause, namely inattention, even though in one case the inattention is produced by brain damage, and in the other the inattention is produced by the task. Thus, evidence of priming by neglected stimuli appears to be additional evidence of the processing and encoding of unattended stimuli.

ATTENTION AND PERCEPTION

IB highlights the intimate link between perception and attention, which is further underscored by recent evidence showing that unattended stimuli that share features with task-relevant stimuli are less likely to suffer IB than those that do not (Most et al., 2001). This new evidence illustrates the power of our intentions in determining what we see and what we do not.

CONCLUDING REMARKS

Although the phenomenon of IB is now well established, it remains surrounded by many unanswered questions. In addition to the almost completely unexplored question concerning whether all unattended, unseen stimuli in a complex scene are fully processed outside of awareness (and if not, which are and which are not), there is the question of whether the observer can locate where in the visual field the information extracted from a single unseen stimulus came from, despite the fact that the observer has failed to perceive it. This possibility is suggested by the proposal that there are two separate visual systems, one dedicated to action, which does not entail consciousness, and the other dedicated to perception, which does entail consciousness (Milner & Goodale, 1995). That is, the action stream may process an unseen stimulus, including its location information, although the perception stream does not. An answer to this question would be informative about the fate of the unseen stimuli.

The pervasiveness of IB raises another unresolved question. Given that people see much less than they think they do, is the visual world a mere illusion? According to one provocative answer to this question, most recently defended by O'Regan and Noe (2001), the outcome of perceptual processing is not the construction of some internal representation; rather, seeing is a way of exploring the environment, and the outside world serves as its own external representation, eliminating the need for internal representations. Whether or not this account turns out to be viable, the phenomenon of IB has raised a host of questions, the answers to which promise to change scientists' understanding of the nature of perception. The phenomenon itself points to the serious dangers of inattention.

Recommended Reading

Mack, A., & Rock, I. (1998). (See References)
Rensink, R. (2002). Change blindness. *Annual Review of Psychology*, 53, 245–277.

Simons, D. (2000). Current approaches to change blindness. *Visual Cognition, 7,* 1–15.
Wilkens, P. (Ed.). (2000). Symposium on Mack and Rock's *Inattentional Blindness. Psyche,* 6 and 7. Retrieved from http://psyche.cs. monash.edu.au/psyche-indexv7.html#ib

Acknowledgments—I am grateful for the comments and suggestions of Bill Prinzmetal and Michael Silverman.

Notes

1. Address correspondence to Arien Mack, Psychology Department, New School University, 65 Fifth Ave., New York, NY 10003.

2. An example of a speeded-up response (facilitation, or positive priming) has already been given. Negative, or inhibition, priming occurs when a stimulus that has been actively ignored is subsequently presented. For example, if a series of superimposed red and green shapes is rapidly presented and subjects are asked to report a feature of the red shapes, later on it is likely to take them longer to identify the green shapes than a shape that has not previously appeared, suggesting that the mental representation of the green shapes has been associated with something like an "ignore me" tag.

References

Haines, R.F. (1991). A breakdown in simultaneous information processing. In G. Obrecht & L.W. Stark (Eds.), *Presbyopia research* (pp. 171–175). New York: Plenum Press.

Lavie, N. (1995). Perceptual load as a necessary condition for selective attention. *Journal of Experimental Psychology: Human Perception and Performance, 21,* 451–468.

Mack, A., Pappas, Z., Silverman, M., & Gay, R. (2002). What we see: Inattention and the capture of attention by meaning. *Consciousness and Cognition, 11,* 488–506.

Mack, A., & Rock, I. (1998). *Inattentional blindness.* Cambridge, MA: MIT Press.

Milner, D., & Goodale, M.A. (1995). *The visual brain in action.* Oxford, England: Oxford University Press.

Moore, C.M., & Egeth, H. (1997). Perception without attention: Evidence of grouping under conditions of inattention. *Journal of Experimental Psychology: Human Perception and Performance, 23,* 339–352.

Most, S.B., Simons, D.J., Scholl, B.J., Jimenez, R., Clifford, E., & Chabris, C.F. (2001). How not to be seen: The contribution of similarity and selective ignoring to sustained inattentional blindness. *Psychological Science, 12,* 9–17.

Neisser, U. (1979). The control of information pickup in selective looking. In A.D. Pick (Ed.), *Perception and its development: A tribute to Eleanor Gibson* (pp. 201–219). Hillsdale, NJ: Erlbaum.

O'Regan, K., & Noe, A. (2001). A sensorimotor account of vision and visual consciousness. *Behavioral and Brain Sciences, 25,* 5.

Rafal, R. (1998). Neglect. In R. Parasuraman (Ed.), *The attentive brain* (pp. 489–526). Cambridge, MA: MIT Press.

Rees, G., Russell, C., Firth, C., & Driver, J. (1999). Inattentional blindness versus inattentional amnesia. *Science, 286,* 849–860.

Scholte, H.S., Spekreijse, H., & Lamme, V.A. (2001). Neural correlates of global scene segmentation are present during inattentional blindness [Abstract]. *Journal of Vision, 1*(3), Article 346. Retrieved from http://journalofvision. org/1/3/346

Simons, D.J., & Chabris, C.F. (1999). Gorillas in our midst: Sustained inattentional blindness for dynamic events. *Perception, 28,* 1059–1074.

Treisman, A. (1969). Strategies and models of selective attention. *Psychological Review, 76,* 282–299.

Wolfe, J. (1999). Inattentional amnesia. In V. Coltheart (Ed.), *Fleeting memories* (pp. 71–94). Cambridge, MA: MIT Press.

Critical Thinking Questions

1. Describe and provide examples of inattentional blindness.

2. What are two competing explanations for inattentional blindness, and what is the supporting research evidence?

3. How have researchers used neural imaging to study visual perception and inattentional blindness?

4. What is the basis for author's question, "Is the visual world a mere illusion?"

Implicit Learning

Peter A. Frensch[1] and Dennis Rünger
Department of Psychology, Humboldt University, Berlin, Germany

Abstract

Implicit learning appears to be a fundamental and ubiquitous process in cognition. Although defining and operationalizing implicit learning remains a central theoretical challenge, scientists' understanding of implicit learning has progressed significantly. Beyond establishing the existence of "learning without awareness," current research seeks to identify the cognitive processes that support implicit learning and addresses the relationship between learning and awareness of what was learned. The emerging view of implicit learning emphasizes the role of associative learning mechanisms that exploit statistical dependencies in the environment in order to generate highly specific knowledge representations.

Keywords

cognitive psychology; learning; consciousness; awareness

Have you ever wondered why it is that you can speak your native language so well without making any grammatical errors although you do not know many of the grammatical rules you follow? Have you ever wondered how it is that you can walk properly although you cannot describe the rules of mechanics your body must certainly follow? These two examples point to an important human property, namely, the ability to adapt to environmental constraints—to learn—in the absence of any knowledge about how the adaptation is achieved. *Implicit learning*—laxly defined as learning without awareness—is seemingly ubiquitous in everyday life.

In this article, we try to provide an overview of the difficulties research on implicit learning has been facing and of the advances that have been made in scientists' understanding of the concept. More specifically, we discuss three separate issues. First, we address what is meant by implicit learning and how the concept has been empirically approached in the recent past. Second, we summarize what is currently known with some certainty about the cognitive processes underlying implicit learning and the mental representations that are acquired through it. Third, we discuss some of the most important current topics of investigation.

DEFINITION AND OPERATIONALIZATION

The one basic theoretical issue that reigns supreme among the difficulties facing researchers concerns the definition and operationalization of implicit learning. Although it seems clear that implicit learning needs to be viewed in opposition to learning that is not implicit (often called explicit, hypothesis-driven learning), it has so far proven extremely difficult to provide a satisfactory definition of implicit learning. At least a dozen different definitions have been offered in the field.

One important consequence of the heterogeneity of definitions is that different researchers have operationalized implicit learning in different ways. For example, Arthur Reber, whose early work in the 1960s rekindled interest in implicit learning, has done most of his empirical work with artificial-grammar-learning tasks. In these tasks, participants are asked to memorize a set of letter strings, such as "XXRTRXV" and "QQWMWQP," that are, unbeknownst to the participants, generated by some rules. After the memorization phase, participants are told that the strings they memorized followed certain rules, and are asked to classify new strings as grammatical (i.e., following the rules) or not. Typically, participants can perform this classification task with accuracy better than would be expected by chance, despite remaining unable to verbally describe the rules.

Thus, in a grammar-learning task, participants learn about permissible and nonpermissible combinations of letters that are presented simultaneously. By comparison, in another task often used to investigate implicit learning, the serial reaction time task (SRTT), participants learn about permissible and nonpermissible combinations of spatial locations that occur over time. In the SRTT, participants are asked to select and depress a key that matches each of the locations at which a stimulus appears on a screen. The sequence of locations at which the stimulus appears is fixed. In general, participants seem to be able to learn the sequence of spatial locations even when they are not able to verbally describe it.

Divergent definitions of implicit learning entail divergent operationalizations of the concept, but even researchers who agree in their definitions might use experimental tasks that differ in what exactly participants might learn. Therefore, it remains an open empirical issue to what extent results from a given task that has been used to probe implicit learning can be generalized to other tasks. This point leads to our first conclusion:

• *Conclusion 1.* Implicit learning of Task A is not necessarily comparable to implicit learning of Task B. Neither the properties of the learning mechanisms involved nor the acquired mental representations need be the same. It is even conceivable that implicit learning of Task A might be possible, but implicit learning of Task B might not.

THE KEY ISSUE

Regardless of how implicit learning is defined and operationalized, the key empirical issue that research needs to address is whether or not learning that is "implicit" is possible, and if it is, whether implicit learning is different from learning that is "not implicit." Many researchers have for practical reasons adopted as their definition of implicit learning "the capacity to learn without awareness of the products of learning." Thus, learning is assumed to be "implicit" when participants are unaware of what they learned. Alternatively, learning is assumed not to be implicit when participants are aware of what they learned. In other words, implicit learning is defined in terms of its product rather than the properties of the learning process.

Various measures have been proposed to assess awareness of the products of learning. The most notable measures are verbal reports and forced-choice tests (such as recognition tests).

Participants in implicit-learning experiments have consistently been shown to be able to acquire knowledge that they cannot verbally describe. This appears to be true for a wide variety of tasks, including the grammar-learning and sequence-learning tasks we described earlier. Thus, if verbal report is used to assess awareness of acquired knowledge, many experimental findings appear to support the conclusion that implicit learning is possible.

However, many authors have argued that verbal reports may have poor validity. First, it has been argued that the verbal-report data do not pass the information criterion; that is, the information assessed by verbal recall tests is not always the same information that has led to the demonstrated learning. Second, verbal recall tests might not pass the sensitivity criterion; that is, they may not provide a level of sensitivity that is comparable to that of tests demonstrating learning in the first place. Many researchers have therefore suggested that awareness should be assessed by forced-choice tests, such as recognition tests, rather than verbal recall.

In the grammar-learning paradigm, participants are sometimes asked to complete recognition tests after they have categorized letter strings as grammatical or nongrammatical. For example, in some studies participants were asked to indicate for each letter string which particular letters they thought made the string grammatical or not. It was found that participants' markings correlated with their classification performance, suggesting at least partial awareness of the knowledge learned.

Similar findings have been obtained in studies that have used other implicit-learning paradigms. For example, after participants had completed the SRTT, they were presented sequence patterns of varying lengths in numerical form. Each sequence (e.g., 123432) denoted a series of locations on the computer screen. Participants were asked to mark patterns that they had encountered during the experiment as true and patterns that they had not seen as false. It was found that participants' recognition scores correlated with their learning scores for the SRTT. In general, many different studies using different experimental paradigms have used forced-choice tests to assess awareness of the acquired knowledge, and these studies appear not to support the existence of implicit learning.

However, it has been argued that this particular interpretation rests on the assumption that the forced-choice tests are pure assessments of awareness (i.e., are process pure). This is almost certainly not the case. Indeed, participants might choose a correct answer on a forced-choice test not because they are aware of the fact that it is the correct answer but because they rely on some intuition that they are not able to express. The growing understanding that tests are rarely process pure has fostered the use of new methodologies that are not based on this assumption. For example, Jacoby's process dissociation procedure offers a measure of awareness that is derived from experimental conditions that are believed to trigger both implicit and nonimplicit processes simultaneously. This consideration of how awareness should be assessed leads to our second conclusion:

- *Conclusion 2.* Many researchers have tried to avoid the difficult issue of how to define implicit learning and have, often without stating so explicitly, adopted the stance that implicit learning is the capacity to learn without awareness of the products of learning. However, it has become clear that the amount of support for implicit learning varies considerably with the specific measure that is selected to assess awareness of what was learned. Thus, by avoiding the issue of how to define implicit learning, researchers have introduced the problem of how to define awareness. In the end, the definitional question has not been resolved, but has merely been transferred from one concept to another.

MECHANISMS OF LEARNING AND AWARENESS

Even when implicit learning (in the sense of learning that yields knowledge the learner is not aware of) is demonstrated conclusively, one learns little about the mechanisms underlying implicit learning. It is helpful to consider the different ways in which, in principle, learning and awareness of the products of learning might be related. Figure 1 depicts five of the many distinct possibilities that have been proposed.

First, it is, of course, conceivable that learning and awareness of what has been learned are perfectly correlated. According to this proposal, implicit learning does not exist. As is shown in Figure 1a, learning might be achieved by a single mechanism that generates memory representations a learner is always aware of.

According to the four remaining possibilities, learning and awareness need not be—but might be—perfectly correlated. According to the second possibil-

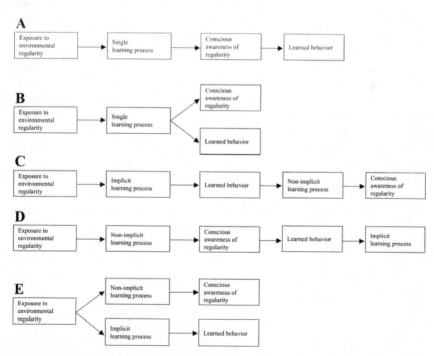

Fig. 1. Possible relations between learning and awareness of what was learned.

ity, depicted in Figure 1b, a single learning mechanism is assumed to create memory representations that control behavior. Some of the learned memory representations might be open to awareness; some might not be.

The last three possibilities (Figs. 1c–1e) allow for truly implicit learning. According to the third possibility, an implicit-learning mechanism might generate memory representations that control behavior. The perception of one's own behavior, in turn, might lead to nonimplicit (i.e., hypothesis-testing) learning that might generate awareness of what was learned (Fig. 1c). Under this view, the effects of implicit learning are an important trigger for nonimplicit learning. For example, a tennis player might perceive an increased accuracy of her serve. She might then conclude that the reason for this improvement is to be found in a slightly higher toss of the ball.

The fourth possibility is that nonimplicit learning might lead to awareness of what was learned, and might control behavior. The expression of behavior, in turn, might provide the input for the operation of an implicit-learning mechanism (Fig. 1d). For example, most tennis players know that solid ground strokes require a player to move toward the approaching ball instead of away from it. The conscious effort to engage in a forward movement may lead to learning within the motor systems that lies largely outside of conscious awareness.

The fifth possibility, shown in Figure 1e, is that there exist two distinct learning mechanisms, with one of the mechanisms generating memory representations that a learner is aware of, and the other mechanism generating representations that a learner is not aware of but that nevertheless control behavior.

Most of the research that has been concerned with the difference between implicit and nonimplicit learning has not addressed which possibility in Figure 1 describes the nature of implicit learning, but rather has tried to demonstrate that learning is possible in the absence of learners' awareness of the acquired knowledge. However, several attempts have been made to distinguish the two-systems hypothesis (i.e., that there are separate systems for implicit and nonimplicit learning), represented by the possibilities depicted in Figures 1c through 1e, from the single-system hypothesis, represented by the possibilities depicted in Figures 1a and 1b. The relative adequacy of these two hypotheses can be assessed by exploring the potentially differing influence of variables such as intention to learn, attention, age of participants, individual differences in intelligence, stimulus complexity, and task demands on learning with awareness and on learning without awareness.

For example, researchers have explored the possibility that implicit and nonimplicit learning might be differentially affected by age. With the SRTT, it has been found that implicit learning is less affected by age than is learning that is based on hypothesis testing. Indeed, implicit learning in the SRTT does not appear to begin to decline until relatively old age, and even then, the elderly display performance levels that are much closer to those of younger adults for implicit-learning tasks than for nonimplicit-learning tasks involving, for example, problem solving, reasoning, and long-term memory. On the whole, this research therefore lends some credibility to the multiple-systems view.

Also, both neuropsychological studies and neuroimaging studies have addressed the adequacy of the multiple-systems and single-system hypotheses.

For example, early studies suggested that even densely amnesic patients can show near-normal implicit learning in both the grammar-learning and the sequence-learning paradigms, although they are specifically impaired on recognition and prediction tasks. More recent critical reexaminations have, however, demonstrated that amnesic patients do seem to show a deficit in implicit learning compared with normal control participants; it is therefore unclear whether or not the findings, on the whole, support the multiple-systems view.

Brain-imaging techniques have increasingly been used to study implicit learning in the SRTT. Although some results suggest that partially distinctive brain areas are involved in implicit and nonimplicit forms of learning, it is, at present, not clear whether these findings should be interpreted as evidence supporting the multiple-systems view or as evidence supporting a "single-system plus awareness" view (depicted in Fig. 1b).

Consideration of the cognitive mechanisms that might be involved in implicit learning leads to our third conclusion:

- *Conclusion 3.* Defining implicit learning with respect to awareness of the products of learning has drawn attention away from the mechanisms that are responsible for the generation of different forms of knowledge. Despite a continuously increasing amount of empirical data, the debate between multiple-systems proponents and single-system proponents has not been settled yet. Furthermore, the question of how exactly awareness and learning might be interrelated has only recently begun to be addressed empirically.

IMPORTANT ADVANCES MADE

If one agrees with the use of verbal-report measures to assess awareness, then recent research on implicit learning has modified earlier theoretical beliefs in important ways. Earlier work had characterized implicit learning as a mechanism by which abstract knowledge of regularities that are present in the environment is acquired automatically and unintentionally by mere exposure to relevant instances. The proposal of a smart unconscious was based, to a large extent, on empirical findings with the grammar-learning task that appeared to show that participants possessed abstract knowledge about the rules of the grammar that went beyond the surface characteristics of the information encountered. This claim seemed further supported by findings indicating that implicitly acquired knowledge may transfer across modalities; for example, learning from a task involving written letters (visual stimuli) can transfer to performance in a task involving letter sounds (auditory stimuli).

This view has been challenged, however, by many recent findings. For example, it has been repeatedly shown that implicitly acquired knowledge might consist of little more than short fragments or chunks of the materials encountered in an implicit-learning situation. In the wake of these findings, neural-network models and fragment-based models that are capable of simulating a great deal of the available experimental findings have been developed. These models utilize representations of elementary stimuli in the learning situation (e.g., representations of letters in a grammar-learning task) and associations between the representations. Learning consists of a continuous, incremental change in the associative pattern that is sensitive to the statistical features of the set of items or events encountered. Thus, a representation of the implicit-learning situation that is shaped by statistical constraints gradually evolves. Although the characterization of implicitly acquired knowledge is still a matter of debate, the current trend is to assume that abstract knowledge might not be implicitly generated.

Many recent studies have explored whether implicit learning, unlike non-implicit learning (i.e., explicit hypothesis testing), proceeds automatically, without the use of attentional resources. By far, most of these studies have used the SRTT, often manipulating the amount of attentional resources available to participants by asking them to perform the SRTT either by itself or together with a secondary task (typically a tone-counting task).

In general, it has been found that implicit learning takes place both in the presence and in the absence of a secondary task. What remains unclear, at present, is the extent to which implicit learning is affected by the attention manipulation. Some researchers argue that the secondary task interferes with task performance rather than with implicit learning proper (i.e., that the secondary task impedes the expression of what has been learned). Under this view, implicit learning does not depend on the availability of attentional resources. Others take the stance that the learning process itself is adversely affected by the presence of a secondary task and thus requires attentional resources.

On the whole, the experiments that have been conducted all suffer from the problem that attention itself is an ill-defined concept that might refer to both mental capacity and selection. In the latter sense, "attention" points to the problem of allocating cognitive resources to a specific item or event. When "attention" is used synonymously with "mental capacity," it instead refers to a limitation of cognitive resources that becomes apparent when resources have to be shared by concurrent cognitive processes. When these two factors are separately and experimentally manipulated, it appears that implicit learning occurs only when stimuli are relevant to the task and are attended to, but that implicit learning may require no or very little mental capacity.

Recent advances in researchers' understanding of implicit learning lead to our fourth conclusion:

- *Conclusion 4.* The early proposal of a smart unconscious capable of acquiring abstract knowledge in an effortless, automatic manner has been replaced recently by the assumption of one or more implicit learning mechanisms that operate mostly associatively. These mechanisms pick up statistical dependencies encountered in the environment and generate highly specific knowledge representations. It is likely that the mechanisms operate only on information that is attended to and that is relevant to the response to be made.

CONCLUSIONS

Researchers' understanding of implicit learning has come a long way. Today, many believe that implicit learning exists, and furthermore that it is based on relatively simple learning mechanisms. These mechanisms associate environmental stimuli that are attended to and that are relevant for behavior. Despite the recent advances, however, the field still suffers from a number of unresolved empirical and theoretical issues. First, there exist conflicting results regarding the role of attention in implicit learning. Second, the exact relation between learning and awareness (see Fig. 1) is very much unknown. Third, the key theoretical issue of how to define implicit learning has still not been resolved.

We strongly believe that progress on the former two (empirical) issues will be made soon and will be based on improved methodology and the joint use of computational modeling and functional brain-imaging techniques. Progress on the key theoretical issue can come, however, only from theoretical advances in understanding of the concepts of "consciousness," "awareness," and "intention." To achieve this progress might require the joint efforts of philosophers, neuroscientists, and cognitive psychologists.

Recommended Reading

Berry, D.C., & Dienes, Z. (1993). *Implicit learning: Theoretical and empirical issues.* Hove, England: Erlbaum.
Cleeremans, A. (1993). *Mechanisms of implicit learning: Connectionist models of sequence processing.* Cambridge, MA: MIT Press.
Reber, A.S. (1993). *Implicit learning and tacit knowledge: An essay on the cognitive unconscious.* New York: Oxford University Press.
Stadler, M.A., & Frensch, P.A. (Eds.). (1998). *Handbook of implicit learning.* Thousand Oaks, CA: Sage.

Note

1. Address correspondence to Peter A. Frensch, Department of Psychology, Humboldt University, Hausvogteiplatz 5-7, D-10177 Berlin, Germany; e-mail: peter.frensch@psychologie.hu-berlin.de.

Critical Thinking Questions

1. Provide a simple definition of implicit learning that captures what researchers have in mind.

2. What are some examples of skills that we have all learned to perform without knowing how we do it?

3. How do researchers determine if a subject's learning is implicit as opposed to explicit?

Language, Learning, and Color Perception

Emre Özgen

University of Surrey, Guildford, Surrey, United Kingdom

Abstract

People perceive colors categorically. But what is the role of the environment (or nurture)—specifically, language—in color perception? The effects of language on the way people categorize and perceive colors have been considered to be minimal, but recent evidence suggests that language may indeed change color perception. Speakers of languages with different color-name repertoires show differences in the way they perceive color. Research shows that categorical effects on color perception can be induced through laboratory training and suggests language can similarly change color perception through the mechanism of perceptual learning.

Keywords

color vision; linguistic relativity; categorical perception

The rainbow is a continuum of light varying smoothly between the shortest and longest wavelengths of the visible spectrum. Yet when we look at it, we do not see a continuum; rather, we see bands (or categories) of hues separated by distinct boundaries. These bands correspond to names like "red," "green," "blue," and so on, a fact that leads to the following question: How would we see the rainbow if our language did not have these particular color names? Languages differ in the parts of the color spectrum for which they have names. For example, some languages have a single name to mean both blue and green. Others can have a name for the color of dying leaves or the color of a certain shape pattern seen on cattle. If you spoke such a language, what would happen when you look at the rainbow? Would you still see a blue band, a green band, and so on? Or instead would you see bands of hues that correspond to the categories mapped out by your own language?

This fundamental question has intrigued many researchers from various disciplines studying human thought and behavior. It is primarily linked to a famous theory called the *linguistic relativity hypothesis* (Whorf, 1940/1956), which proposes that language influences and even shapes thought.

Color perception, or more specifically, color categorization, was an obvious choice for investigating the linguistic relativity hypothesis. Researchers observed that languages vary in the way they encode color space. Studying how speakers of different languages perceive and think about color could provide insight into the relationship between language and thought. Indeed, early studies showed effects of language on memory for and recognition of colors. However, a major shift of opinion came with a seminal study by Berlin and Kay (1969). These

Address correspondence to Emre Özgen, Psychology Department, University of Surrey, Guildford, Surrey, GU2 7XH, United Kingdom; e-mail: e.ozgen@surrey.ac.uk.

58

researchers observed that although languages vary in the way they encode color space with basic color terms, there are also strong similarities that suggest a universal pattern. For example, Berlin and Kay proposed that the basic color terms in a language evolve over time, and that differences in the color terminologies of different languages arise from differences in evolutionary stage; all languages eventually (evolve to) end up with the same 11 "universal" basic color terms. A theory of universal color perception emerged from this study. However, its far-reaching conclusions seemed somewhat premature as more complex evidence accumulated.

More recently, researchers began to focus on another aspect of color perception: categorical perception (CP). Figure 1 demonstrates what is meant by CP. The figure shows four colors that are separated from each other by equal intervals, distance d. Two of these colors (B1 and B2) are examples of blue. The remaining two (G2 and G1) are members of the category green. The vertical dashed line represents the category boundary. It is harder to discriminate between B1 and B2 or between G1 and G2 than between B2 and G2. In other words, people find it easier to distinguish between two colors (or find them less similar) when they are from separate categories than when both are from the same category. The *perceptual distance* (indicated by Pd in Fig. 1) is greater for the pair that crosses the boundary than for the pairs that do not.

Such a perceptual property provides a very good operationalization for the question at hand. Because color categories are created by language, if the linguistic relativity hypothesis is true, CP of color should be a function of the perceiver's language. Researchers have been studying CP of color both in the field and in the laboratory to test such predictions. In this article, I briefly review some of the findings and focus on the recent advances made in such studies.

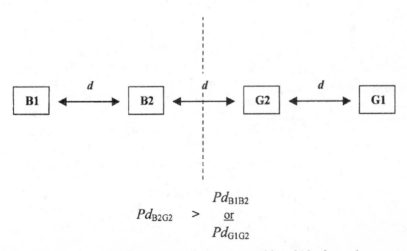

$$Pd_{B2G2} \quad > \quad \begin{array}{c} Pd_{B1B2} \\ \text{or} \\ Pd_{G1G2} \end{array}$$

Fig. 1. Diagram demonstrating categorical perception. Although the four colors are separated by equal distances, d, the perceptual distance (Pd) is greater for the pair that crosses the blue-green boundary (dashed line) than for the pairs that do not cross this boundary.

LANGUAGE EFFECTS IN PERCEPTION

Some African languages provide a good opportunity for the crosscultural study of color CP. The main feature that makes them useful in this regard is that they use a single color term to indicate a region of color space that English (as well as many other Western languages) encodes using two, or sometimes three, terms. For example, certain languages use a single term to mean both blue and green, or red and pink, or yellow and orange. In other words, there is no linguistic category boundary between these colors in these languages. The question is, do speakers of such languages lack these boundaries perceptually as well?

This question can be answered using a visual search task. Participants are shown a target color and then an array of stimuli in different colors. The task is to point to stimuli that are the same color as the target. CP effects can be studied by manipulating whether the target and distractors are from the same or different categories. In studies using this task, comparisons of English speakers with speakers of African languages that do not have a blue-green boundary reveal language effects. English speakers are faster than Africans when the target is blue and the distractors are green, or vice versa (cross-category trials for English speakers but not for Africans). However, when target and distractors are in the same category (both blue or both green), English speakers are slower than Africans. Similar effects are shown on a triad task, in which participants are shown three colors and asked to "pick the odd one out," on the basis of similarity. Although English speakers tend to pick the color that is from a different English category than the other two colors, Africans tend to show no such bias because all three colors are in the same African category.

Berlin and Kay's theory of the evolution of basic color terms has been challenged by the fact that some languages appear to have 12 such terms (1 more than Berlin and Kay's maximum number). Russian and Turkish are the strongest such candidates (Özgen & Davies, 1998). In both languages, the blue region is divided into two basic color terms, mainly on the basis of lightness. Although the best examples of the terms are quite different in Russian and Turkish, both languages encode light and dark blue colors using separate basic terms. Exploiting the difference between Turkish and English, my colleagues and I asked Turkish and English speakers to rate the similarity between pairs of colors. Compared with English speakers, Turkish speakers exaggerated the differences between colors straddling the boundary between the Turkish terms *mavi* (*"blue"*) and *lacivert* (*"dark blue"*). In a free-grouping task ("place these colors into groups on the basis of similarity"), the Turks tended to group *mavi* and *lacivert* colors separately, whereas English speakers mostly grouped these colors together. Similar effects were found in a task involving color discrimination. We also found differences in Turkish and English speakers' CP on the visual search task: Turkish speakers were faster and more accurate than English speakers in finding the target color if the target and distractors were from different Turkish categories but the same English category.

Further evidence for language effects has recently come from a study comparing speakers of English and Berinmo, a language spoken in Papua New Guinea. Berinmo has just five basic color terms (Roberson, Davies, & Davidoff,

2000). Further, these terms seem to have unusual referents, such as the color of dead leaves (what some English speakers call "khaki"). The study showed that Berinmo speakers discriminated two colors better if they were from separate Berinmo categories than if they were in the same category. However, English speakers showed no such cross-category advantage for the same stimuli, presumably because the Berinmo category boundary involved does not exist in English. Conversely, English speakers were better at discriminating colors that crossed the blue-green boundary than those that did not, whereas Berinmo speakers showed no such advantage, as would be predicted because their language does not have a blue-green boundary. However, the English speakers, and not the Berinmo speakers, showed better discrimination for colors in different English categories than for colors in the same English category.

These examples of language effects on color CP imply that perhaps the categorical nature of color perception is not innate but learned. However, research on infant color perception seems to reveal contradictory findings. Studies with 4-month-old infants reveal that after they view a color for a sufficient time to lose interest in it (i.e., to habituate), they start looking again (i.e., dishabituate) when shown a new color from a different universal category, but not when shown a new color from the same category. Thus, they seem to treat colors from the same category as being the same. These findings suggest that infants as young as 4 months perceive colors categorically even though they have not yet developed any language skills. However, preschool and school-age African children do not seem to show these "universal" CP effects on tasks like visual search or on measures of perceived similarity, whereas children who speak English (which has basic color terms for all 11 universal categories) do. It is almost as if the basic category structure (i.e., best examples and rough boundaries of colors) is there to begin with and then somehow "unlearned" among African children. Or perhaps boundary effects (or CP effects) on color discrimination are indeed learned from very early on, not just through language but also through continually perceiving common categories of colors that surround people from birth (red toy, blue dress, etc.).

Recent evidence (Roberson & Davidoff, 2000) suggests that language can have a direct effect on CP through the use of verbal labeling and rehearsal strategies. Roberson and Davidoff proposed that in a discrimination task that has memory demands, people strategically label colors with one category name or another, and keep these labels in memory. In order to discriminate between colors, people then compare the labels. It is easier to say that the colors are different if the labels do not match than if they do. However, although this may be one way in which language can influence judgments, it is restricted to the way people remember colors, not the way people "perceive" them. Is it possible that speakers of different languages actually see colors differently?

The answer to this question can be "yes" only if it is possible that real change in color perception can occur at low levels (early, fundamental stages) of visual processing. If there is no way in which color perception can be changed, then it would be impossible to argue that it varies across cultures and language communities. Is color perception plastic, or modifiable? Or is adults' color perception identical to their color perception as infants?

A well-known phenomenon called perceptual learning is widely accepted as good evidence that perception in general can indeed be modified. Perceptual learning refers to improvement in a given perceptual skill through repeated practice. For example, as a result of practice, people get better at discriminating between very slightly different line orientations, detecting tiny gaps between two offset lines (vernier acuity), and detecting very low-contrast patterns. Through practice, people can improve their performance on just about any perceptual task you can think of. Evidence suggests that this learning takes place at the earliest (most fundamental) stages of visual processing, in the brain area referred to as the primary visual cortex.

Research in neuroscience and psychophysics shows that the brain is a plastic, adaptive organ that is ever changing to meet the demands of the environment. Reorganization of neuronal connections is at its highest levels during infancy, but certainly continues throughout adulthood. Perceptual learning is one way in which the brain adapts to the demands of the environment, resulting in such physiological change. It seems unlikely that color perception is a special case—a rigid mechanism that is the same regardless of the environment.

A well-known form of perceptual learning is category learning. Participants who practice a novel perceptual categorization task repeatedly show perceptual effects of the new categories on subsequent tests. Recently, we tested whether perceptual learning in general, and category learning specifically, could modify color perception (Özgen & Davies, 2002). In one experiment, we required participants to discriminate pairs of colors within the same region (either blue or green). The two colors in a pair were displayed one after the other, separated by 500 ms. The task was to indicate whether or not the second color was identical to the first color. Our participants had to perform thousands of these judgments across several days. Their discrimination of colors improved steadily.

In our main experiment, we trained participants to categorize colors across a new category boundary, separating two kinds of hue that are referred to by the same basic term in English. After participants learned this new hue categorization correctly, we tested their discrimination skills and found that their ability to discriminate between colors improved only for colors that were on different sides of the learned category boundary. In other words, CP effects were induced through training, simulating the effects of color categories in natural language.

However, in our test of discrimination, the colors to be judged were presented separately, with a 5-s interval in between, so the task put demands on memory as well as perception. As mentioned earlier, when memory is involved, people tend to use verbal labels, and this leads to CP effects. Thus, the improved discrimination we found may have been due to a simple learned strategy rather than a newly acquired perceptual skill. To examine this issue further, in a recent experiment we tested whether participants would show CP effects in a discrimination test that required no memory involvement because the two colors were shown simultaneously. We observed the same findings; color discrimination improved across the new category boundary only.

Currently, we are investigating whether category learning leads to changes in color-difference detection thresholds (i.e., how much of a difference is necessary for the difference to be perceived). Preliminary results suggest a dramatic improvement in thresholds only for hues falling on the learned boundary. This is the strongest indication yet that color perception is changed by learning hue categories.

When people learn a new color category, they pay special attention to the boundary regions, and performance improves in these regions alone. It is as if learning has the effect of "warping" perceptual space at these locations in order to enable correct categorization. Although the experimental results I have summarized do not necessarily support the strongest form of the linguistic relativity hypothesis (that language determines thought), they do indicate that a somewhat less strong form of the hypothesis may be true: Language may affect perception. When children learn the color terms of their language, they go through a perceptual learning process that is very similar to the one experienced by the participants in our laboratory studies, except that it takes place earlier in life and lasts much longer (recall that the degree of brain plasticity is higher in infancy than in adulthood). The resulting change in perceptual space might thus manifest itself in patterns of performance on various laboratory tasks, such as the ones my colleagues and I have used in our investigations.

CONCLUSIONS AND ISSUES

The demonstration that color perception can be modified through learning indicates that the process of learning a language may influence or even shape the way people perceive colors. However, observed differences between speakers of different languages when they perform various cognitive tasks such as similarity judgments and even visual search do not provide sufficient evidence that this is actually what happens. As mentioned earlier, these differences might be attributable to differences in verbal labeling as opposed to pure perception. Therefore, it is necessary to carry out studies focusing on low-level perception of color by speakers of different languages. For example, the color-difference detection thresholds of speakers of languages with different color-term repertoires could be compared. Any observed differences in thresholds for an area that is around a linguistic boundary in one language but not the other would most likely reflect differences in low-level perceptual sensitivities. Such investigations are currently under way in our laboratory. Demonstrating such low-level differences between speakers of different languages using this or similar methods would be compelling evidence for the strong form of the linguistic relativity hypothesis.

Another issue that needs to be resolved concerns infants' color perception. As mentioned, after habituating to a color, 4-month-old infants seem to prefer looking at a color from a different universal category over looking at another color from the habituated category. This suggests that the universal categories may be "hardwired." However, on some tasks, school-age African children show evidence that their own language influences their perception of a color (a linguistic relativity effect). The most compelling way of resolving these apparently conflicting findings might be to use direct measures of perceptual sensitivity (such as color-difference detection thresholds), adapted for preschool children or even infants. Infant studies of color perception have mainly used "preferential looking" (i.e., amount of time spent looking at one stimulus compared with another) as a measure. However, it is difficult to know exactly what perceptual ability this measure taps into; it is conceivable that infants are able to discriminate between many colors but "prefer" to look at certain stimuli rather than others for a reason that is not related to perceptual sensitivity. A measure suitable for assessing infants' ability to discriminate colors would be likely to provide crucial insight into the origin of color CP.

It is remarkable to think that even the most fundamental perceptual mechanisms, such as those involved in the perception of colors, can be influenced by the environment, including culture and language. The evidence reviewed here suggests just such an influence. So, to go back to my initial example, it is just possible that what you see when you look at the rainbow actually depends on the language you speak.

Recommended Reading

Fahle, M., & Poggio, T. (Eds.). (2002). *Perceptual learning.* London: MIT Press.
Hardin, C.L., & Maffi, L. (Eds.). (1997). *Color categories in thought and language.* New York: Cambridge University Press.
Kaiser, P.K., & Boynton, R.M. (Eds.). (1996). *Human color vision.* Washington, DC: Optical Society of America.

References

Berlin, B., & Kay, P. (1969). *Basic color terms: Their universality and evolution.* Berkeley: University of California Press.
Özgen, E., & Davies, I.R.L. (1998). Turkish color terms: Tests of Berlin and Kay's theory of color universals and linguistic relativity. *Linguistics, 36,* 919–956.
Özgen, E., & Davies, I.R.L. (2002). Acquisition of categorical color perception: A perceptual learning approach to the linguistic relativity hypothesis. *Journal of Experimental Psychology: General, 131,* 477–493.
Roberson, D., & Davidoff, J. (2000). The categorical perception of colours and facial expressions: The effect of verbal interference. *Memory & Cognition, 28,* 977–986.
Roberson, D., Davies, I., & Davidoff, J. (2000). Color categories are not universal: Replications and new evidence in favor of linguistic relativity. *Journal of Experimental Psychology: General, 129,* 369–398.
Whorf, B.L. (1956). *Language, thought and reality.* Cambridge, MA: MIT Press. (Original work published 1940)

Critical Thinking Questions

1. What is the linguistic relativity hypothesis, and why does color perception offer a means of testing this hypothesis?

2. Why does the author refer to color perception as a process of categorization?

3. What evidence supports or fails to support the idea that there are eleven basic and universal color terms?

4. What does the research on the role of language suggest about whether color categorization is innate or learned?

Tricks of Memory

Henry L. Roediger, III,[1] and Kathleen B. McDermott
Department of Psychology, Washington University, St. Louis, Missouri

Abstract

Remembering an episode from even the recent past may involve a blend of fiction and fact. We discuss a straightforward laboratory paradigm that is proving useful in the study of false memories of simple episodes. In this paradigm, subjects study lists of 15 related words *(bed, rest, awake . . .)* that are all related to a critical word that is not presented *(sleep)*. Later, subjects recall and recognize the critical missing word with about the same probability that they remember words from the list. This memory illusion is resistant to people's attempts to avoid it. We argue that similar memory errors are commonplace and are a natural outcome of an intelligent cognitive system, which makes inferences about incoming information. Therefore, memory illusions, like perceptual illusions, are a consequence of normal human information processing and offer a window for examining basic cognitive processes.

Keywords

memory; false memory; memory illusions; illusions; associative errors

There are two fundamental errors of remembering: forgetting events that occurred previously and remembering those that did not occur (or remembering them differently from the way in which they occurred). The first error, forgetting, hardly needs documentation; the experience is embarrassingly familiar to everyone. The other major class of memory errors, errors of commission, strikes most people as a curious one: How could a memory that seems vivid and clear be anything but accurate?

This article focuses on these tricks of memory. Sources of error can arise at several stages in the encoding-storage-retrieval sequence. People can perceive (and therefore encode) events differently from the way they occur; stored memories can be influenced by intervening events; and conditions during the retrieval stage can lead to reports that bear little relation to the original occurrences.

We believe that distortions of memory provide a fertile ground for studying interesting and important psychological phenomena. The experimental techniques used to induce illusory memories have typically involved the presentation of complex material (e.g., prose or videotapes), the introduction of misleading information between the time when the material is first presented (the study phase) and the time when memory is tested (the test phase), and the use of long delays between study and test (see Roediger, 1996). The work described here provides a new procedure for inducing illusory memories. This procedure differs from typical ones used in false memory research in that it uses a standard list-learning paradigm, no misleading information, immediate testing, and warnings to subjects to be cautious and accurate. Despite these features, the illusory memories obtained are among the strongest ever reported in the literature on human memory.

AN ASSOCIATIVE MEMORY ILLUSION

In our first studies (Roediger & McDermott, 1995), we created illusory memories by adapting a procedure used by Deese (1959) for other purposes. In our typical experiment, subjects hear lists of 15 words presented at the rate of 1 word every 1.5 s. Each list consists of a set of words associated to a single word that is not itself presented. For example, subjects may hear *bed, rest, awake, tired, dream, wake, snooze, blanket, doze, slumber, snore, nap, peace, yawn,* and *drowsy;* immediately afterward, they are asked to recall the list. The subjects are instructed not to guess—to be certain that they recall only items that were actually on the list. In this example, the list words are all associates of *sleep,* which does not appear on the list. The results from one experiment (averaged over 24 such associative lists) are shown in Figure 1. The graph shows strong primacy and recency effects, or high probabilities of recall of words from the beginning and the end of the lists. However, the most striking finding is represented by the dashed line, which indicates the level of recall for the critical nonpresented words (e.g., *sleep*) from which the lists were derived. The probability of recall of these missing words was somewhat greater than the probability of recall of words that actually had been presented in the middle of the lists!

After subjects had studied and recalled numerous lists, they were given a recognition test in which studied items were mixed with two types of nonstudied words (often called lures or distractors): the critical items (e.g., *sleep*) and unrelated distractors (e.g., *spider*). Subjects classified each word as *old* (studied) or *new* (nonstudied). If they classified a test word as old, they made a further judgment: whether they remembered or just knew the item had been studied (Tulving, 1985). That is, if they could recollect something specific about the moment of occurrence of the word during list presentation, they were to assign

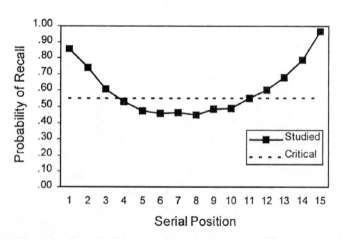

Fig. 1. Example of results from an experiment testing recall of semantically associated words presented in lists. The probability of accurate recall is graphed as a function of serial position in the list (solid line). The dashed line shows the probability that a non-presented word associated with the list words was falsely recalled (from Roediger & McDermott, 1995, Experiment 2).

a *remember* judgment to the test word. If they knew the word had been in the list but could not recollect its exact moment of occurrence, they were to assign a *know* judgment.

Results for the three types of items (studied, unrelated nonstudied, and critical nonstudied) are shown in Figure 2. Examining the two left-most bars reveals no surprises: About 80% of the studied words were recognized, and most of these words were deemed to be remembered (the shaded part of the bar) rather than known (the white part). For unrelated lures, the false alarm rate (i.e., the frequency of recognizing them even though they were not presented) was low, and most of these falsely recognized words were deemed to be known, not remembered. This latter result makes intuitive sense in that there was no original event to be remembered. The right-most bar shows recognition of critical items like *sleep*; the false alarm rate for these words approximated the hit rate (i.e., rate of correct recognition) for studied items (i.e., about .80). In addition, subjects claimed to remember (i.e., to vividly recollect) the presentation of these words as frequently as they did items that had been studied! This procedure demonstrates robust false remembering because subjects are saying not simply that a critical word seems familiar, but that they actually remember some specific aspect about the moment of its occurrence.

MANIPULATING THE FALSE MEMORY EFFECT

How robust is the illusion? If subjects are informed about the effect, can they prevent its occurrence? The instructions we used in the original experiments, widely adopted by other researchers, caution subjects to be accurate. However,

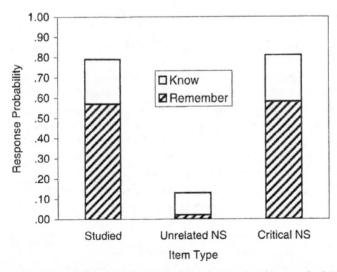

Fig. 2. Recognition performance for studied words, unrelated nonstudied (NS) words, and critical nonstudied (NS) words (from Roediger & McDermott, 1995, Experiment 2). Subjects indicated whether they remembered studying or simply "knew" they had studied each item they classified as "old."

we and other researchers have subsequently gone further and fully informed subjects as to the nature of the false memory phenomenon, even giving a sample trial. In a recent study (McDermott & Roediger, 1998), we gave such instructions and then tested recognition when the critical items (like *sleep*) were sometimes present in the list and sometimes not. Subjects who were informed about the nature of the false memory phenomenon and instructed to attempt to avoid it did reduce both their hit rates and their false alarm rates (i.e., they became generally more cautious). However, the decrease in the false alarm rate was somewhat greater than the decrease in the hit rate, which indicates that subjects (to some extent) can selectively attenuate the effect. Nonetheless, informing subjects about the nature of the effect and asking them to avoid false recognition does not come close to eliminating the effect.

Another technique that might be expected to reduce the false memory effect is simply to make memory for the list items very accurate by some experimental manipulation. One might imagine the effect would then decrease, because it seems reasonable to assume that more accurate recall of events would decrease errors. However, some reflection (and some theories) can also lead to the opposite prediction: If the processes involved in list recall are the same as those that cause false recall, then increasing list recall should make it more likely that the critical lure will be activated and recalled.

There is no simple answer to the question of how accurate and illusory memories are related: Both positive and negative correlations between veridical and false recall or recognition have been reported—even in the same experiment. For example, in McDermott's (1996) Experiment 2, one variable increased both veridical and false recall, whereas another variable increased veridical recall and decreased false recall. Clearly, the relations between veridical and false recall (and veridical and false recognition) are complex and represent a crucial puzzle for theories of the false memory phenomenon.

INDIVIDUAL DIFFERENCES

Another interesting arena of research concerns individual differences among people in susceptibility to the false memory effect. Balota et al. (1999) tested patients diagnosed with early stages of Alzheimer's disease, which has a pernicious effect on remembering. These subjects were compared with healthy older and younger adults in a simplified version of the paradigm. As shown in the white bars in Figure 3, older adults recalled fewer list items than did younger adults, and Alzheimer's patients recalled fewer still. Of course, this outcome is not a surprise because it is well known that free recall is worse in older adults than younger adults and that Alzheimer's disease has a profound negative effect on memory for episodes. The interesting pattern in the figure is in the probability of false recall of critical items, shown in the shaded bars. Despite the older adults' and Alzheimer's patients' sharp decrease in accurate recall relative to younger adults, false recall of critical items was approximately equivalent across subject groups. Older adults and Alzheimer's patients actually showed a slight increase in false recall, and other researchers have also reported an increased tendency to false recall for older adults relative to young adults.

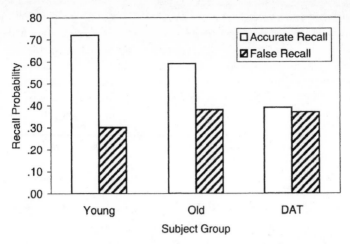

Fig. 3. Probability of veridical and false recall for young and old subjects and patients with Alzheimer's disease (Dementia of the Alzheimer Type, or DAT; from Balota et al., 1999).

Other studies reveal interesting patterns involving other individual difference variables. For example, Winograd, Peluso, and Glover (1998) showed that self-reports of high degrees of dissociative experiences, hypnotizability, and vivid mental imagery correlated with enhanced false recall and false recognition. In addition, women who believed they had recovered once-repressed memories of abuse were reported to exhibit greater false recognition than control subjects (Clancy, Schacter, McNally, & Pitman, 2000). In sum, there is growing evidence that the tendency to exhibit false memories varies as a function of individual differences.

ACTIVATION-MONITORING THEORY

Probably the most widely endorsed theory of this associative memory illusion is some version of an activation-monitoring account, which was discussed in our original report (Roediger & McDermott, 1995). While subjects listen to a list, the critical nonpresented item may be mentally activated, coming to mind either consciously (with the person thinking *sleep*) or unconsciously (a representation of *sleep* may be activated without coming consciously to mind). In some sense, the 15 list items prime the concept of sleep (Roediger, Balota, & Watson, in press). If the critical item is repeatedly aroused during study, then at retrieval subjects are faced with a classic reality-monitoring problem (Johnson & Raye, 1981): "Did I hear *sleep*, or does it seem familiar for some other reason?" According to this activation-monitoring framework, processes for both encoding and monitoring retrieval must be specified to explain the illusion.

There is considerable evidence for the applicability of activation theories in understanding this associative illusion, although other perspectives are also quite promising (e.g., Reyna & Brainerd, 1995). For example, McDermott (1997) showed that presentation of the associative lists used in our previous work creates priming on perceptual implicit memory tests. That is, when asked to complete word stems (e.g., "sle-") or word fragments (e.g., "s l _ _ p") with the first word that came to mind, subjects responded with "sleep" more often if they had seen the list related to this word (i.e., *bed, rest, awake*, etc., but not the word *sleep* itself) than if this list had not been presented. Because verbal perceptual implicit memory tests show priming only following lexical activation of words, these results suggest that the false memory phenomenon is partly due to conscious activation of the critical words during list presentation. Such conscious activation would also explain the very high levels of *remember* responses to the critical lures on recognition tests: Subjects remember the experience of hearing a critical word because the concept consciously came to mind during list presentation.

The importance of retrieval factors has been highlighted by other reports. For example, Israel and Schacter (1997) showed that if studied items are made distinctive, then retrieved words that bear no specific marks of distinction may be rejected as lures. They presented some lists of words auditorily, as in the standard paradigm, but in other lists they showed a picture when each word was heard (e.g., a picture of a bed as people heard the word "bed"). They found that false recall was reduced in the latter condition, presumably because during recall subjects could reject items such as *sleep* as having occurred on the list if they could not remember a picture having been presented at the same time. In short, a growing body of evidence is consistent with an account drawing upon both activation and monitoring processes.

IMPLICATIONS

Our paradigm for studying false memories has been faulted by some researchers as being artificial and unlike conditions in which false memories are likely to arise in the outside world. However, in our opinion, this paradigm captures one prevalent source of false memories that arise routinely. Whenever people engage in conversation, listen to a talk, read a newspaper article, or watch a television program, they recode events from the outside world as they try to understand them. By "recode," we mean that people interpret events and make inferences about them on the basis of their past experience. Part and parcel of the recoding process is activation of a person's own knowledge structures, or schemata (Bartlett, 1932). The information may spark related thoughts, and these thoughts may later be remembered as having been made as explicit statements. Our paradigm provides a tractable laboratory situation for studying the cognitive processes creating these sorts of false memories. Memories are not recordings but rather recodings; that is, they are not audio or video recordings but a recoded blend of events from the external world, as interpreted by each person's unique schemata.

CONCLUSION

Does the fact that false memories can be easily created mean that humans are irrational, or have disturbingly poor memories? We think not. Although memories are prone to errors in predictable ways, these can be viewed as intelligent errors, or errors made by an intelligent cognitive system. Part of what makes humans clever is the ability to make inferences. People make inferences routinely in comprehending their surroundings, and these inferences are a critically important feature of human cognition. The fact that such inferences can lead one astray, and that people can recollect vividly events that they only inferred, is a small price to pay for the inventiveness and adaptiveness of the human mind.

Recommended Reading

McDermott, K.B. (1996). (See References)

Payne, D.G., Elie, C.J., Blackwell, J.M., & Neuschatz, J.S. (1996). Memory illusions: Recalling, recognizing, and recollecting events that never occurred. *Journal of Memory and Language, 35*, 261–285.

Roediger, H.L., & McDermott, K.B. (2000). Distortions of memory. In F.I.M. Craik & E. Tulving (Eds.), *The Oxford handbook of memory* (pp. 149–162). Oxford, England: Oxford University Press.

Roediger, H.L., McDermott, K.B., & Robinson, K.J. (1998). The role of associative processes in producing false remembering. In M. Conway, S. Gathercole, & C. Cornoldi (Eds.), *Theories of memory II* (pp. 187–245). Hove, England: Psychology Press.

Schacter, D.L. (1995). Memory distortion: History and current status. In D.L. Schacter (Ed.), *Memory distortion* (pp. 1–43). Cambridge, MA: Harvard University Press.

Note

1. Address correspondence to Henry L. Roediger, III, Department of Psychology, Campus Box 1125, Washington University, One Brookings Dr., St. Louis, MO 63130-4899; e-mail: roediger@artsci.wustl.edu.

References

Balota, D.A., Cortese, M.J., Duchek, J.M., Adams, D., Roediger, H.L., McDermott, K.B., & Yerys, B.E. (1999). Veridical and false memories in healthy older adults and in dementia of the Alzheimer's type. *Cognitive Neuropsychology, 16*, 361–384.

Bartlett, F.C. (1932). *Remembering: A study in experimental and social psychology.* Cambridge, England: University Press.

Clancy, S.A., Schacter, D.L., McNally, R.J., & Pitman, R.K. (2000). False recognition in women reporting recovered memories of sexual abuse. *Psychological Science, 11*, 26–31.

Deese, J. (1959). On the prediction of occurrence of particular verbal intrusions in immediate recall. *Journal of Experimental Psychology, 58*, 17–22.

Israel, L., & Schacter, D.L. (1997). Pictorial encoding reduces false recognition of semantic associates. *Psychonomic Bulletin & Review, 4*, 577–581.

Johnson, M.K., & Raye, C.L. (1981). Reality monitoring. *Psychological Review, 88*, 67–85.

McDermott, K.B. (1996). The persistence of false memories in list recall. *Journal of Memory and Language, 35*, 212–230.

McDermott, K.B. (1997). Priming on perceptual implicit memory tests can be achieved through presentation of associates. *Psychonomic Bulletin & Review, 4*, 582–586.

McDermott, K.B., & Roediger, H.L. (1998). Attempting to avoid illusory memories: Robust false recognition of associates persists under conditions of explicit warnings and immediate testing. *Journal of Memory and Language, 39*, 508–520.

Reyna, V.F., & Brainerd, C.J. (1995). Fuzzy trace theory: An interim synthesis. *Learning and Individual Differences, 7*, 1–75.

Roediger, H.L. (1996). Memory illusions. *Journal of Memory and Language, 35*, 76–100.

Roediger, H.L., Balota, D.A., & Watson, J.M. (in press). Priming and the arousal of false memories. In H.L. Roediger, J.S. Nairne, I. Neath, & A.M. Surprenant (Eds.), *The nature of remembering: Essays in honor of Robert G. Crowder.* Washington, DC: American Psychological Association.

Roediger, H.L., & McDermott, K.B. (1995). Creating false memories: Remembering words not presented in lists. *Journal of Experimental Psychology: Learning, Memory, and Cognition, 21,* 803–814.

Tulving, E. (1985). Memory and consciousness. *Canadian Psychologist, 26,* 1–12.

Winograd, E., Peluso, J.P., & Glover, T.A. (1998). Individual differences in susceptibility to memory illusions. *Applied Cognitive Psychology, 12,* S5–S27.

Critical Thinking Questions

1. What are the two fundamental types of errors in remembering?

2. Describe the word list procedure that researchers have used to create illusory memories.

3. How robust is the false memory effect? What evidence is there that some individuals are more susceptible to it than others?

4. What is the activation-monitoring theory of the false memory effect, and what evidence is there to support it?

The Confidence of Eyewitnesses in Their Identifications From Lineups

Gary L. Wells,[1] Elizabeth A. Olson,
and Steve D. Charman
Psychology Department, Iowa State University, Ames, Iowa

Abstract

The confidence that eyewitnesses express in their lineup identifications of criminal suspects has a large impact on criminal proceedings. Many convictions of innocent people can be attributed in large part to confident but mistaken eyewitnesses. Although reasonable correlations between confidence and accuracy can be obtained under certain conditions, confidence is governed by some factors that are unrelated to accuracy. An understanding of these confidence factors helps establish the conditions under which confidence and accuracy are related and leads to important practical recommendations for criminal justice proceedings.

Keywords

eyewitness testimony; lineups; eyewitness memory

Mistaken identification by eyewitnesses was the primary evidence used to convict innocent people whose convictions were later overturned by forensic DNA tests (Scheck, Neufeld, & Dwyer, 2000; Wells et al., 1998). The eyewitnesses in these cases were very persuasive because on the witness stand they expressed extremely high confidence that they had identified the actual perpetrator. Long before DNA exoneration cases began unfolding in the 1990s, however, eyewitness researchers in psychology were finding that confidence is not a reliable indicator of accuracy and warning the justice system that heavy reliance on eyewitness's confidence in their identifications might lead to the conviction of innocent people.

Studies have consistently demonstrated that the confidence an eyewitness expresses in an identification is the major factor determining whether people will believe that the eyewitness made an accurate identification. The confidence an eyewitness expresses is also enshrined in the criteria that the U.S. Supreme Court used 30 years ago (and that now guide lower courts) for deciding the accuracy of an eyewitness's identification in a landmark case. Traditionally, much of the experimental work examining the relation between confidence and accuracy in eyewitness identification tended to frame the question as "What is the correlation between confidence and accuracy?" as though there were some single, true correlation value. Today, eyewitness researchers regard the confidence-accuracy relation as something that varies across circumstances. Some of these circumstances are outside the control of the criminal justice system, but some are determined by the procedures that criminal justice personnel control.

A GENERAL FRAMEWORK FOR CONFIDENCE-ACCURACY RELATIONS

It has been fruitful to think about eyewitness accuracy and eyewitness confidence as variables that are influenced by numerous factors, some of which are the same and some of which are different. We expect confidence and accuracy to be more closely related when the variables that are influencing accuracy are also influencing confidence than when the variables influencing accuracy are different from those influencing confidence. Consider, for instance, the variable of exposure duration (i.e., how long the eyewitness viewed the culprit while the crime was committed). An eyewitness who viewed the culprit for a long time during the crime should be more accurate than one who had only a brief view. Furthermore, the longer view could be a foundation for the eyewitness to feel more confident in the identification, either because the witness has a more vivid and fluent memory from the longer duration or because the witness infers his or her accuracy from the long exposure duration. Hence, the correlation between confidence and accuracy should be higher the more variation there is in the exposure duration across witnesses (Read, Vokey, & Hammersley, 1990). Suppose, however, that some eyewitnesses were reinforced after their identification decision (e.g., "Good job. You are a good witness."), whereas others were given no such reinforcement. Such postidentification reinforcement does nothing to make witnesses more accurate, but dramatically inflates their confidence (Wells & Bradfield, 1999).

Eyewitness confidence can be construed simply as the eyewitness's belief, which varies in degree, about whether the identification was accurate or not. This belief can have various sources, both internal and external, that need not be related to accuracy. Shaw and his colleagues, for example, have shown that repeated questioning of eyewitnesses about mistaken memories does not make the memories more accurate but does inflate the eyewitnesses' confidence in those memories (Shaw, 1996; Shaw & McLure, 1996). Although the precise mechanisms for the repeated-questioning effect are not clear (e.g., increased commitment to the mistaken memory vs. increased fluidity of the response), these results illustrate a dissociation between variables affecting confidence and variables affecting accuracy.

It is useful to think about broad classes of variables that could be expected to drive confidence and not accuracy, or to drive accuracy and not confidence, or to drive both variables. It is even possible to think about variables that could decrease accuracy while increasing confidence. Consider, for instance, coincidental resemblance. Mistaken identifications from lineups occur primarily when the actual culprit is not in the lineup. Suppose there are two such lineups, one in which the innocent suspect does not highly resemble the real culprit and a second in which the innocent suspect is a near clone (coincidental resemblance) of the real culprit. The second lineup will result not only in an increased rate of mistaken identification compared with the first lineup, but also in higher confidence in that mistake. In this case, a variable that decreases accuracy (resemblance of an innocent suspect to the actual culprit) serves to increase confidence.

THE CORRELATION, CALIBRATION, AND INFLATION OF CONFIDENCE

Although many individual studies have reported little or no relation between eye-witnesses' confidence in their identifications and the accuracy of their identifications, an analysis that statistically combined individual studies indicates that the confidence-accuracy correlation might be as high as +.40 when the analysis is restricted to individuals who make an identification (vs. all witnesses; see Sporer, Penrod, Read, & Cutler, 1995). How useful is this correlation for predicting accuracy from confidence? In some ways, a correlation of .40 could be considered strong. For instance, when overall accuracy is 50%, a .40 correlation would translate into 70% of the witnesses with high confidence being accurate and only 30% of the witnesses with low confidence being accurate. As accuracy deviates from 50%, however, differences in accuracy rates between witnesses with high and low confidence will diminish even though the correlation remains .40.

Another way to think about a .40 correlation is to compare it with something that people experience in daily life, namely the correlation between a person's height and a person's gender. Extrapolating from males' and females' average height and standard deviation (69.1, 63.7, and 5.4 in., respectively; Department of Health and Human Services, n.d.) yields a correlation between height and gender of +.43. Notice that the correlation between height and gender is quite similar to the correlation between eyewitnesses' identification confidence and accuracy. Thus, if eyewitnesses' identifications are accurate 50% of the time, we would expect to encounter a highly confident mistaken eyewitness (or a nonconfident accurate eyewitness) about as often as we would encounter a tall female (or a short male).

Although the eyewitness-identification literature has generally used correlation methods to express the statistical association between confidence and accuracy, it is probably more forensically valid to use calibration and overconfidence/underconfidence measures rather than correlations (Brewer, Keast, & Rishworth, 2002; Juslin, Olson, & Winman, 1996). In effect, the correlation method (specifically, point-biserial correlation) expresses the degree of statistical association by calculating the difference in confidence (expressed in terms of the standard deviation) between accurate and inaccurate witnesses. Calibration, on the other hand, assesses the extent to which an eyewitness's confidence, expressed as a percentage, matches the probability that the eyewitness is correct. Overconfidence reflects the extent to which the percentage confidence exceeds the probability that the eyewitness is correct (e.g., 80% confidence and 60% probability correct), and underconfidence reflects the extent to which the percentage confidence underestimates the probability that the eyewitness is correct (e.g., 40% confidence and 60% probability correct). Juslin et al. pointed out that the confidence-accuracy correlation can be quite low even when calibration is high.

Work by Juslin et al. (1996) indicates that eyewitnesses can be well calibrated at times, but recent experiments (Wells & Bradfield, 1999) illustrate a problem that can arise when trying to use percentage confidence expressed by witnesses to infer the probability that their identifications are accurate. In a series of experiments, eyewitnesses were induced to make mistaken identifications from lineups in which the culprit was absent and were then randomly assigned to receive confirming "feedback" telling them that they identified the actual suspect or to receive no feedback at all. Later, these witnesses were asked how certain they were at the time of their identification (i.e., how certain they were before the feedback). Those who did not receive confirming feedback gave average confidence ratings of less than 50%, but those receiving confirming feedback gave average confidence ratings of over 70%. Because all of these eyewitnesses had made mistaken identifications, even the no-feedback witnesses were overconfident, but the confirming-feedback witnesses were especially overconfident. Confidence inflation is a difficult problem in actual criminal cases because eyewitnesses are commonly given feedback about whether their identification decisions agree with the investigator's theory of the case. In these cases, it is the detective, rather than the eyewitness, who determines the confidence of the eyewitness.

Confirming feedback not only inflates confidence, thereby inducing overconfidence, but also harms the confidence-accuracy correlation. When eyewitnesses are given confirming feedback following their identification decisions, the confidence of inaccurate eyewitnesses is inflated more than is the confidence of accurate eyewitnesses, and the net result is a reduction in the confidence-accuracy correlation (Bradfield, Wells, & Olson, 2002). Hence, although the confidence of an eyewitness can have utility if it is assessed independently of external influences (e.g., comments from the detective, learning about what other eyewitnesses have said), the legal system rarely assesses confidence in this way.

IMPACT ON POLICIES AND PRACTICES

What impact has research on the confidence-accuracy problem had on the legal system? Until relatively recently, the impact has been almost nil. However, when DNA exoneration cases began unfolding in the mid-1990s, U.S. Attorney General Janet Reno initiated a study of the causes of these miscarriages of justice. More than three fourths of these convictions of innocent persons involved mistaken eyewitness identifications, and, in every case, the mistaken eyewitnesses were extremely confident and, therefore, persuasive at trial (Wells et al., 1998). A Department of Justice panel used the psychological literature to issue the first set of national guidelines on collecting eyewitness identification evidence (Technical Working Group for Eyewitness Evidence, 1999). One of the major recommendations was that the confidence of the eyewitness be assessed at the time of the identification, before there is any chance for it to be influenced by external factors.

The state of New Jersey has gone even further in adopting the recommendations of eyewitness researchers. Based on findings from the psychological literature, guidelines from the attorney general of New Jersey now call for double-blind testing with lineups. Double-blind lineup testing means that the person who administers the lineup does not know which person in the lineup is the suspect and which ones are merely fillers. Under the New Jersey procedures, the confidence expressed by the eyewitness will be based primarily on the eyewitness's memory, not on the expectations of or feedback from the lineup administrator.

There is growing evidence that the legal system is now beginning to read and use the psychological literature on eyewitnesses to formulate policies and procedures. The 2002 report of Illinois Governor George Ryan's Commission on Capital Punishment is the latest example of this new reliance on the psychological literature. The commission specifically cited the literature on the problem with confidence inflation and recommended double-blind testing and explicit recording of confidence statements at the time of the identification to prevent or detect confidence inflation (Illinois Commission on Capital Punishment, 2002).

NEW DIRECTIONS

Although the psychological literature on eyewitness identification has done much to clarify the confidence-accuracy issue and specify some conditions under which confidence might be predictive of accuracy, research has started to turn to other indicators that might prove even more predictive of accuracy. One of the most promising examples is the relation between the amount of time an eyewitness takes to make an identification and the accuracy of the identification. Eyewitnesses who make their identification decision quickly (in 10 s or less) are considerably more likely to be accurate than are eyewitnesses who take longer (e.g., Dunning & Perretta, in press). Confidence is a self-report that is subject to distortion (e.g., from postidentification feedback), whereas decision time is a behavior that can be directly observed. Hence, decision time might prove more reliable than confidence as an indicator of eyewitness accuracy. Yet another new direction in eyewitness identification research concerns cases in which there are multiple eyewitnesses. Recent analyses show that the behaviors of eyewitnesses who do not identify the suspect from a lineup can be used to assess the likely accuracy of the eyewitnesses who do identify the suspect from a lineup (Wells & Olson, in press). The future of eyewitness identification research is a bright one, and the legal system now seems to be paying attention.

Recommended Reading

Cutler, B.L., & Penrod, S.D. (1995). *Mistaken identification: The eyewitness, psychology, and the law.* New York: Cambridge University Press.
Scheck, B., Neufeld, P., & Dwyer, J. (2000). (See References)
Wells, G.L., Malpass, R.S., Lindsay, R.C.L., Fisher, R.P., Turtle, J.W., & Fulero, S. (2000). From the lab to the police station: A successful application of eyewitness research. *American Psychologist, 55,* 581–598.

Note

1. Address correspondence to Gary L. Wells, Psychology Department, Iowa State University, Ames, IA 50011; e-mail: glwells@iastate.edu.

References

Bradfield, S.L., Wells, G.L., & Olson, E.A. (2002). The damaging effect of confirming feedback on the relation between eyewitness certainty and identification accuracy. *Journal of Applied Psychology, 87,* 112–120.

Brewer, N., Keast, A., & Rishworth, A. (2002). Improving the confidence-accuracy relation in eyewitness identification: Evidence from correlation and calibration. *Journal of Experimental Psychology: Applied, 8*, 44–56.

Department of Health and Human Services, National Center for Health Statistics. (n.d.). *National Health and Nutrition Examination Survey*. Retrieved May 22, 2002, from http://www.cdc.gov/ nchs/about/major/nhanes/datatblelink.htm#unpubtab

Dunning, D., & Perretta, S. (in press). Automaticity and eyewitness accuracy: A 10 - to - 12 second rule for distinguishing accurate from inaccurate positive identifications. *Journal of Applied Psychology*.

Illinois Commission on Capital Punishment. (2002, April). *Report of the Governor's Commission on Capital Punishment*. Retrieved April 23, 2002, from http://www.idoc.state.il.us/ccp/ccp/ reports/commission_report/

Juslin, P., Olson, N., & Winman, A. (1996). Calibration and diagnosticity of confidence in eyewitness identification: Comments on what can and cannot be inferred from a low confidence-accuracy correlation. *Journal of Experimental Psychology: Learning, Memory, and Cognition, 5*, 1304–1316.

Read, J.D., Vokey, J.R., & Hammersley, R. (1990). Changing photos of faces: Effects of exposure duration and photo similarity on recognition and the accuracy-confidence relationship. *Journal of Experimental Psychology: Learning, Memory, and Cognition, 16*, 870–882.

Scheck, B., Neufeld, P., & Dwyer, J. (2000). *Actual innocence*. New York: Random House.

Shaw, J.S., III. (1996). Increases in eyewitness confidence resulting from postevent questioning. *Journal of Experimental Psychology: Applied, 2*, 126–146.

Shaw, J.S., III, & McClure, K.A. (1996). Repeated postevent questioning can lead to elevated levels of eyewitness confidence. *Law and Human Behavior, 20*, 629–654.

Sporer, S., Penrod, S., Read, D., & Cutler, B.L. (1995). Choosing, confidence, and accuracy: A meta-analysis of the confidence-accuracy relation in eyewitness identification studies. *Psychological Bulletin, 118*, 315–327.

Technical Working Group for Eyewitness Evidence. (1999). *Eyewitness evidence: A guide for law enforcement*. Washington, DC: U.S. Department of Justice, Office of Justice Programs.

Wells, G.L., & Bradfield, A.L. (1999). Distortions in eyewitnesses' recollections: Can the postidentification-feedback effect be moderated? *Psychological Science, 10*, 138–144.

Wells, G.L., & Olson, E.A. (in press). Eyewitness identification: Information gain from incriminating and exonerating behaviors. *Journal of Experimental Psychology: Applied*.

Wells, G.L., Small, M., Penrod, S., Malpass, R.S., Fulero, S.M., & Brimacombe, C.A.E. (1998). Eyewitness identification procedures: Recommendations for lineups and photospreads. *Law and Human Behavior, 22*, 603–647.

Critical Thinking Questions

1. Why is an eyewitness's confidence an important variable?

2. What is the correlation between eyewitness accuracy and confidence? Is it more or less than you would have anticipated?

3. What do the authors mean when they say that sometimes the detective rather than the eyewitness determines the eyewitness's level of confidence?

Human Motivation and Emotion

While cognitive psychologists portray human beings as computerlike processors of information, other researchers study the ways in which we passionate, warm-blooded creatures are driven by various motives (such as the need for food, sleep, sex, affiliation, achievement, and self-esteem) and emotions (such as joy, sadness, fear, anger, surprise, and disgust).

In the opening article of this section, Arne Öhman and Susan Mineka (2003) speculate on the evolutionary origins of an intense fear of snakes that is prevalent and readily learned among humans and other primates. Martin Covington (2000) describes the distinction between intrinsic and extrinsic motivation and reviews research on the question of whether or when grades and other tangible inducements undermine the love of learning in school children. Addressing different aspects of human sexual motivation, Letitia Anne Peplau (2003) describes pervasive gender differences in sexuality—ways in which men and women differ regardless of whether they are straight or gay. Moving from motivation in the bedroom to the workplace, Christina Maslach (2003) reviews recent research on "job burnout," a social problem that plagues teachers, nurses, and others who work in human services. Focusing on unconscious emotion, Piotr Winkielman and Kent Berridge (2004) describe how positive and negative emotional states can be triggered in us by subliminal stimuli, and can even influence our preferences and actions, without awareness.

The Malicious Serpent: Snakes as a Prototypical Stimulus for an Evolved Module of Fear

Arne Öhman[1] and Susan Mineka
Department of Clinical Neuroscience, Karolinska Institute,
Stockholm, Sweden (A.Ö.), and Department of Psychology,
Northwestern University, Evanston, Illinois (S.M.)

Abstract

As reptiles, snakes may have signified deadly threats in the environment of early mammals. We review findings suggesting that snakes remain special stimuli for humans. Intense snake fear is prevalent in both humans and other primates. Humans and monkeys learn snake fear more easily than fear of most other stimuli through direct or vicarious conditioning. Neither the elicitation nor the conditioning of snake fear in humans requires that snakes be consciously perceived; rather, both processes can occur with masked stimuli. Humans tend to perceive illusory correlations between snakes and aversive stimuli, and their attention is automatically captured by snakes in complex visual displays. Together, these and other findings delineate an evolved fear module in the brain. This module is selectively and automatically activated by once-threatening stimuli, is relatively encapsulated from cognition, and derives from specialized neural circuitry.

Keywords

evolution; snake fear; fear module

Snakes are commonly regarded as shiny, slithering creatures worthy of fear and disgust. If one were to believe the Book of Genesis, humans' dislike for snakes resulted from a divine intervention: To avenge the snake's luring of Eve to taste the fruit of knowledge, God instituted eternal enmity between their descendants. Alternatively, the human dislike of snakes and the common appearances of reptiles as the embodiment of evil in myths and art might reflect an evolutionary heritage. Indeed, Sagan (1977) speculated that human fear of snakes and other reptiles may be a distant effect of the conditions under which early mammals evolved. In the world they inhabited, the animal kingdom was dominated by awesome reptiles, the dinosaurs, and so a prerequisite for early mammals to deliver genes to future generations was to avoid getting caught in the fangs of Tyrannosaurus rex and its relatives. Thus, fear and respect for reptiles is a likely core mammalian heritage. From this perspective, snakes and other reptiles may continue to have a special psychological significance even for humans, and considerable evidence suggests this is indeed true. Furthermore, the pattern of findings appears consistent with the evolutionary premise.

THE PREVALENCE OF SNAKE FEARS IN PRIMATES

Snakes are obviously fearsome creatures to many humans. Agras, Sylvester, and Oliveau (1969) interviewed a sample of New Englanders about fears, and found snakes to be clearly the most prevalent object of intense fear, reported by 38% of females and 12% of males.

Fear of snakes is also common among other primates. According to an exhaustive review of field data (King, 1997), 11 genera of primates showed fear-related responses (alarm calls, avoidance, mobbing) in virtually all instances in which they were observed confronting large snakes. For studies of captive primates, King did not find consistent evidence of snake fear. However, in direct comparisons, rhesus (and squirrel) monkeys reared in the wild were far more likely than lab-reared monkeys to show strong phobiclike fear responses to snakes (e.g., Mineka, Keir, & Price, 1980). That this fear is adaptive in the wild is further supported by independent field reports of large snakes attacking primates (M. Cook & Mineka, 1991).

This high prevalence of snake fear in humans as well as in our primate relatives suggests that it is a result of an ancient evolutionary history. Genetic variability might explain why not all individuals show fear of snakes. Alternatively, the variability could stem from differences in how easily individuals learn to fear reptilian stimuli when they are encountered in aversive contexts. This latter possibility would be consistent with the differences in snake fear between wild- and lab-reared monkeys.

LEARNING TO FEAR SNAKES

Experiments with lab-reared monkeys have shown that they can acquire a fear of snakes vicariously, that is, by observing other monkeys expressing fear of snakes. When nonfearful lab-reared monkeys were given the opportunity to observe a wild-reared "model" monkey displaying fear of live and toy snakes, they were rapidly conditioned to fear snakes, and this conditioning was strong and persistent. The fear response was learned even when the fearful model monkey was shown on videotape (M. Cook & Mineka, 1990).

When videos were spliced so that identical displays of fear were modeled in response to toy snakes and flowers, or to toy crocodiles and rabbits (M. Cook & Mineka, 1991), the lab-reared monkeys showed substantial conditioning to toy snakes and crocodiles, but not to flowers and toy rabbits. Toy snakes and flowers served equally well as signals for food rewards (M. Cook & Mineka, 1990), so the selective effect of snakes appears to be restricted to aversive contexts. Because these monkeys had never seen any of the stimuli used prior to these experiments, the results provide strong support for an evolutionary basis to the selective learning.

A series of studies published in the 1970s (see Öhman & Mineka, 2001) tested the hypothesis that humans are predisposed to easily learn to fear snakes. These studies used a discriminative Pavlovian conditioning procedure in which various pictures served as conditioned stimuli (CSs) that predicted the presence and absence of mildly aversive shock, the unconditioned stimulus (US). Participants for whom snakes (or spiders) consistently signaled shocks showed stronger and more lasting conditioned skin conductance responses (SCRs; palmar sweat responses that index emotional activation) than control participants for whom flowers or mushrooms signaled shocks. When a nonaversive US was used, however, this difference disappeared. E.W. Cook, Hodes, and Lang (1986) demonstrated that qualitatively different responses were conditioned to snakes (heart rate acceleration, indexing fear) than to flowers and mushrooms (heart rate deceleration, indexing attention to the eliciting stimulus). They also reported superior conditioning to snakes than to gun stimuli paired with loud noises. Such results suggest that the selective association between snakes and aversive USs reflects evolutionary history rather than cultural conditioning.

NONCONSCIOUS CONTROL OF RESPONSES TO SNAKES

If the prevalence and ease of learning snake fear represents a core mammalian heritage, its neural machinery must be found in brain structures that evolved in early mammals. Accordingly, the fear circuit of the mammalian brain relies heavily on limbic structures such as the amygdala, a collection of neural nuclei in the anterior temporal lobe. Limbic structures emerged in the evolutionary transition from reptiles to mammals and use preexisting structures in the "reptilian brain" to control emotional output such as flight/fight behavior and cardiovascular changes (see Öhman & Mineka, 2001).

From this neuroevolutionary perspective, one would expect the limbically controlled fear of snakes to be relatively independent of the most recently evolved control level in the brain, the neocortex, which is the site of advanced cognition. This hypothesis is consistent with the often strikingly irrational quality of snake phobia. For example, phobias may be activated by seeing mere pictures of snakes. Backward masking is a promising methodology for examining whether phobic responses can be activated without involvement of the cortex. In this method, a brief visual stimulus is blanked from conscious perception by an immediately following masking stimulus. Because backward masking disrupts visual processing in the primary visual cortex, responses to backward-masked stimuli reflect activation of pathways in the brain that may access the fear circuit without involving cortical areas mediating visual awareness of the stimulus.

In one study (Öhman & Soares, 1994), pictures of snakes, spiders, flowers, and mushrooms were presented very briefly (30 ms), each time immediately followed by a masking stimulus (a randomly cut and reassembled picture). Although the participants could not recognize the intact pictures, participants who were afraid of snakes showed enhanced SCRs only to masked snakes, whereas participants who were afraid of spiders responded only to spiders. Similar results were obtained (Öhman & Soares, 1993) when nonfearful participants, who had been conditioned to unmasked snake pictures by shock USs, were exposed to masked pictures without the US. Thus, responses to conditioned snake pictures survived backward masking; in contrast, masking eliminated conditioning effects in another group of participants conditioned to neutral stimuli such as flowers or mushrooms.

Furthermore, subsequent experiments (Öhman & Soares, 1998) also demonstrated conditioning to masked stimuli when masked snakes or spiders (but not masked flowers or mushrooms) were used as CSs followed by shock USs. Thus, these masking studies show that fear responses (as indexed by SCRs) can be learned and elicited when backward masking prevents visually presented snake stimuli from accessing cortical processing. This is consistent with the notion that responses to snakes are organized by a specifically evolved primitive neural circuit that emerged with the first mammals long before the evolution of neocortex.

ILLUSORY CORRELATIONS BETWEEN SNAKES AND AVERSIVE STIMULI

If expression and learning of snake fear do not require cortical processing, are people's cognitions about snakes and their relationships to other events biased and irrational? One example of such biased processing occurred in experiments on illusory correlations: Participants (especially those who were afraid of snakes) were more likely to perceive that slides of fear-relevant stimuli (such as snakes) were paired with shock than to perceive that slides of control stimuli (flowers and mushrooms) were paired with shock. This occurred even though there were no such relationships in the extensive random sequence of slide stimuli and aversive and nonaversive outcomes (tones or nothing) participants had experienced (Tomarken, Sutton, & Mineka, 1995).

Similar illusory correlations were not observed for pictures of damaged electrical equipment and shock even though they were rated as belonging together better than snakes and shock (Tomarken et al., 1995). In another experiment, participants showed exaggerated expectancies for shock to follow both snakes and damaged electrical equipment before the experiment began (Kennedy, Rapee, & Mazurski, 1997), but reported only the illusory correlation between snakes and shock after experiencing the random stimulus series. Thus, it appears that snakes have a cognitive affinity with aversiveness and danger that is resistant to modification by experience.

AUTOMATIC CAPTURE OF ATTENTION BY SNAKE STIMULI

People who encounter snakes in the wild may report that they first froze in fear, only a split second later realizing that they were about to step on a snake. Thus, snakes may automatically capture attention. A study supporting this hypothesis (Öhman, Flykt, & Esteves, 2001) demonstrated shorter detection latencies for a discrepant snake picture among an array of many neutral distractor stimuli (e.g., flower pictures) than vice versa. Furthermore, "finding the snake in the grass" was not affected by the number of distractor stimuli, whereas it took longer to detect discrepant flowers and mushrooms among many than among few snakes when the latter served as distractor stimuli. This suggests that snakes, but not flowers and mushrooms, were located by an automatic perceptual routine that effortlessly found target stimuli that appeared to "pop out" from the matrix independently of the number of distractor stimuli. Participants who were highly fearful of snakes showed even superior performance in detecting snakes. Thus, when snakes elicited fear in participants, this fear state sensitized the perceptual apparatus to detect snakes even more efficiently.

THE CONCEPT OF A FEAR MODULE

The evidence we have reviewed shows that snake stimuli are strongly and widely associated with fear in humans and other primates and that fear of snakes is relatively independent of conscious cognition. We have proposed the concept of an evolved fear module to explain these and many related findings (Öhman & Mineka, 2001). The fear module is a relatively independent behavioral, mental, and neural system that has evolved to assist mammals in defending against threats such as snakes. The module is selectively sensitive to, and automatically activated by, stimuli related to recurrent survival threats, it is relatively encapsulated from more advanced human cognition, and it relies on specialized neural circuitry.

This specialized behavioral module did not evolve primarily from survival threats provided by snakes during human evolution, but rather from the threat that reptiles have provided through mammalian evolution. Because reptiles have been associated with danger throughout evolution, it is likely that snakes represent a prototypical stimulus for activating the fear module. However, we are not arguing that the human brain has a specialized module for automatically generating fear of snakes. Rather, we propose that the blueprint for the fear module was built around the deadly threat that ancestors of snakes provided to our distant ancestors, the early mammals. During further mammalian evolution, this blueprint was modified, elaborated, and specialized for the ecological niches occupied by different species. Some mammals may even prey on snakes, and new stimuli and stimulus features have been added to reptiles as preferential activators of the module. For example, facial threat is similar to snakes when it comes to activating the fear module in social primates (Öhman & Mineka, 2001). Through Pavlovian conditioning, the fear module may come under the control of a very wide range of stimuli signaling pain and danger. Nevertheless, evolutionarily derived constraints have afforded stimuli once related to recurrent survival threats easier access for gaining control of the module through fear conditioning (Öhman & Mineka, 2001).

ISSUES FOR FURTHER RESEARCH

The claim that the fear module can be conditioned without awareness is a bold one given that there is a relative consensus in the field of human conditioning that awareness of the CS-US contingency is required for acquiring conditioned responses. However, as we have extensively argued elsewhere (Öhman & Mineka, 2001; Wiens & Öhman, 2002), there is good evidence that conditioning to nonconsciously presented CSs is possible if they are evolutionarily fear relevant. Other factors that might promote such nonconscious learning include intense USs, short CS-US intervals, and perhaps temporal overlap between the CS and the US. However, little research on these factors has been reported, and there is a pressing need to elaborate their relative effectiveness in promoting conditioning of the fear module outside of awareness.

One of the appeals of the fear module concept is that it is consistent with the current understanding of the neurobiology of fear conditioning, which gives a central role to the amygdala (e.g., Öhman & Mineka, 2001). However, this understanding is primarily based on animal data. Even though the emerging brain-imaging literature on human fear conditioning is consistent with this database, systematic efforts are needed in order to tie the fear module more convincingly to human brain mechanisms. For example, a conspicuous gap in knowledge concerns whether the amygdala is indeed specially tuned to conditioning contingencies involving evolutionarily fear-relevant CSs such as snakes.

An interesting question that can be addressed both at a psychological and at a neurobiological level concerns the perceptual mechanisms that give snake stimuli privileged access to the fear module. For example, are snakes detected at a lower perceptual threshold relative to non-fear-relevant objects? Are they identified faster than other objects once detected? Are they quicker to activate the fear module and attract attention once identified? Regardless of the locus of perceptual privilege, what visual features of snakes make them such powerful fear elicitors and attention captors? Because the visual processing in pathways preceding the cortical level is crude, the hypothesis that masked presentations of snakes directly access the amygdala implies that the effect is mediated by simple features of snakes rather than by the complex configuration of features defining a snake. Delineating these features would allow the construction of a "super fear stimulus." It could be argued that such a stimulus would depict "the archetypical evil" as represented in the human brain.

Recommended Reading

Mineka, S. (1992). Evolutionary memories, emotional processing, and the emotional disorders. *The Psychology of Learning and Motivation, 28*, 161–206.

Öhman, A., Dimberg, U., & Öst, L.-G. (1985). Animal and social phobias: Biological constraints on learned fear responses. In S. Reiss & R.R. Bootzin (Eds.), *Theoretical issues in behavior therapy* (pp. 123–178). New York: Academic Press.

Öhman; A., & Mineka, S. (2001). (See References)

Note

1. Address correspondence to Arne Öhman, Psychology Section, Department of Clinical Neuroscience, Karolinska Institute and Hospital, Z6:6, S-171 76 Stockholm, Sweden; e-mail: arne.ohman@cns.ki.se.

References

Agras, S., Sylvester, D., & Oliveau, D. (1969). The epidemiology of common fears and phobias. *Comprehensive Psychiatry, 10*, 151–156.

Cook, E.W., Hodes, R.L., & Lang, P.J. (1986). Preparedness and phobia: Effects of stimulus content on human visceral conditioning. *Journal of Abnormal Psychology, 95*, 195–207.

Cook, M., & Mineka, S. (1990). Selective associations in the observational conditioning of fear in rhesus monkeys. *Journal of Experimental Psychology: Animal Behavior Processes, 16*, 372–389.

Cook, M., & Mineka, S. (1991). Selective associations in the origins of phobic fears and their implications for behavior therapy. In P. Martin (Ed.), *Handbook of behavior therapy and psychological science: An integrative approach* (pp. 413–434). Oxford, England: Pergamon Press.

Kennedy, S.J., Rapee, R.M., & Mazurski, E.J. (1997). Covariation bias for phylogenetic versus ontogenetic fear-relevant stimuli. *Behaviour Research and Therapy, 35*, 415–422.

King, G.E. (1997, June). *The attentional basis for primate responses to snakes.* Paper presented at the annual meeting of the American Society of Primatologists, San Diego, CA.

Mineka, S., Keir, R., & Price, V. (1980). Fear of snakes in wild- and laboratory-reared rhesus monkeys (*Macaca mulatta*). *Animal Learning and Behavior, 8*, 653–663.

Öhman, A., Flykt, A., & Esteves, F. (2001). Emotion drives attention: Detecting the snake in the grass. *Journal of Experimental Psychology: General, 131*, 466–478.

Öhman, A., & Mineka, S. (2001). Fear, phobias and preparedness: Toward an evolved module of fear and fear learning. *Psychological Review, 108*, 483–522.

Öhman, A., & Soares, J.J.F. (1993). On the automatic nature of phobic fear: Conditioned electro-dermal responses to masked fear-relevant stimuli. *Journal of Abnormal Psychology, 102,* 121–132.

Öhman, A., & Soares, J.J.F. (1994). "Unconscious anxiety": Phobic responses to masked stimuli. *Journal of Abnormal Psychology, 103,* 231–240.

Öhman, A., & Soares, J.J.F. (1998). Emotional conditioning to masked stimuli: Expectancies for aversive outcomes following nonrecognized fear-irrelevant stimuli. *Journal of Experimental Psychology: General, 127,* 69–82.

Sagan, C. (1977). *The dragons of Eden: Speculations on the evolution of human intelligence.* London: Hodder and Stoughton.

Tomarken, A.J., Sutton, S.K., & Mineka, S. (1995). Fear-relevant illusory correlations: What types of associations promote judgmental bias? *Journal of Abnormal Psychology, 104,* 312–326.

Wiens, S., & Öhman, A. (2002). Unawareness is more than a chance event: Comment on Lovibond and Shanks (2002). *Journal of Experimental Psychology: Animal Behavior Processes, 28,* 27–31.

Critical Thinking Questions

1. Why are the authors uniquely interested in the fear of snakes as opposed to other objects?

2. How do experiments on fear conditioning support the notion that humans are predisposed, or "hardwired" to fear snakes?

3. How do experiments on attention support the notion that humans are predisposed to fear snakes?

4. What is a fear module and why do the authors propose that it exists?

Intrinsic Versus Extrinsic Motivation in Schools: A Reconciliation

Martin V. Covington[1]

Department of Psychology, University of California at Berkeley, Berkeley, California

Abstract

This article explores the nature of the relationship between intrinsic and extrinsic motivation in schools, and in particular examines critically the assertion that these processes are necessarily antagonistic. The weight of evidence suggests that rewards in the form of school grades and the focus of many students on doing well, grade-wise, need not necessarily interfere with learning for its own sake. Educational implications of these findings are considered. One such implication is that focusing on students' interests can be a valuable motivational strategy.

Keywords

motivation; achievement; appreciation

When psychologists speak of motivation, they typically refer to the reasons that individuals are aroused to action. Over the past 50 years, two quite different kinds of reasons have emerged in the thinking of psychologists: intrinsic and extrinsic reasons. Individuals are said to be driven to act for extrinsic reasons when they anticipate some kind of tangible payoff, such as good grades, recognition, or gold stars. These rewards are said to be extrinsic because they are unrelated to the action. In effect, the activity becomes a means to an end. By contrast, individuals are said to be intrinsically motivated when they engage in activities for their own sake. In this instance, the rewards reside in the actions themselves; that is, the actions are their own reinforcement. Put differently, in the case of intrinsic motivation, the repetition of an action does not depend as much on some external inducement as on the satisfaction derived from overcoming a personal challenge, learning something new, or discovering things of personal interest.

For generations, observers have extolled the virtues of learning for its own sake, not only because of the benefits of personal growth or enhanced well-being, but also because intrinsically based learning is the handmaiden to better, more efficient learning. For example, intrinsically engaged students are more likely than extrinsically driven students to employ deep-level, sophisticated study strategies in their work (Ames & Archer, 1988). Perhaps most noteworthy for establishing causal, not merely correlational, relationships are studies (e.g., Schunk, 1996) in which students were randomly assigned to varying achievement conditions. Those students who were directed to work for the goals of mastery, exploration, and appreciation demonstrated greater task involvement and used more effective learning strategies than children who were directed to focus on their performance alone.

At the same time, experts also lament the prospects of encouraging intrinsic engagement in a world controlled by extrinsic rewards (e.g., Kohn, 1993). My purpose here is to explore briefly the nature of the relationship between intrinsic and extrinsic motivation in schools, and in particular to examine critically the assertion that these processes are necessarily antagonistic, such that the will to learn for its own sake is inhibited or even destroyed by the offering of extrinsic rewards and incentives like school grades.

It is important to be clear about what the issue is. The issue is not that offering tangible rewards will necessarily interfere with learning. To the contrary, offering students tangible rewards sometimes actually increases learning, especially if the assignment is seen as a chore or boring. Rather, the issue is whether offering rewards focuses undue attention on the tangible payoffs, thereby decreasing students' appreciation of what they are learning.

OBSTACLES TO INTRINSIC ENGAGEMENT

The potentially destructive impact of tangible rewards on the will to learn for its own sake has been documented in several ways. First, there is the prospect that once these rewards are no longer available, students will show little or no inclination to continue in their studies (Covington, 1998). Second, there is the possibility that offering rewards to students for doing what already interests them may also undercut personal task involvement. For example, if a teacher tries to encourage intrinsic values directly, say, by praising students for pursuing a hobby, then, paradoxically, these interests may actually be discouraged. This phenomenon is the so-called overjustification effect (Lepper, Greene, & Nisbett, 1973). According to one interpretation, such discouragement occurs because the value of an already justifiable activity becomes suspect by the promise of additional rewards—hence the term overjustification—so that the individual reasons, "If someone has to pay me to do this, then it must not be worth doing for its own sake."

The goal of fostering a love of learning is complicated not only by offering or withholding tangible rewards, but also by the scarcity of these rewards. In many classrooms, an inadequate supply of rewards (e.g., good grades) is distributed by teachers unequally, with the greatest number of rewards going to the best performers or to the fastest learners. This arrangement is based on the false assumption that achievement is maximized when students compete for a limited number of rewards. Although this may maximize motivation, students are aroused for the wrong reasons—to win over others and to avoid losing—and these reasons eventually lead to failure and resentment (Covington, 1998). In this competitive context, grades stand as a mark of worthiness, because it is widely assumed in our society that one is only as worthy as one's ability to achieve competitively.

If high grades not only are important for the tangible future benefits they bestow—being the gateway to prestigious occupations—but also serve as an indication of one's personal worth, then what becomes of the valuing of learning in the scramble for grades? Is not the valuing and appreciation of learning marginalized? No, apparently not. There can be little doubt that students also value learning, irrespective of the grades they receive (see Covington, 1999).

A RECONCILIATION

How can we resolve this apparent contradiction? The observations of students themselves provide some answers (Covington, 1999; Covington & Wiedenhaupt, 1997).

First, students readily acknowledge that they strive for the highest grades possible, but—and this is the important point—different students have different reasons for a grade focus. It is these reasons that in turn determine the degree to which students become intrinsically engaged. For instance, when students strive for high grades as a mark of approval, to impress other people, or to avoid failure, they will value learning only to the extent that it serves to aggrandize their ability status, not for any inherent attraction of the material itself. If, by contrast, students have a task-oriented purpose in striving for high grades (e.g., if they use grades as feedback for how they can improve and learn more), then they will appreciate their accomplishments for their positive properties. In effect, it is not necessarily the presence of grades per se, or even a dominant grade focus, that influences the degree to which learning is appreciated. Rather, students' valuing of what they learn depends on their initial reasons for learning and the meaning they attach to their grades. This implies that striving for good grades and caring for learning are not necessarily incompatible goals. The degree of compatibility of these goals is influenced by the reasons for learning.

Second, the degree to which students become intrinsically engaged in their schoolwork depends in part on whether they are achieving their grade goals, that is, whether they feel successful. On the one hand, being successful in one's studies promotes an appreciation for what one is learning. On the other hand, falling short of one's grade goals may intensify one's concentration on doing better (to the point that appreciation of the subject matter is excluded), divert attention to protecting one's sense of worth, or cause feelings of hopelessness about ever succeeding, feelings that bode ill for both the goal of appreciation and the goal of achievement. Thus, the degree of goal compatibility is also influenced by experiences of success and failure.

Third, students also indicate that they often manipulate academic circumstances to create a tolerable balance between grades and caring. The most frequent strategies involve making school more interesting by deliberately seeking out what is of interest to them, even in the case of boring assignments, or arranging a course of study, or even a college major, around personal interests. Thus, the compatibility of grades and caring is also influenced by personal interests.

From these observations, we can conclude that students are more likely to value what they are learning, and to enjoy the process, (a) when they are achieving their grade goals; (b) when the dominant reasons for learning are task-oriented reasons, not self-aggrandizing or failure-avoiding reasons; and (c) when what they are studying is of personal interest.

The role of personal interest in this equation is especially noteworthy. Although it is not surprising that people enjoy learning more about what already interests them, what is intriguing is the extent to which pursuing one's own interests offsets the potentially negative effects of receiving a disappointing grade. In fact, the evidence suggests that a student's appreciation for what he or she is learning is far greater when the student is failing but interested in the task than when the same student is succeeding, gradewise, but has little interest in the subject-matter content.

A related point concerning this equation also deserves comment. Receiving a good grade, especially for interesting work, increases, not decreases, intrinsic engagement. This finding seems to contradict the previously mentioned expectation that providing people with tangible payoffs for pursuing what already interests them will dampen their enthusiasm. Students themselves offer several plausible explanations for why these worries may be exaggerated, if not groundless. Based on their experiences, some students report anecdotally that doing well causes positive feelings like pride, which in turn increases their enthusiasm for learning. Other anecdotal observations suggest that doing well reduces worry about failing, so that students are freer to explore what is most interesting. And, according to yet other students, being successful stimulates them to study more, and the more they learn, the more interesting the material is likely to become. Whatever the explanation, it seems that the effects of tangible payoffs on intrinsic processes are far from simple.

EDUCATIONAL IMPLICATIONS

What practical steps do these findings suggest for how schools can serve both the goal of disseminating knowledge and the goal of promoting an appreciation of what is learned in the face of an ever-present grade focus?

First, the most obvious implication is that a major instructional goal should be to arrange schooling around the personal interests of students. Second, obviously learning cannot always be arranged around personal preferences, nor can students always succeed. Nonetheless, instructional practices can alter the meaning of failure when it occurs. Basically, this step involves eliminating the climate of scarcity of rewards by defining success not in the relative sense of outperforming others, but rather absolutely, that is, in terms of whether students measure up to a given standard of performance, irrespective of how many other students do well or poorly (Covington & Teel, 1996). When well-defined standards of performance are provided, the failure to achieve them tends to motivate students to try harder because failure implies falling short of a goal, not falling short as a person.

Third, in addition to creating grading systems that encourage intrinsic reasons for learning, teachers should provide payoffs that actively strengthen and reward these positive reasons. Although students focus primarily on the prospects of getting a good grade, they are also more likely to invest greater time and energy (beyond what is necessary for the grade) in those tasks for which there are additional tangible, yet intrinsically oriented payoffs. These payoffs include the opportunity to share the results of their work with others, or the chance to explain more deeply and personally why what they learned was important to them. This suggestion implies that, far from being incompatible, intrinsic and extrinsic reasons for learning are both encouraged by tangible rewards, but by different kinds of tangible rewards. This proposition sheds an entirely new light on the concerns raised by many experts regarding the overjustification effect. It is not the offering of tangible rewards that undercuts personal task engagement so much as it is the absence of those kinds of payoffs that encourage and recognize the importance of being involved in and caring about what one is learning.

Finally, students are the first to acknowledge a conflict between the goals of striving for high grades and enjoying learning. However, the conflict arises, they say, not out of any incompatibility of goals. Rather, the demands of school leave little room to pursue either goal fully, let alone to pursue the two goals together. As a result, students must prioritize these objectives, a process that typically favors the goal of striving for grades, and they lament what they forfeit. But prioritizing is not the same as incompatibility. The recommendations made in this review can act to balance these priorities more in favor of intrinsic engagement and a love of learning.

Recommended Reading

Cameron, J., & Pierce, W.D. (1994). Reinforcement, reward and intrinsic motivation: A meta-analysis. *Review of Educational Research, 64*, 363–423.

Condry, J., & Koslowski, B. (1979). Can education be made "intrinsically interesting" to children? In D. Katz (Ed.), Current topics in early childhood education (Vol. II, pp. 227ñ260). Norwood, NJ: Ablex.

Cordova, D.I., & Lepper, M.R. (1996). Intrinsic motivation and the process of learning: Beneficial effects of contextualization, personalization and choice. *Journal of Educational Psychology, 88*, 715–730.

Covington, M.V. (1992). *Making the grade: A self-worth perspective on motivation and school reform.* New York: Cambridge University Press.

Elliot, A.J., & Harackiewicz, J.M. (1996). Approach and avoidance achievement goals and intrinsic motivation: A mediational analysis. *Journal of Personality and Social Psychology, 70*, 461–475.

Note

1. Address correspondence to Martin V. Covington, Department of Psychology, 3210 Tolman Hall, University of California at Berkeley, Berkeley, CA 94720-1650.

References

Ames, C., & Archer, J. (1988). Achievement goals in the classroom: Student learning strategies and motivation processes. *Journal of Educational Psychology, 80*, 260–267.

Covington, M.V. (1998). *The will to learn: A guide for motivating young people.* New York: Cambridge University Press.

Covington, M.V. (1999). Caring about learning: The nature and nurturing of subject-matter appreciation. *Educational Researcher, 34*, 127–136.

Covington, M.V., & Teel, K.M. (1996). *Overcoming student failure: Changing motives and incentives for learning.* Washington, DC: American Psychological Association.

Covington, M.V., & Wiedenhaupt, S. (1997). Turning work into play: The nature and nurturing of intrinsic task engagement. In R. Perry & J.C. Smart (Eds.), *Effective teaching in higher education: Research and practice, special edition* (pp. 101–114). New York: Agathon Press.

Kohn, A. (1993). *Punished by rewards.* New York: Houghton Mifflin.

Lepper, M.R., Greene, D., & Nisbett, R.E. (1973). Undermining children's intrinsic interest with extrinsic rewards: A test of the "overjustification" hypothesis. *Journal of Personality and Social Psychology, 28*, 129–137.

Schunk, D.H. (1996). Goal and self-evaluative influences during children's cognitive skill learning. *American Educational Research Journal, 33*, 359–382.

Critical Thinking Questions

1. What is intrinsic motivation, what is extrinsic motivation, and why is it important to make this distinction?

2. Why do grades and other tangible rewards pose a threat to intrinsic motivation?

3. How can grades and other tangible rewards enhance intrinsic motivation?

4. What educational implications does the author draw for using reward in the classroom?

Human Sexuality: How Do Men and Women Differ?

Letitia Anne Peplau[1]

Psychology Department, University of California, Los Angeles, Los Angeles, California

Abstract

A large body of scientific research documents four important gender differences in sexuality. First, on a wide variety of measures, men show greater sexual desire than do women. Second, compared with men, women place greater emphasis on committed relationships as a context for sexuality. Third, aggression is more strongly linked to sexuality for men than for women. Fourth, women's sexuality tends to be more malleable and capable of change over time. These male-female differences are pervasive, affecting thoughts and feelings as well as behavior, and they characterize not only heterosexuals but lesbians and gay men as well. Implications of these patterns are considered.

Keywords

human sexuality; sexual desire; sexual orientation; sexual plasticity

A century ago, sex experts confidently asserted that men and women have strikingly different sexual natures. The rise of scientific psychology brought skepticism about this popular but unproven view, and the pendulum swung toward an emphasis on similarities between men's and women's sexuality. For example, Masters and Johnson (1966) captured attention by proposing a human sexual response cycle applicable to both sexes. Feminist scholars cautioned against exaggerating male-female differences and argued for women's sexual equality with men. Recently, psychologists have taken stock of the available scientific evidence. Reviews of empirical research on diverse aspects of human sexuality have identified four important male-female differences. These gender differences are pervasive, affecting thoughts and feelings as well as behavior, and they characterize not only heterosexuals but lesbians and gay men as well.

SEXUAL DESIRE

Sexual desire is the subjective experience of being interested in sexual objects or activities or wishing to engage in sexual activities (Regan & Berscheid, 1999). Many lines of research demonstrate that men show more interest in sex than women (see review by Baumeister, Catanese, & Vohs, 2001). Compared with women, men think about sex more often. They report more frequent sex fantasies and more frequent feelings of sexual desire. Across the life span, men rate the strength of their own sex drive higher than do their female age-mates. Men are more interested in visual sexual stimuli and more likely to spend money on such sexual products and activities as X-rated videos and visits to prostitutes.

Men and women also differ in their preferred frequency of sex. When heterosexual dating and marriage partners disagree about sexual frequency, it is usually the man who wants to have sex more often than the woman does. In heterosexual couples, actual sexual frequency may reflect a compromise between the desires of the male and female partners. In gay and lesbian relationships, sexual frequency is decided by partners of the same gender, and lesbians report having sex less often than gay men or heterosexuals. Further, women appear to be more willing than men to forgo sex or adhere to religious vows of celibacy.

Masturbation provides a good index of sexual desire because it is not constrained by the availability of a partner. Men are more likely than women to masturbate, start masturbating at an earlier age, and do so more often. In a review of 177 studies, Oliver and Hyde (1993) found large male-female differences in the incidence of masturbation. In technical terms, the meta-analytic effect size[2] (d) for masturbation was 0.96, which is smaller than the physical sex difference in height (2.00) but larger than most psychological sex differences, such as the performance difference on standardized math tests (0.20). These and many other empirical findings provide evidence for men's greater sexual interest.

SEXUALITY AND RELATIONSHIPS

A second consistent difference is that women tend to emphasize committed relationships as a context for sexuality more than men do. When Regan and Berscheid (1999) asked young adults to define sexual desire, men were more likely than women to emphasize physical pleasure and sexual intercourse. In contrast, women were more likely to "romanticize" the experience of sexual desire, as seen in one young woman's definition of sexual desire as "longing to be emotionally intimate and to express love for another person" (p. 75). Compared with women, men have more permissive attitudes toward casual premarital sex and toward extramarital sex. The size of these gender differences is relatively large, particularly for casual premarital sex (d = 0.81; Oliver & Hyde, 1993). Similarly, women's sexual fantasies are more likely than men's to involve a familiar partner and to include affection and commitment. In contrast, men's fantasies are more likely to involve strangers, anonymous partners, or multiple partners and to focus on specific sex acts or sexual organs.

A gender difference in emphasizing relational aspects of sexuality is also found among lesbians and gay men (see review by Peplau, Fingerhut, & Beals, in press). Like heterosexual women, lesbians tend to have less permissive attitudes toward casual sex and sex outside a primary relationship than do gay or heterosexual men. Also like heterosexual women, lesbians have sex fantasies that are more likely to be personal and romantic than the fantasies of gay or heterosexual men. Lesbians are more likely than gay men to become sexually involved with partners who were first their friends, then lovers. Gay men in committed relationships are more likely than lesbians or heterosexuals to have sex with partners outside their primary relationship.

In summary, women's sexuality tends to be strongly linked to a close relationship. For women, an important goal of sex is intimacy; the best context for pleasurable sex is a committed relationship. This is less true for men.

SEXUALITY AND AGGRESSION

A third gendered pattern concerns the association between sexuality and aggression. This link has been demonstrated in many domains, including individuals' sexual self-concepts, the initiation of sex in heterosexual relationships, and coercive sex.

Andersen, Cyranowski, and Espindle (1999) investigated the dimensions that individuals use to characterize their own sexuality. Both sexes evaluated themselves along a dimension of being romantic, with some individuals seeing themselves as very passionate and others seeing themselves as not very passionate. However, men's sexual self-concepts were also characterized by a dimension of aggression, which concerned the extent to which they saw themselves as being aggressive, powerful, experienced, domineering, and individualistic. There was no equivalent aggression dimension for women's sexual self-concepts.

In heterosexual relationships, men are commonly more assertive than women and take the lead in sexual interactions (see review by Impett & Peplau, 2003). During the early stages of a dating relationship, men typically initiate touching and sexual intimacy. In ongoing relationships, men report initiating sex about twice as often as their female partners or age-mates. To be sure, many women do initiate sex, but they do so less frequently than their male partners. The same pattern is found in people's sexual fantasies. Men are more likely than women to imagine themselves doing something sexual to a partner or taking the active role in a sexual encounter.

Rape stands at the extreme end of the link between sex and aggression. Although women use many strategies to persuade men to have sex, physical force and violence are seldom part of their repertoire. Physically coercive sex is primarily a male activity (see review by Felson, 2002). There is growing recognition that stranger and acquaintance rape are not the whole story; some men use physical force in intimate heterosexual relationships. Many women who are battered by a boyfriend or husband also report sexual assaults as part of the abuse.

In summary, aggression is more closely linked to sexuality for men than for women. Currently, we know little about aggression and sexuality among lesbians and gay men; research on this topic would provide a valuable contribution to our understanding of gender and human sexuality.

SEXUAL PLASTICITY

Scholars from many disciplines have noted that, in comparison with men's sexuality, women's sexuality tends to have greater plasticity. That is, women's sexual beliefs and behaviors can be more easily shaped and altered by cultural, social, and situational factors. Baumeister (2000) systematically reviewed the scientific evidence on this point. In this section, I mention a few of the many supportive empirical findings.

One sign of plasticity concerns changes in aspects of a person's sexuality over time. Such changes are more common among women than among men. For example, the frequency of women's sexual activity is more variable than men's. If a woman is in an intimate relationship, she might have frequent sex with her partner. But following a breakup, she might have no sex at all, including masturbation, for several months. Men show less temporal variability: Following a romantic breakup, men may substitute masturbation for interpersonal sex and so maintain a more constant frequency of sex. There is also growing evidence that women are more likely than men to change their sexual orientation over time. In an illustrative longitudinal study (Diamond, 2003), more than 25% of 18- to 25-year-old women who initially identified as lesbian or bisexual changed their sexual identity during the next 5 years. Changes such as these are less common for men.

A further indication of malleability is that a person's sexual attitudes and behaviors are responsive to social and situational influences. Such factors as education, religion, and acculturation are more strongly linked to women's sexuality than to men's. For example, moving to a new culture may have more impact on women's sexuality than on men's. The experience of higher education provides another illustration. A college education is associated with more liberal sexual attitudes and behavior, but this effect is greater for women than for men. Even more striking is the association between college education and sexual orientation shown in a recent national survey (Laumann, Gagnon, Michael, & Michaels, 1994). Completing college doubled the likelihood that a man identified as gay or bisexual (1.7% among high school graduates vs. 3.3% among college graduates). However, college was associated with a 900% increase in the percentage of women identifying as lesbian or bisexual (0.4% vs. 3.6%).

CONCLUSION AND IMPLICATIONS

Diverse lines of scientific research have identified consistent male-female differences in sexual interest, attitudes toward sex and relationships, the association between sex and aggression, and sexual plasticity. The size of these gender differences tends to be large, particularly in comparison to other male-female differences studied by psychologists. These differences are pervasive, encompassing thoughts, feelings, fantasies, and behavior. Finally, these male-female differences apply not only to heterosexuals but also to lesbians and gay men.

Several limitations of the current research are noteworthy. First, much research is based on White, middle-class American samples. Studies of other populations and cultural groups would be valuable in assessing the generalizability of findings. Second, although research findings on lesbians and gay men are consistent with patterns of male-female difference among heterosexuals, the available empirical database on homosexuals is relatively small. Third, differences between women and men are not absolute but rather a matter of degree. There are many exceptions to the general patterns described. For instance, some women show high levels of sexual interest, and some men seek sex only in committed relationships. Research documenting male-female differences has advanced further than research systematically tracing the origins of these differences. We are only beginning to understand the complex ways in which biology, experience, and culture interact to shape men's and women's sexuality.

These four general differences between women's and men's sexuality can illuminate specific patterns of sexual interaction. For example, in heterosexual couples, it is fairly common for a partner to engage in sex when he or she is not really interested or "in the mood." Although both men and women sometimes consent to such unwanted sexual activity, women are more often the compliant sexual partner (see review by Impett & Peplau, 2003). Each of the gender differences I have described may contribute to this pattern. First, the stage is set by a situation in which partners have differing desires for sex, and the man is more often the partner desiring sex. Second, for compliant sex to occur, the more interested partner must communicate his or her desire. Men typically take the lead in expressing sexual interest. Third, the disinterested partner's reaction is pivotal: Does this partner comply or, instead, ignore or reject the request? If women view sex as a way to show love and caring for a partner, they may be more likely than men to resolve a dilemma about unwanted sex by taking their partner's welfare into account. In abusive relationships, women may fear physical or psychological harm from a male partner if they refuse. Finally, sexual compliance illustrates the potential plasticity of female sexuality. In this case, women are influenced by relationship concerns to engage in a sexual activity that goes against their personal preference at the time.

The existence of basic differences between men's and women's sexuality has implications for the scientific study of sexuality. Specifically, an adequate understanding of human sexuality may require separate analyses of sexuality in women and in men, based on the unique biology and life experiences of each sex. Currently, efforts to reconceptualize sexual issues have focused on women's sexuality. Three examples are illustrative.

Rethinking Women's Sexual Desire

How should we interpret the finding that women appear less interested in sex than men? One possibility is that researchers have inadvertently used male standards (e.g., penile penetration and orgasm) to evaluate women's sexual experiences and consequently ignored activities, such as intimate kissing, cuddling, and touching, that may be uniquely important to women's erotic lives. Researchers such as Wallen (1995) argue that it is necessary to distinguish between sexual desire (an intrinsic motivation to pursue sex) and arousability (the capacity to become sexually aroused in response to situational cues). Because women's sexual desire may vary across the menstrual cycle, it may be more appropriate to describe women's desire as periodic rather than weak or limited. In contrast, women's receptivity to sexual overtures and their capacity for sexual response may depend on situational rather than hormonal cues. Other researchers (e.g., Tolman & Diamond, 2001) argue that more attention must be paid to the impact of hormones that may have special relevance for women, such as the neuropeptide oxytocin, which is linked to both sexuality and affectional bonding.

Rethinking Women's Sexual Orientation

Some researchers have proposed new paradigms for understanding women's sexual orientation (e.g., Peplau & Garnets, 2000). Old models either assumed commonalities among homosexuals, regardless of gender, or hypothesized similarities between lesbians and heterosexual men, both of whom are attracted to women. In contrast, empirical research has documented many similarities in women's sexuality, regardless of their sexual orientation. A new model based on women's experiences might highlight the centrality of relationships to women's sexual orientation, the potential for at least some women to change their sexual orientation over time, and the importance of sociocultural factors in shaping women's sexual orientation.

Rethinking Women's Sexual Problems

Finally, research on women's sexuality has led some scientists to question current systems for classifying sexual dysfunction among women. The widely used *Diagnostic and Statistical Manual of Mental Disorders (DSM)* of the American Psychiatric Association categorizes sexual dysfunction on the basis of Masters and Johnson's (1966) model of presumed normal and universal sexual functioning. Critics (e.g., Kaschak & Tiefer, 2001) have challenged the validity of this model, its applicability to women, and its use as a basis for clinical assessment. They have also faulted the *DSM* for ignoring the relationship context of sexuality for women. Kaschak and Tiefer have proposed instead a new "woman-centered" view of women's sexual problems that gives prominence to partner and relationship factors that affect women's sexual experiences, and also to social, cultural, and economic factors that influence the quality of women's sexual lives.

Recommended Reading

Baumeister, R.F., & Tice, D.M. (2001). *The social dimension of sex*. Boston: Allyn and Bacon.
Kaschak, E., & Tiefer, L. (Eds.). (2001). (See References)
Peplau, L.A., & Garnets, L.D. (2000). (See References)
Regan, P.C., & Berscheid, 18. (1999). (See References)

Notes

1. Address correspondence to Letitia Anne Peplau, Psychology Department, Franz 1285, University of California, Los Angeles, CA 90095-1563; e-mail: lapeplau@ucla.edu.
2. In a meta-analysis, the findings of multiple studies are analyzed quantitatively to arrive at an overall estimate of the size of a difference between two groups, in this case, between men and women. This effect size (known technically as d) is reported using a common unit of measurement. By convention in psychological research, 0.2 is considered a small effect size, 0.5 is a moderate effect size, and 0.8 is a large effect size.

References

Andersen, B.L., Cyranowski, J.M., & Espindle, D. (1999). Men's sexual self-schema. *Journal of Personality and Social Psychology, 76*, 645–661.
Baumeister, R.F. (2000). Gender differences in erotic plasticity. *Psychological Bulletin, 126*, 347–374.
Baumeister, R.F., Catanese, K.R., & Vohs, K.D. (2001). Is there a gender difference in strength of sex drive? *Personality and Social Psychology Review, 5*, 242–273.
Diamond, L.M. (2003). Was it a phase? Young women's relinquishment of lesbian/bisexual identities over a 5-year period. *Journal of Personality and Social Psychology, 84*, 352–364.
Felson, R.B. (2002). *Violence and gender reexamined*. Washington, DC: American Psychological Association.
Impett, E., & Peplau, L.A. (2003). Sexual compliance: Gender, motivational, and relationship perspectives. *Journal of Sex Research, 40*, 87–100.

Kaschak, E., & Tiefer, L. (Eds.). (2001). *A new view of women's sexual problems*. New York: Haworth Press.

Laumann, E., Gagnon, J., Michael, R., & Michaels, S. (1994). *The social organization of sexuality.* Chicago: University of Chicago Press.

Masters, W.H., & Johnson, V.E. (1966). *Human sexual response.* Boston: Little, Brown, & Co.

Oliver, M.B., & Hyde, J.S. (1993). Gender differences in sexuality: A meta-analysis. *Psychological Bulletin, 114,* 29–51.

Peplau, L.A., Fingerhut, A., & Beals, K. (in press). Sexuality in the relationships of lesbians and gay men. In J. Harvey, A. Wenzel, & S. Sprecher (Eds.), *Handbook of sexuality in close relationships.* Mahwah, NJ: Erlbaum.

Peplau, L.A., & Garnets, L.D. (Eds.). (2000). Women's sexualities: New perspectives on sexual orientation and gender [Special issue]. *Journal of Social Issues, 56*(2).

Regan, P.C., & Berscheid, E. (1999). *Lust: What we know about human sexual desire.* Thousand Oaks, CA: Sage.

Tolman, D.L., & Diamond, L.M. (2001). Desegregating sexuality research: Cultural and biological perspectives on gender and desire. *Annual Review of Sex Research, 12,* 33–74.

Wallen, K. (1995). The evolution of female sexual desire. In P. Abramson & S.D. Pinkerton (Eds.), *Sexual nature/sexual culture* (pp. 57–79). Chicago: University of Chicago Press.

Critical Thinking Questions

1. Do men and women differ in their sexual desire?

2. How do men and women differ when it comes to sexuality and aggression?

3. Compare men and women in terms of their sexual "plasticity."

4. What are some implications of the differences in human sexuality between men and women?

Job Burnout: New Directions in Research and Intervention

Psychology Department, University of California at Berkeley, Berkeley, California

Abstract

Job burnout is a prolonged response to chronic emotional and interpersonal stressors on the job and is defined here by the three dimensions of exhaustion, cynicism, and sense of inefficacy. Its presence as a social problem in many human services professions was the impetus for the research that is now taking place in many countries. That research has established the complexity of the problem and has examined the individual stress experience within a larger social and organizational context of people's response to their work. The framework, which focuses attention on the interpersonal dynamics between the worker and other people in the workplace, has yielded new insights into the sources of stress, but effective interventions have yet to be developed and evaluated.

Keywords

work stress; organizational behavior; job engagement; job-person fit

Job burnout is a psychological syndrome that involves a prolonged response to stressors in the workplace. Specifically, it involves the chronic strain that results from an incongruence, or misfit, between the worker and the job. Perhaps the best-known fictional example of job burnout comes from the novel *A Burnt Out Case* (Greene, 1961), in which a spiritually tormented and disillusioned architect quits his job and withdraws into the African jungle. Other literature, both fictional and nonfictional, has described similar phenomena, including extreme fatigue and the loss of idealism and passion for one's job. What is noteworthy is that the importance of burnout as a social problem was identified by both workers and social commentators long before it became a focus of systematic study by researchers.

Thus, the trajectory of burnout research began with a real social problem rather than with derivations from scholarly theory. In other words, it followed a grassroots, bottom-up path rather than a top-down one. The origin of this research had some initial liabilities, as early studies were dismissed as flimsy popular psychology. However, a substantial, international body of empirical work and theoretical models has now laid to rest early questions about research scholarship in this field (see Schaufeli & Enzmann, 1998, for the most recent comprehensive citation of this research literature). The advantage of this trajectory has been that burnout research has been clearly grounded in the realities of people's experiences in the workplace, and this has led to a comprehensive understanding of the environmental context of this phenomenon, as well as to new ideas for intervention.

A MULTIDIMENSIONAL MODEL OF JOB BURNOUT

To study the problem of job burnout, my colleagues and I began with extensive interviews of workers in many human service occupations, and then developed a multidimensional model of the burnout phenomenon. The three key dimensions of this stress response are an overwhelming exhaustion, feelings of cynicism and detachment from the job, and a sense of ineffectiveness and lack of accomplishment. This multidimensional model stands in contrast to more typical unidimensional conceptions of stress because it goes beyond the individual stress experience (exhaustion) to encompass the person's response to the job (cynicism) and to him- or herself (feelings of inefficacy). The cynicism dimension, in particular, is not found in the traditional job-stress literature, but it represents a basic hallmark of the burnout experience—the negative, callous, or excessively detached response to other people and other aspects of the job.

The exhaustion dimension represents the basic stress response that is studied in other stress research, and it shows the expected positive correlation with workload demands and with stress-related health outcomes. However, the fact that exhaustion is a necessary criterion for defining burnout does not mean it is sufficient. Rather, exhaustion leads workers to engage in other actions to distance themselves emotionally and cognitively from their work, presumably as a way to cope with work demands. In burnout research, a strong relationship between exhaustion and cynicism is found consistently, across a wide range of organizational and occupational settings. The relationship of a sense of inefficacy to the other two dimensions of burnout is more complex. In some cases, feelings of inefficacy appear to be a consequence of exhaustion or cynicism, but in other cases, such feelings seem to develop in parallel with the other two dimensions, rather than sequentially. Although there have been several hypotheses about how burnout develops within the individual over time, there has been little research to test them, given the inherent difficulties of conducting longitudinal studies.

The three dimensions of burnout are related to workplace variables in different ways. In general, exhaustion and cynicism tend to emerge from the presence of work overload and social conflict, whereas a sense of inefficacy arises more clearly from a lack of resources to get the job done (e.g., lack of critical information, lack of necessary tools, or insufficient time). The combinations of variations on these three dimensions can result in different patterns of work experience and risk of burnout. For example, one job situation might involve a lot of difficult working relationships with co-workers (leading to exhaustion and cynicism) but provide good opportunities to achieve success (leading to a sense of efficacy). In another case, the job might involve a lot of heavy work demands (leading to exhaustion and cynicism) but a lack of clear goals (leading to a sense of inefficacy). These and other possible patterns underscore the complexity of the work environment and its differential impact on people. Our model also suggests that effective interventions to deal with burnout should be framed in terms of these three dimensions (e.g., what changes will reduce the risk of exhaustion? what changes will promote the sense of efficacy?).

After we identified the three dimensions of burnout in the early exploratory phases of our research, we developed a measure to assess them, the Maslach

Burnout Inventory (MBI). The MBI was originally designed for use with people working in the human services and health care, because burnout appeared to be a particularly significant problem in these occupations. We then developed a slightly revised version for people working in educational settings. More recently, given the increasing interest in burnout within occupations that are not so clearly people oriented, we developed a general version of the MBI for use with any occupation (see Maslach, Jackson, & Leiter, 1996, for the most recent edition). The MBI has been translated into many languages, and is the common tool used internationally in research on burnout.

Another new development in the conceptualization of burnout has been a focus on its positive antithesis—job engagement. Some researchers define engagement as the opposite end of the three burnout dimensions—energy, involvement, and sense of efficacy. Others conceptualize engagement in its own terms, rather than as an opposite to burnout, and so define it as a persistent, positive motivational state of fulfillment in employees that is characterized by vigor, dedication, and absorption (see Maslach, Schaufeli, & Leiter, 2001, for a comparison of these approaches). Regardless of the definition adopted, one of the important implications of the research on engagement is that interventions may be more effective if they are framed in terms of building engagement rather than reducing burnout.

THE INTERPERSONAL CONTEXT OF JOB STRESS

The significance of the multidimensional model of burnout is that it goes beyond the traditional focus on just the individual stress experience by embedding it within a social context. This interpersonal framework emerged from the early research on caregiving and service occupations, in which the core of the job was the relationship between provider and recipient. This interpersonal context of the job meant that, from the beginning, burnout was studied not so much as an individual stress response, but rather in terms of an individual's transactions with other people in the workplace. Moreover, this interpersonal context focused attention on the individual's emotions, and on the motives and values underlying his or her work with service recipients.

The conceptual impact of this interpersonal framework is perhaps best seen in the cynicism dimension of burnout. People's attempts to distance themselves from aspects of their job can be viewed as individual coping responses to stress. However, when viewed through the lens of interpersonal context, such responses can be seen to have dysfunctional or negative consequences for other people (such as a worker's clients or colleagues). The person who is experiencing a high level of cynicism tends to withdraw from the job and do the bare minimum, rather than strive to do the very best.

Because of this emphasis on the context of the job environment, burnout researchers have focused more on situational variables (e.g., workload demands, social support from colleagues) than on individual variables such as personality (e.g., Type A) and physical health (e.g., cardiovascular disease), which were the focus of prior research on stress. Consequently, burnout research has contributed little to current understanding of the connection between stress and health, but has had more to say about the connection between stress and various job factors. It is worthy of note that the primary researchers in the burnout field have come from social and organizational psychology, and that their theoretical perspectives have shaped the contextual framework of the research to a large degree.

Among the general public, the conventional wisdom about burnout is that the problem lies within the person. Some people argue that the person who burns out is trying too hard and doing too much, whereas others believe that the weak and incompetent burn out. However, research results have not supported the argument that burnout is related to a person's disposition. Although there are some personal variables that have been linked to burnout, the demonstrated relationships have not been large in size and sometimes vary from one study to another. Demographic analyses show that burnout tends to be higher for people who are single than for people who are married and for younger employees than for older employees. In addition, men score slightly higher on cynicism than do women. Burnout has also been linked to the personality dimension of neuroticism (which is defined as anxiety and emotional instability) and to lower levels of hardiness and self-esteem.

The research case is much stronger for the contrasting argument that burnout is more a function of the situation than of the person. Many studies, across many occupations and in different countries, have identified the consistent impact on employee burnout of a range of job characteristics (see Schaufeli & Enzmann, 1998). For example, chronically difficult job demands, an imbalance between high demands and low resources, and the presence of conflict (whether between people, between role demands, or between important values) are consistently found in situations in which employees experience burnout.

Recently, we have attempted to bring some conceptual order to the literature on burnout and job stress by analyzing burnout in terms of six key domains of work life: workload, control, reward, community, fairness, and values. The first two areas are reflected in the demand-control model of job stress (Karasek & Theorell, 1990), according to which job stress results from the combination of a high level of workload demands and a low level of autonomy and control over the job. Reward refers to the power of positive reinforcements to shape behavior. The area of community refers to social relationships in the workplace, and the impact they can have on the worker in terms of social support or interpersonal conflict. Fairness includes any work policies or procedures that affect people's sense of equity and social justice. Finally, the area of values picks up the cognitive-emotional power of job goals and expectations (see Leiter & Maslach, in press).

A consistent theme throughout the burnout literature is the problematic relationship between the person and the work environment, which is often described in terms of imbalance or misfit. For example, the demands of the job may exceed the capacity of the individual to cope effectively, or the person's efforts may not be met with equitable rewards. Within the field of psychology, there is a long history of trying to explain behavior in terms of the interaction of person and environment, and this work has included models of job-person fit. Such a model might be a better framework for understanding job burnout than are approaches that consider personal and situational factors separately.

APPROACHES TO INTERVENTION

As noted earlier, the work on burnout began with a focus on a social problem in the workplace. An underlying theme of that pragmatic framework has been to discover solutions to that problem. From the beginning, the growing research literature was matched (or even outstripped) by a parallel literature of workshop and self-help materials. As burnout became more clearly identified as a form of job stress, it received increasing attention from administrators and policymakers in the workplace. It is thus fair to say that the field of job burnout has always had a primary thrust toward application, in addition to scholarship.

Nevertheless, research on interventions to deal with burnout has been limited. The primary reason for the small number of such studies has been not a lack of interest, but the major difficulties involved in designing an intervention, finding an opportunity to implement it, and being able to do longitudinal follow-up studies.

Interestingly, most discussions of burnout interventions focus primarily on individual-centered approaches, such as removing an individual worker from the job or training the individual to change work behaviors or strengthen his or her internal resources. This type of approach is paradoxical given that researchers have found that situational and organizational factors play a bigger role in burnout than do individual ones. Individually oriented approaches may help alleviate exhaustion, but may not affect the other dimensions of burnout. In addition, individual strategies are relatively ineffective in the workplace, where people have much less control over stressors than in other domains of their life. However, there are both philosophical and pragmatic reasons for the predominant focus on the individual, including notions of individual causality and responsibility and the assumption that it is easier and cheaper to change people than organizations (Maslach & Goldberg, 1998).

Recently, however, we have attempted to develop an organizational approach to assessing burnout and developing strategies for change (Leiter & Maslach, 2000). The program is based on our applied research on burnout and utilizes tools that can be used by both researchers and organizational practitioners—the former to study hypotheses within the context of field studies and the latter to assess the workplace within the context of organizational interventions. The program builds on the latest research developments in the field, such as the positive focus on job engagement, the six areas of work life, and a model of job-person fit. It is still too early to evaluate the effectiveness of this program, but the potential exists to translate the research on job burnout into successful application.

Recommended Reading

Maslach, C., Schaufeli, W.B., & Leiter, M.P. (2001). (See References)
Schaufeli, W.B., & Enzmann, D. (1998). (See References)
Schaufeli, W.B., Maslach, C., & Marek, T. (Eds.). (1993). *Professional burnout: Recent developments in theory and research*. Washington, DC: Taylor & Francis.

Note

1. Address correspondence to Christina Maslach, Office of the Chancellor, 200 California Hall, University of California, Berkeley, CA 94720-1500.

References

Greene, G. (1961). *A burnt out case*. New York: Viking Press.

Karasek, R., & Theorell, T. (1990). *Stress, productivity, and the reconstruction of working life*. New York: Basic Books.

Leiter, M.P., & Maslach, C. (2000). *Preventing burnout and building engagement: A complete program for organizational renewal*. San Francisco: Jossey-Bass.

Leiter, M.P., & Maslach, C. (in press). Areas of worklife: A structured approach to organizational predictors of job burnout. In P.L. Perrewe & D.C. Ganster (Eds.), *Research in occupational stress and well-being* (Vol. 3). Oxford, England: Elsevier.

Maslach, C., & Goldberg, J. (1998). Prevention of burnout: New perspectives. *Applied and Preventive Psychology, 7*, 63–74.

Maslach, C., Jackson, S.E., & Leiter, M.P. (1996). *The Maslach Burnout Inventory* (3rd ed.). Palo Alto, CA: Consulting Psychologists Press.

Maslach, C., Schaufeli, W.B., & Leiter, M.P. (2001). Job burnout. *Annual Review of Psychology, 52*, 397–422.

Schaufeli, W.B., & Enzmann, D. (1998). *The burnout companion to study and practice: A critical analysis*. London: Taylor & Francis.

Critical Thinking Questions

1. What is job burnout and what causes it?

2. What are the key dimensions in the multidimensional model of job burnout?

3. Why does the author view burnout within an interpersonal framework?

Unconscious Emotion

Piotr Winkielman[1] and Kent C. Berridge[2]

[1]University of California, San Diego, and [2]University of Michigan

Abstract

Conscious feelings have traditionally been viewed as a central and necessary ingredient of emotion. Here we argue that emotion also can be genuinely unconscious. We describe evidence that positive and negative reactions can be elicited subliminally and remain inaccessible to introspection. Despite the absence of subjective feelings in such cases, subliminally induced affective reactions still influence people's preference judgments and even the amount of beverage they consume. This evidence is consistent with evolutionary considerations suggesting that systems underlying basic affective reactions originated prior to systems for conscious awareness. The idea of unconscious emotion is also supported by evidence from affective neuroscience indicating that subcortical brain systems underlie basic "liking" reactions. More research is needed to clarify the relations and differences between conscious and unconscious emotion, and their underlying mechanisms. However, even under the current state of knowledge, it appears that processes underlying conscious feelings can become decoupled from processes underlying emotional reactions, resulting in genuinely unconscious emotion.

Keywords

affect; automaticity; consciousness; emotion; neuroscience

To say that people are conscious of their own emotions sounds like a truism. After all, emotions are feelings, so how could one have feelings that are not felt? Of course, people sometimes may be mistaken about the cause of their emotion or may not know why they feel a particular emotion, as when they feel anxious for what seems no particular reason. On occasion, people may even incorrectly construe their own emotional state, as when they angrily deny that they are angry. But many psychologists presume that the emotion itself is intrinsically conscious, and that with proper motivation and attention, it can be brought into the full light of awareness. So, at least, goes the traditional view.

Our view goes a bit further. We suggest that under some conditions an emotional process may remain entirely unconscious, even when the person is attentive and motivated to describe his or her feelings correctly (Berridge & Winkielman, 2003; Winkielman, Berridge, & Wilbarger, in press). Such an emotional process may nevertheless drive the person's behavior and physiological reactions, even while remaining inaccessible to conscious awareness. In short, we propose the existence of genuinely unconscious emotions.

Address correspondence to Piotr Winkielman, Department of Psychology, University of California, San Diego, 9500 Gilman Dr., La Jolla, CA 92093-0109, e-mail: pwinkiel@ucsd.edu, or to Kent Berridge, Department of Psychology, University of Michigan, 525 East University, Ann Arbor, MI 48109-1109, e-mail: berridge@umich.edu.

THE TRADITIONAL VIEW: EMOTION AS A CONSCIOUS EXPERIENCE

The assumption that emotions are always conscious has been shared by some of the most influential psychologists in history. In his famous article "What Is an Emotion," James (1884) proposed that emotion is a perception of bodily changes. This perception forms a conscious feeling, which is a necessary ingredient of both simple affective states, such as pleasure and pain, and more complex emotions, such as love or pride. Conscious feeling is exactly what distinguishes emotion from other mental states. Without it, "we find that we have nothing left behind, no 'mind-stuff' out of which the emotion can be constituted . . ." (p. 193). For Freud (1950), too, emotions themselves were always conscious, even if their underlying causes sometimes were not: "It is surely of the essence of an emotion that we should feel it, i.e. that it should enter consciousness" (pp. 109–110).

The assumption that affective reactions are conscious is widely shared in the contemporary literature on emotion. Explaining how most researchers use the term "affect," Frijda (1999) said that the term "primarily refers to hedonic experience, the experience of pleasure and pain" (p. 194). Clore (1994) unequivocally titled one of his essays "Why Emotions Are Never Unconscious" and argued that subjective feeling is a necessary (although not a sufficient) condition for emotion. In short, psychologists past and present generally have agreed that a conscious feeling is a primary or even a necessary ingredient of affect and emotion.

IMPLICIT EMOTION AND UNCONSCIOUS AFFECT

By contrast, it is now widely accepted that cognitive processes and states can be unconscious (occurring below awareness) or implicit (occurring without attention or intention). So, it may not require much of a leap to consider the possibility of unconscious or implicit emotion. As Kihlstrom (1999) put it,

> Paralleling the usage of these descriptors in the cognitive unconscious, "explicit emotion" refers to the person's conscious awareness of an emotion, feeling, or mood state; "implicit emotion", by contrast, refers to changes in experience, thought, or action that are attributable to one's emotional state, independent of his or her conscious awareness of that state. (p. 432)

Unconscious Elicitation of Conscious Affective Reactions

Research advances in the past few years challenge the traditional view by demonstrating "unconscious emotion," at least in a limited sense of unconscious causation. Several studies have shown that stimuli presented below awareness can elicit an affective reaction that is itself consciously felt. An example is subliminal induction of the mere-exposure effect, that is, a positive response to repeatedly presented items. In one study, some participants were first subliminally exposed to several repeated neutral stimuli consisting of random visual patterns. Later, those participants reported being in a better mood—a conscious feeling state—than participants who had been subliminally exposed to neutral stimuli that had not been repeatedly presented (Monahan, Murphy, & Zajonc, 2000). In other studies, changes in self-reported mood have been elicited by subliminal presentation of positive or negative images, such as pictures of snakes and spiders presented to phobic individuals (Öhman, Flykt, & Lundqvist, 2000).

But asserting that subliminal stimuli may cause emotion is different from asserting that emotional reactions themselves can ever be unconscious (Berridge & Winkielman, 2003; Kihlstrom, 1999). The research we just mentioned still fits into the conventional view that once emotions are caused, they are always conscious. In fact, these studies relied on introspective reports of conscious feelings to demonstrate the presence of emotion once it was unconsciously caused.

So the question remains: Can one be unconscious not only of the causes of emotion, but also of one's own emotional reaction itself—even if that emotional reaction is intense enough to alter one's behavior? Studies from our lab suggest that the answer is yes. Under some conditions, people can have subliminally triggered emotional reactions that drive judgment and behavior, even in the absence of any conscious feelings accompanying these reactions.

Uncorrected and Unremembered Emotional Reactions

In an initial attempt to demonstrate unconscious emotion, a series of studies examined participants' ratings of neutral stimuli, such as Chinese ideographs, preceded by subliminally presented happy or angry faces (Winkielman, Zajonc, & Schwarz, 1997). Some participants in those studies were asked to monitor changes in their conscious feelings, and told not to use their feelings as a source of their preference ratings. Specifically, experimental instructions informed those participants that their feelings might be "contaminated" by irrelevant factors, such as hidden pictures (Study 1) or music playing in the background (Study 2). Typically, such instructions eliminate the influence of conscious feelings on evaluative judgments (Clore, 1994). However, even for participants told to disregard their feelings, the subliminally presented happy faces increased and subliminally presented angry faces decreased preference ratings of the neutral stimuli. This failure to correct for invalid feelings indicates that participants might not have experienced any conscious reactions in the first place. Indeed, after the experiment, participants did not remember experiencing any mood changes when asked about what they had felt during the rating task. Still, memory is not infallible. A skeptic could argue that participants had conscious feelings immediately after subliminal exposure to emotional faces, but simply failed to remember the feelings later. Thus, it is open to debate whether these studies demonstrate unconscious emotion.

Unconscious Emotional Reactions Strong Enough to Change Behavior

We agreed that stronger evidence was needed. Proof of unconscious emotion requires showing that participants are unable to report a conscious feeling at the same time their behavior reveals the presence of an emotional reaction. Ideally, the emotional reaction should be strong enough to change behavior with some consequences for the individual. To obtain such evidence, we assessed participants' pouring and drinking of a novel beverage after they were subliminally exposed to several emotional facial expressions (Berridge & Winkielman, 2003; Winkielman et al., in press). The general procedure of these experiments can be seen in Figure 1. Participants were first asked if they were thirsty. Next, they were subliminally exposed to several emotional expressions (happy, neutral, or angry) embedded in a cognitive task requiring participants to classify a clearly visible neutral face as male or female. Immediately afterward, some participants rated their feelings on scales assessing emotional experience and then were given a novel lemon-lime beverage to consume and evaluate. Other participants consumed and evaluated the beverage before rating their feelings. Specifically, in Study 1, participants were asked to pour themselves a cup of the beverage from a pitcher and then drink from the cup, whereas in Study 2, participants were asked to take a small sip of the beverage from a prepared cup and then rate it on various dimensions, including monetary value.

In both studies, conscious feelings were not influenced by subliminal presentation of emotional faces, regardless of whether participants rated their feelings on a simple scale from positive to negative mood or from high to low arousal, or on a multi-item scale asking about specific emotions, such as contentment or irritation. That is, participants did not feel more positive after subliminally presented happy expressions than after subliminally presented neutral expressions. Nor did they feel more negative after angry expressions than after neutral expressions. Yet participants' consumption and ratings of the drink were influenced by those subliminal stimuli—especially when participants were thirsty. Specifically, thirsty participants poured significantly more drink from the pitcher and drank more from their cup after happy faces than after angry faces (Study 1). Thirsty

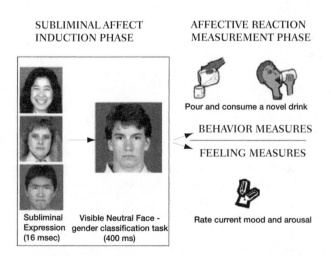

SUBLIMINAL AFFECT
INDUCTION PHASE

AFFECTIVE REACTION
MEASUREMENT PHASE

Pour and consume a novel drink

BEHAVIOR MEASURES

FEELING MEASURES

Rate current mood and arousal

Subliminal   Visible Neutral Face -
Expression   gender classification task
(16 msec)   (400 ms)

Fig. 1. Sequence of events in research investigating the impact of subliminally presented emotional facial expressions. First, participants are subliminally exposed to several expressions of the same valence (happy, neutral, or angry). The expressions are hidden by a visible neutral face that participants classify as male or female. Second, participants pour and drink a beverage and report their conscious feelings (in counterbalanced order).

participants were also willing to pay about twice as much for the drink after happy than after angry expressions (Study 2). The modulating role of thirst indicates that unconscious emotional reactions acted through basic biopsychological mechanisms that determine reactions to incentives, such as a drink, rather than through cognitive mechanisms influencing interpretation of the stimulus (Berridge & Winkielman, 2003; Winkielman et al., 2002).

In summary, the studies just described show that subliminally presented emotional faces can cause affective reactions that alter consumption behavior, without eliciting conscious feelings at the moment the affective reactions are caused. Because the influence of emotional faces on consumption behavior was observed also for those participants who rated their feelings immediately after the subliminal presentation of the faces, these results cannot be explained by failures of memory. Thus, we propose that these results demonstrate unconscious affect in the strong sense of the term—affect that is powerful enough to alter behavior, but that people are simply not aware of, even when attending to their feelings.

Support From Evolution and Neuroscience

From the standpoint of evolution and neuroscience, there are good reasons to suppose that at least some forms of emotional reaction can exist independently of subjective correlates. Evolutionarily speaking, the ability to have conscious feelings is probably a late achievement compared with the ability to have behavioral affective reactions to emotional stimuli (LeDoux, 1996). Basic affective reactions are widely shared by animals, including reptiles and fish, and at least in some species may not involve conscious awareness comparable to that in humans. The original function of emotion was to allow the organism to react appropriately to positive or negative events, and conscious feelings might not always have been required.

The neurocircuitry needed for basic affective responses, such as a "liking" reaction[1] to a pleasant sensation or a fear reaction to a threatening stimulus, is largely contained in emotional brain structures that lie below the cortex, such as the nucleus accumbens, amygdala, hypothalamus, and even lower brain stem (Berridge, 2003; LeDoux, 1996). These subcortical structures evolved early and may carry out limited operations that are essentially preconscious, compared with the elaborate human cortex at the top of the brain, which is more involved in conscious emotional feelings. Yet even limited subcortical structures on their own are capable of some basic affective reactions. A dramatic demonstration of this point comes from affective neuroscience studies with anencephalic human infants. The brain of such infants is congenitally malformed, possessing only a brain stem, and lacking nearly all structures at the top or front of the brain, including the entire cortex. Yet sweet tastes of sugar still elicit positive facial expressions of liking from anencephalic infants, whereas bitter tastes elicit negative facial expressions of disgust (Steiner, 1973).

---

[1]We use the term "liking" to indicate an unconscious reaction, not a conscious feeling of pleasure.

Even in normal brains, the most effective "brain tweaks" so far discovered for enhancing liking and related affective reactions all involve deep brain structures below the cortex. Thus, animal studies have shown that liking for sweetness increases after a drug that activates opioid receptors is injected into the nucleus accumbens (a reward-related structure at the base of the front of the brain). Liking reactions to sugar can even be enhanced by injecting a drug that activates other receptors into the brain stem, which is perhaps the most basic component of the brain. Such examples reflect the persisting importance of early-evolved neurocircuitry in generating behavioral emotional reactions in modern mammalian brains (Berridge, 2003; LeDoux, 1996). In short, evidence from affective neuroscience suggests that basic affective reactions are mediated largely by brain structures deep below the cortex, raising the possibility that these reactions might not be intrinsically accessible to conscious awareness.

KEY QUESTIONS FOR FUTURE RESEARCH

As we have argued, there are good theoretical reasons why some emotional reactions might be unconscious, and we suggest that our recent empirical evidence actually provides an example. However, several critical issues need to be addressed by future research.

The studies discussed here focused only on basic liking-disliking, so it is possible that the crucial property of unconscious emotion is simply positive-negative valence, rather than qualitative distinctions associated with categorical emotion (fear, anger, disgust, joy, etc.). However, evidence suggests that subcortical circuitry may be capable of some qualitative differentiation. For example, human neuroimaging studies reveal differential activation of the amygdala in response to consciously presented facial expressions of fear versus anger (Whalen, 1998). If future research shows that subliminally presented expressions of fear, anger, disgust, and sadness can create qualitatively different physiological and behavioral reactions, all without conscious experience, then there may indeed exist implicit affective processes deserving the label "unconscious emotion" in its strongest sense. Studies that simultaneously measure psychophysiology, behavior, and self-reports of emotion could be particularly useful to address such issues (Winkielman, Berntson, & Cacioppo, 2001).

The studies discussed here employed basic affective stimuli, such as subliminally presented facial expressions, to influence emotional behavior without eliciting conscious feelings. Future studies might address whether more complex stimuli that derive their positive or negative value from a person's cultural environment can also influence emotional behavior without eliciting any accompanying feelings. A related question concerns whether stimuli presented above the threshold of awareness can also change emotional behavior and physiology without influencing feelings.

The studies described here suggest that under some conditions emotional reactions are genuinely unconscious. But obviously many emotional states are conscious, even when elicited with subliminal stimuli (Monahan et al., 2000; Öhman et al., 2000). What determines when a basic emotional reaction is accompanied by conscious feelings? Is it possible for even a strong emotional reaction to be unconscious? What are the neural mechanisms by which emotion is made conscious? How do behavioral consequences of conscious and unconscious reactions differ?

Finally, a question of practical importance to many emotion researchers, as well as clinicians, concerns the meaning of people's reports of their own emotions. The existence of verifiable but unconscious emotional reactions does not mean that subjective feelings are merely "icing on the emotional cake." At least, that is not our view. We believe that self-reports of feelings have a major place in emotion research and treatment. However, it is also clear that psychologists should not limit themselves to subjective experiences. A combination of approaches and techniques, from psychology and human and animal affective neuroscience, will best lead to understanding the relation between conscious and unconscious emotions.

Recommended Reading

Bargh, J.A., & Ferguson, M.L. (2000). Beyond behaviorism: On the automaticity of higher mental processes. *Psychological Bulletin, 126,* 925–945.
Berridge, K.C., & Winkielman, P. (2003). (See References)
Damasio, A.R. (1999). *The feeling of what happens: Body and emotion in the making of consciousness.* New York: Harcourt Brace.
Wilson, T.D. (2002). *Strangers to ourselves: Discovering the adaptive unconscious.* Cambridge, MA: Harvard University Press.
Zajonc, R.B. (2000). Feeling and thinking: Closing the debate over the independence of affect. In J.P. Forgas (Ed.), *Feeling and thinking: The role of affect in social cognition* (pp. 31–58). New York: Cambridge University Press.

REFERENCES

Berridge, K.C. (2003). Pleasures of the brain. *Brain and Cognition, 52,* 106–128.
Berridge, K.C., & Winkielman, P. (2003). What is an unconscious emotion: The case for unconscious 'liking.' *Cognition and Emotion, 17,* 181–211.
Clore, G.L. (1994). Why emotions are never unconscious. In P. Ekman & R.J. Davidson (Eds.), *The nature of emotion: Fundamental questions* (pp. 285–290). New York: Oxford University Press.
Freud, S. (1950). *Collected papers, Vol. 4* (J. Riviere, Trans.). London: Hogarth Press and Institute of Psychoanalysis.
Frijda, N.H. (1999). Emotions and hedonic experience. In D. Kahneman, E. Diener, & N. Schwarz (Eds.), *Well-being: The foundations of hedonic psychology* (pp. 190–210). New York: Russell Sage Foundation.
James, W. (1884). What is an emotion. *Mind, 9,* 188–205.
Kihlstrom, J.F. (1999). The psychological unconscious. In L.A. Pervin & O.P. John (Eds.), *Handbook of personality: Theory and research* (2nd ed., pp. 424–442). New York: Guilford Press.
LeDoux, J. (1996). *The emotional brain: The mysterious underpinnings of emotional life.* New York: Simon & Schuster.
Monahan, J.L., Murphy, S.T., & Zajonc, R.B. (2000). Subliminal mere exposure: Specific, general, and diffuse effects. *Psychological Science, 11,* 462–466.
Öhman, A., Flykt, A., & Lundqvist, D. (2000). Unconscious emotion: Evolutionary perspectives, psychophysiological data and neuropsychological mechanisms. In R.D. Lane, L. Nadel, & G. Ahern (Eds.), *Cognitive neuroscience of emotion* (pp. 296–327). New York: Oxford University Press.
Steiner, J.E. (1973). The gustofacial response: Observation on normal and anencephalic newborn infants. *Symposium on Oral Sensation and Perception, 4,* 254–278.

Whalen, P.J. (1998). Fear, vigilance, and ambiguity: Initial neuroimaging studies of the human amygdala. *Current Directions in Psychological Science, 7,* 177–188.

Winkielman, P., Berntson, G.G., & Cacioppo, J.T. (2001). The psychophysiological perspective on the social mind. In A. Tesser & N. Schwarz (Eds.), *Blackwell handbook of social psychology: Intraindividual processes* (pp. 89–108). Oxford, England: Blackwell.

Winkielman, P., Berridge, K.C., & Wilbarger, J. (in press). Unconscious affective reactions to masked happy versus angry faces influence consumption behavior and judgments of value. *Personality and Social Psychology Bulletin.*

Winkielman, P., Zajonc, R.B., & Schwarz, N. (1997). Subliminal affective priming resists attributional interventions. *Cognition and Emotion, 11,* 433–465.

Critical Thinking Questions

1. What is the traditional view of emotion?

2. What evidence is there for the proposition that an emotion can be elicited without a person's awareness?

3. How have the authors shown that people have emotional reactions they cannot report on?

4. What evidence is there in brain research that people can experience emotion without conscious thought?

Nature, Nurture, and Human Development

Are you programmed by nature, or is your fate molded by nurturing forces in the environment? This question animates much of developmental psychology, the study of how people grow, mature, and change as they get older. By comparing people of different ages, and by following individuals over time, developmental psychologists study all aspects of the human life cycle—from prenatal development to infancy, childhood, adolescence, adulthood, and old age. The articles in this section cover some of the new and exciting research.

This section opens with an article by Janet DiPietro (2004) in which she reviews animal experiments showing that maternal stress in pregnancy can affect development of the offspring and speculates on whether human mothers and children are similarly at risk. Renee Baillargeon (2004) then reviews some of the recent and clever studies (infants can't talk, so researchers come up with indirect ways to assess what they know) on how infants perceive the physical world around them. Interested in the nature and nurture of childhood, Eleanor Maccoby (2002) describes her classic research on the tendency for boys and girls to play in segregated same-sex groups, leading them to form male and female "subcultures." Wyndol Furman (2002) writes about research on adolescent romantic relationships, how they change over the course of adolescence, and the ways in which they are influenced by parents and peers. Advancing into adulthood, Arthur Kramer and Sherry Willis (2002) review what is known about the declines in old age of various intellectual functions and, in particular, how these declines can be reduced through cognitive training, practice, and other interventions.

The Role of Prenatal Maternal Stress in Child Development

Janet A. DiPietro
Johns Hopkins University

Abstract

The notion that a woman's psychological state during pregnancy affects the fetus is a persistent cultural belief in many parts of the world. Recent results indicate that prenatal maternal distress in rodents and nonhuman primates negatively influences long-term learning, motor development, and behavior in their offspring. The applicability of these findings to human pregnancy and child development is considered in this article. Potential mechanisms through which maternal psychological functioning may alter development of the fetal nervous system are being identified by current research, but it is premature to conclude that maternal prenatal stress has negative consequences for child development. Mild stress may be a necessary condition for optimal development.

Keywords

pregnancy; fetus; fetal development; stress

"Ay ay, for this I draw in many a tear,
And stop the rising of blood-sucking sighs,
Lest with my sighs or tears I blast or drown
King Edward's fruit, true heir to the English Crown"

—Queen Elizabeth's response upon learning of her husband's imprisonment in Shakespeare's *King Henry VI* (Part 3), Act IV, Scene IV

Since antiquity, people have thought that the emotions and experiences of a pregnant woman impinge on her developing fetus. Some of these notions, such as the idea that a severe fright marks a child with a prominent birthmark, no longer persist. However, the premise that maternal psychological distress has deleterious effects on the fetus is the focus of active scientific inquiry today. A resurgence of interest in the prenatal period as a staging period for later diseases, including psychiatric ones, has been fostered by the enormous attention devoted to the hypothesis of fetal programming advanced by D.J. Barker and his colleagues. Fetal programming implies that maternal and fetal factors that affect growth impart an indelible impression on adult organ function, including functioning of the brain and nervous system. That earlier circumstances, including those during the prenatal period, might affect later development is hardly newsworthy to developmentalists. In the 1930s, the Fels Research Institute initiated a longitudinal study of child development that commenced with intensive investigation of the fetal period.

Address correspondence to Janet DiPietro, Department of Population and Family Health Sciences, 624 N. Broadway, Johns Hopkins University, Baltimore, MD 21205; e-mail: jdipietr@jhsph.edu.

Possible effects of maternal psychological distress during pregnancy range along a continuum from the immediate and disastrous (e.g., miscarriage) to the more subtle and long term (e.g., developmental disorders). Most existing research has focused on the effects of maternal distress on pregnancy itself. For example, there are numerous comprehensive reviews of research indicating that women who express greater distress during pregnancy give birth somewhat earlier to somewhat lighter babies than do women who are less distressed. The focus of this report is on the potential for maternal stress to generate more far-reaching effects on behavioral and cognitive development in childhood.

MECHANISMS AND EVIDENCE FROM ANIMAL STUDIES

There are no direct neural connections between the mother and the fetus. To have impact on the fetus, maternal psychological functioning must be translated into physiological effects. Three mechanisms by which this might occur are considered most frequently: alteration in maternal behaviors (e.g., substance abuse), reduction in blood flow such that the fetus is deprived of oxygen and nutrients, and transport of stress-related neurohormones to the fetus through the placenta. Stress-related neurohormones, such as cortisol, are necessary for normal fetal maturation and the birth process. However, relatively slight variations in these hormones, particularly early in pregnancy, have the potential to generate a cascade of effects that may result in changes to the fetus's own stress response system.

The most compelling evidence of a link between maternal psychological functioning and later development in offspring is found in animal studies. Stress responses in rodents can be reliably induced by a variety of experimental methods. Deliberate exposure of pregnant laboratory animals to stressful events (e.g., restraint) produces effects on offspring. These include deficits in motor development, learning behavior, and the ability to cope effectively in stressful situations. There is a tendency for the effects to be greater in female than in male offspring. Changes in brain structure and function of prenatally stressed animals have also been documented (Welberg & Seckl, 2001). Yet not all documented effects of prenatal stress are negative; mild stress has been observed to benefit, not damage, later learning in rats (Fujioka et al., 2001).

In a series of studies, pregnant rhesus monkeys that were exposed to repeated periods of loud noise were shown to bear offspring with delayed motor development and reduced attention in infancy. A constellation of negative behaviors, including enhanced responsiveness to stress and dysfunctional social behavior with peers, persisted through adolescence (Schneider & Moore, 2000). In general, studies of stress in nonhuman primates find males to be more affected than females. However, although a study comparing offspring of pregnant pigtailed macaques that were repeatedly stressed with offspring of nonstressed mothers did find that the behavior of prenatally stressed males was less mature than the behavior of non-prenatally stressed males, for females the results were reversed. The females born to the stressed mothers displayed more mature behavior than non-prenatally stressed females (Novak & Sackett, 1996). Thus, although most studies have reported detrimental consequences, reports of either no effects or beneficial ones make it clear that much is left to be learned about the specific characteristics of stressors that either accelerate or retard development.

DOES MATERNAL STRESS AFFECT DEVELOPMENT IN HUMANS?

Several important factors make it difficult to generalize results based on animal studies to humans. First, there are substantial physiological differences inherent to pregnancies in different species. Second, researchers are unable to control the events that transpire after birth in humans. Women who are psychologically stressed before pregnancy are also likely to be stressed after pregnancy, so it is critical that the role of social influences after birth be carefully distinguished from pregnancy effects that are transmitted biologically. Finally, the nature of the prenatal stress studied in animals and humans is very different, and this may pose the greatest barrier to the ability to generalize. In animal research, stressors are external events that are controlled in terms of duration, frequency, and intensity. The closest parallel in human studies is found in the few studies that have taken advantage of specific events, including an earthquake and the World Trade Center disaster, to study the effects on pregnancy in women residing in physical proximity. No such study has examined children's cognitive or behavioral outcomes. However, what is measured in virtually all human studies of "stress" during pregnancy is women's affect, mood, and emotional responses to daily circumstances in their lives. Maternal anxiety and, to a lesser extent, depression are prominent foci of research. Both may reflect emotional responses to stressful circumstances, but they also represent more persistent features of personality. Thus, not only are the physiological consequences and nature of prenatal stress different between animal and human studies, but when human studies detect an association between mothers' prenatal anxiety, for example, and their children's later behavior, it may be the result of shared genes or childrearing practices related to maternal temperament.

Despite these concerns, there is a small but growing literature indicating that there is a relation between pregnant women's psychological distress and their children's behavioral outcomes. In one study, the ability of 8-month-old infants to pay attention during a developmental assessment was negatively correlated with the amount of anxiety their mothers reported about their pregnancy (Huizink, Robles de Medina, Mulder, Visser, & Buitelaar, 2002). This study is one of the few in which infants' behavior was rated by an independent observer and not a parent. Two separate studies with large numbers of participants found positive associations between maternal distress (primarily anxiety) in the first half of pregnancy and behavioral disorders or negative emotionality at preschool age (Martin, Noyes, Wisenbaker, & Huttunen, 2000; O'Connor, Heron, Golding, Beveridge, & Glover, 2002). Unfortunately, both relied on mothers' reports of their children's problems, so it is impossible to know whether the results simply indicate that anxious mothers perceive their children to be more difficult than nonanxious mothers do. However, new information about potential mechanisms whereby maternal stress might affect fetal development gives plausibility to these results. Maternal anxiety is associated with reduced blood flow to the fetus (Sjostrom, Valentin, Thelin, & Marsal, 1997), and fetal levels of stress hormones reflect those of their mothers (Gitau, Cameron, Fisk, & Glover, 1998).

Remarkably, this handful of published studies represents most of what we know about the effects of maternal distress on child development. There are several additional reports in the literature, but because of problems in methods or analysis, their results are not compelling. As the field matures, methodological, analytical, and interpretational standards will emerge over time.

THE NEXT LEVEL OF INVESTIGATION

The implicit assumption has been that prenatal stress and emotions have consequences for child development after birth because they have more immediate effects on the development of the nervous system before birth. Until recently, the fetal period of development was a black box. Although fetuses remain one of the few categories of research participants who can be neither directly viewed nor heard, opportunities to measure fetal development now exist. As pregnancy advances, the behavioral capabilities of the fetus become similar to those of a newborn infant, although the fetus is limited by the constraints of the uterus. Nonetheless, measurement of fetal motor activity, heart rate, and their relation to each other provides a fairly complete portrait of fetal development. New techniques present an opportunity to examine the manner in which the psychological state of the pregnant woman may affect development prior to birth, and perhaps permanently change the offspring's course of development.

In our first efforts to examine the link between fetal behavior and maternal stress, my colleagues and I relied on commonly used paper-and-pencil questionnaires to measure maternal psychological attributes. In a small study, we found that mothers' perception of experiencing daily hassles in everyday life was inversely related to the degree to which their fetuses' movement and heart rate were in synchrony. Such synchrony is an indicator of developing neural integration (DiPietro, Hodgson, Costigan, Hilton, & Johnson, 1996). In a second study, we found that mothers' emotional intensity, perception of their lives as stressful, and, in particular, feelings that they were more hassled than uplifted by their pregnancy were positively related to the activity level of their fetuses (DiPietro, Hilton, Hawkins, Costigan, & Pressman, 2002). We had previously reported that active fetuses tend to be active 1-year-olds, so fetal associations portend postnatal ones.

Measures of maternal stress and emotions that are based on mothers' self-reports are important only to the extent that they correspond to physiological signals that can be transmitted to the fetus; thus, they provide limited information. We turned to investigating the degree to which maternal physiological arousal, as measured by heart rate and electrical conductance of the skin, a measure of emotionality, is associated with fetal behavior. The results were unexpected in that fetal motor activity, even when it was imperceptible to women, stimulated transient increases in their heart rate and skin conductance.

It became apparent to us that the only way to truly examine the effect of stress on the fetus was to subject women to a standard, noninvasive stressor and measure the fetal response. The stressor we selected was a common cognitive challenge known as the Stroop Color-Word Test. In this test, subjects are asked to read color names that are printed in various colors and so must dissociate the color of the words from their meaning. The test is not aversive but reliably induces physiological arousal. In general, when pregnant women engaged in this task, fetal motor activity was suppressed, although individual responses varied. The degree to which individual women and fetuses responded to the Stroop test was similar from the middle to the end of pregnancy. These results lead us to propose three hypotheses. First, women respond to stress in characteristic ways that fetuses are repeatedly exposed to over the course of pregnancy. This experience serves to sensitize the developing nervous system. Second, there are both short-term and longer-term adaptive responses to stress by the fetus, depending on the intensity and repetitiveness of the stimulation. Finally, the immediacy of the fetal response to the Stroop, as well as to maternal viewing of graphic scenes from a movie on labor and delivery, suggest an additional mechanism whereby maternal stress might affect the fetus. We propose that the fetus responds to changes in the sensory environment of the uterus that occur when maternal heart rate, blood pressure, and other internal functions are abruptly altered. This proposal cannot be readily tested, but hearing is among the first perceptual systems to develop prenatally, and it is well documented that the fetus can perceive sounds that emanate from both within and outside the uterus.

Our final foray into this area of inquiry has been to follow children who participated in our studies as fetuses. Recently, we completed developmental testing on approximately one hundred 2-year-old children. The results, as is often the case in fetal research, surprised us. Higher maternal anxiety midway through pregnancy was strongly associated with better motor and mental development scores on the Bayley Scales of Infant Development, a standard developmental assessment. These associations remained even after controlling statistically for other possible contributing factors, including level of maternal education and both anxiety and stress after giving birth. This finding is in the direction opposite to that which would be predicted on the basis of most, but not all, of the animal research. Yet it is consistent with what is known about the class of neurohormones known as glucocorticoids, which are produced during the stress response and also play a role in the maturation of body organs. Our results are also consistent with findings from a series of studies on physical stress. The newborns of pregnant women who exercised regularly were somewhat smaller than the newborns of women who did not exercise much, but showed better ability to remain alert and track stimuli; the children of the regular exercisers also had higher cognitive ability at age 5 (Clapp, 1996). Exercise and psychological distress do not necessarily have the same physiological consequences to the fetus, but the parallel is intriguing.

CONCLUSIONS

At this time, there is too little scientific evidence to establish that a woman's psychological state during pregnancy affects her child's developmental outcomes. It is premature to extend findings from animal studies to women and children, particularly given the disparity in the way the animal and human studies are designed. The question of whether maternal stress and affect serve to accelerate or inhibit maturation of the fetal nervous system, and postnatal development in turn, remains open. It has been proposed that a certain degree of stress during early childhood is required for optimal organization of the brain, because stress provokes periods of disruption to existing structures (Huether, 1998), and this may be true for the prenatal period as well.

The relation between maternal stress and children's development may ultimately be found to mirror the relation between arousal and performance, which is characterized by an inverted U-shaped curve. This function, often called the Yerkes-Dodson law, posits that both low and high levels of arousal are associated with performance decrements, whereas a moderate level is associated with enhanced performance. This model has been applied to a spectrum of psychological observations, and a parallel with prenatal maternal stress may exist as well. In other words, too much or too little stress may impede development, but a moderate level may be formative or optimal. The current intensive investigation in this research area should provide better understanding of the importance of the prenatal period for postnatal life as investigators direct their efforts toward determining how maternal psychological signals are received by the fetus.

Recommended Reading

Kofman, O. (2002). The role of prenatal stress in the etiology of developmental behavioral disorders. *Neuroscience and Biobehavioral Reviews, 26*, 457–470.

Mulder, E., Robles de Medina, P., Huizink, A., Van den Bergh, B., Buitelaar, J., & Visser, G. (2002). Prenatal maternal stress: Effects on pregnancy and the (unborn) child. *Early Human Development, 70*, 3–14.

Paarlberg, K.M., Vingerhoets, A., Passchier, J., Dekker, G., & van Geijn, H. (1995). Psychosocial factors and pregnancy outcome: A review with emphasis on methodological issues. *Journal of Psychosomatic Research, 39*, 563–595.

Wadhwa, P., Sandman, C., & Garite, T. (2001). The neurobiology of stress in human pregnancy: Implications for prematurity and development of the fetal central nervous system. *Progress in Brain Research, 133*, 131–142.

Acknowledgments—This work has been supported by Grant R01 HD5792 from the National Institute of Child Health and Development.

References

Clapp, J. (1996). Morphometric and neurodevelopmental outcome at age five years of the offspring of women who continued to exercise regularly throughout pregnancy. *Journal of Pediatrics, 129*, 856–863.

DiPietro, J., Hilton, S., Hawkins, M., Costigan, K., & Pressman, E. (2002). Maternal stress and affect influence fetal neurobehavioral development. *Developmental Psychology, 38*, 659–668.

DiPietro, J.A., Hodgson, D.M., Costigan, K.A., Hilton, S.C., & Johnson, T.R.B. (1996). Development of fetal movement-fetal heart rate coupling from 20 weeks through term. *Early Human Development, 44*, 139–151.

Fujioka, T., Fujioka, A., Tan, N., Chowdhury, G., Mouri, H., Sakata, Y., & Nakamura, S. (2001). Mild prenatal stress enhances learning performance in the non-adopted rat offspring. *Neuroscience, 103*, 301–307.

Gitau, R., Cameron, A., Fisk, N., & Glover, V. (1998). Fetal exposure to maternal cortisol. *Lancet, 352*, 707–708.

Huether, G. (1998). Stress and the adaptive self-organization of neuronal connectivity during early childhood. *International Journal of Neuroscience, 16*, 297–306.

Huizink, A., Robles de Medina, P., Mulder, E., Visser, G., & Buitelaar, J. (2002). Psychological measures of prenatal stress as predictors of infant temperament. *Journal of the American Academy of Child & Adolescent Psychiatry, 41*, 1078–1085.

Martin, R., Noyes, J., Wisenbaker, J., & Huttunen, M. (2000). Prediction of early childhood negative emotionality and inhibition from maternal distress during pregnancy. *Merrill-Palmer Quarterly, 45*, 370–391.

Novak, M., & Sackett, G. (1996). Reflexive and early neonatal development in offspring of pigtailed macaques exposed to prenatal psychosocial stress. *Developmental Psychobiology, 29*, 294.

O'Connor, T., Heron, J., Golding, J., Beveridge, M., & Glover, V. (2002). Maternal antenatal anxiety and children's behavioural/emotional problems at 4 years. *British Journal of Psychiatry, 180*, 502–508.

Schneider, M., & Moore, C. (2000). Effects of prenatal stress on development: A non-human primate model. In C. Nelson (Ed.), *Minnesota Symposium on Child Psychology: Vol. 31. The effects of early adversity on neurobehavioral development* (pp. 201–244). Mahwah, NJ: Erlbaum.

Sjostrom, K., Valentin, L., Thelin, T., & Marsal, K. (1997). Maternal anxiety in late pregnancy and fetal hemodynamics. *European Journal of Obstetrics and Gynecology, 74*, 149–155.

Welberg, L., & Seckl, J. (2001). Prenatal stress, glucocorticoids and the programming of the brain. *Journal of Neuroendocrinology, 13*, 113–128.

Critical Thinking Questions

1. What leads the author to believe that maternal stress can cause development changes in a fetus?

2. Summarize the findings from animal studies on the role of prenatal maternal stress.

3. Describe the challenges and approaches for conducting research on prenatal stress in humans.

4. What does the author conclude about the state of the science when it comes to the role of prenatal maternal stress in humans?

Infants' Physical World

Renée Baillargeon

University of Illinois

Abstract

Investigations of infants' physical world over the past 20 years have revealed two main findings. First, even very young infants possess expectations about physical events. Second, these expectations undergo significant developments during the first year of life, as infants form event categories, such as occlusion, containment, and covering events, and identify the variables relevant for predicting outcomes in each category. A new account of infants' physical reasoning integrates these findings. Predictions from the account are examined in change-blindness and teaching experiments.

Keywords

infant cognition; physical reasoning; explanation-based learning

Over the past 20 years, my collaborators and I have been studying how infants use their developing physical knowledge to predict and interpret the outcomes of events. This article focuses on infants' knowledge about three event categories: occlusion events, which are events in which an object is placed or moves behind a nearer object, or occluder; containment events, which are events in which an object is placed inside a container; and covering events, which are events in which a rigid cover is lowered over an object (Baillargeon & Wang, 2002). I first summarize two relevant bodies of developmental findings, and then point out discrepancies between these findings. Next, I outline a new account of infants' physical reasoning that attempts to make sense of these discrepancies. Finally, I describe new lines of research that test predictions from this account.

All of the research reviewed here used the violation-of-expectation method. In a typical experiment, infants see an expected event, which is consistent with the expectation examined in the experiment, and an unexpected event, which violates this expectation. With appropriate controls, evidence that infants look reliably longer at the unexpected than at the expected event indicates that they possess the expectation under investigation, detect the violation in the unexpected event, and respond to this violation with increased attention.

PRIOR FINDINGS

Beginnings

Infants as young as 2.5 months of age (the youngest tested to date) can detect some violations in occlusion, containment, and covering events (see Fig. 1). For

---

Address correspondence to Renée Baillargeon, Psychology Department, University of Illinois, 603 E. Daniel, Champaign, IL 61820; e-mail: rbaillar@s.psych.uiuc.edu.

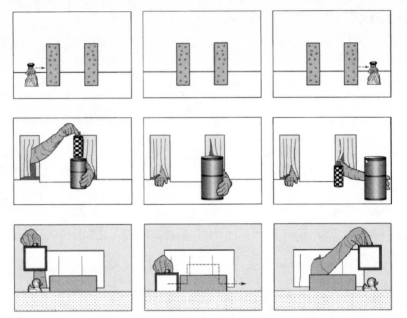

Fig. 1. Examples of violations detected by very young infants. The top row illustrates an occlusion violation: The toy mouse disappears behind one screen and reappears from behind the other screen without appearing in the gap between them (Aguiar & Baillargeon, 1999). The middle row illustrates a containment violation: The checkerboard object is lowered inside the container, which is then slid forward and to the side to reveal the object standing in the container's initial position (Hespos & Baillargeon, 2001b). The bottom row illustrates a covering violation: The cover is lowered over the toy duck, slid behind the left half of the screen, lifted above the screen, moved to the right, lowered behind the right half of the screen, slid past the screen, and finally lifted to reveal the duck (Wang, Baillargeon, & Paterson, in press).

example, in one occlusion experiment, 2.5-month-old infants saw a toy mouse disappear behind one screen and reappear from behind another screen. The infants detected the violation in this event, suggesting that they believed that the mouse continued to exist after it became hidden, and realized that it could not disappear behind one screen and reappear from behind another screen without appearing in the gap between them (Aguiar & Baillargeon, 1999).

In a containment experiment, 2.5-month-old infants saw an experimenter lower an object inside a container; the experimenter then slid the container forward and to the side to reveal the object standing in the container's initial position. The infants responded to this event with increased attention, suggesting that they believed that the object continued to exist after it became hidden, and realized that it could not pass through the closed walls of the container (Hespos & Baillargeon, 2001b).

In a covering experiment, infants aged 2.5 to 3 months saw a toy duck resting on the left end of a platform; the middle of the platform was hidden by a screen slightly taller than the duck. An experimenter lowered a cover over the duck, slid the cover behind the left half of the screen, lifted it above the screen, moved it to the right, lowered it behind the right half of the screen, slid it past the screen, and finally lifted it to reveal the duck. The infants detected the violation in this event, suggesting that they believed that the duck continued to exist after it became hidden, and expected it to move with the cover when the cover was slid but not lifted to a new location (Wang, Baillargeon, & Paterson, in press).

How do 2.5-month-old infants detect these and other (e.g., Luo & Baillargeon, in press; Spelke, Breinlinger, Macomber, & Jacobson, 1992; Wilcox, Nadel, & Rosser, 1996) occlusion, containment, and covering violations? It does not seem likely that very young infants would have repeated opportunities to observe all of these (or similar) events and to learn to associate each event with its outcome. Rather, it seems more likely, as suggested by Spelke (1994), that from an early age infants interpret physical events in accord with general principles of *continuity* (objects exist continuously in time and space) and *solidity* (for two objects to each exist continuously, the two cannot exist at the same time in the same space). Later in this review, I return to the question of whether these principles are likely to be innate or learned.

Developments

Although by 2.5 months of age infants already possess expectations about occlusion, containment, and covering events, much development must still take place in these expectations. Recent research has revealed two main findings. First, for each event category, infants identify a series of variables that enables them to predict outcomes more and more accurately over time. For example, at about 3.5 months of age, infants identify height as an occlusion variable: They now expect tall objects to remain partly visible when behind short occluders (Baillargeon & DeVos, 1991). At about 7.5 months of age, infants identify another occlusion variable, transparency: They now expect an object to remain visible when behind a clear, transparent occluder (Luo & Baillargeon, 2004).

Second, infants do not generalize variables across event categories: They learn separately about each category. When infants identify a variable in one event category weeks or months before they identify it in another category, striking lags can be observed in their responses to similar events from the two categories (see Fig. 2). For example, in one series of experiments, 4.5-month-old infants saw an experimenter lower a tall object either behind (occlusion condition) or inside (containment condition) a short container until only the knob at the top of the object remained visible above the container. The infants detected the violation in the occlusion but not the containment condition; further results indicated that only infants ages 7.5 months and older detected the violation in the containment condition (Hespos & Baillargeon, 2001a). In other experiments, 9-month-old infants watched an experimenter either lower a tall object inside a short container until it became fully hidden (containment condition) or lower a short cover—the container turned upside down—over the same object until it became fully hidden (covering condition). The infants detected the violation in the containment but not the covering condition; further results revealed that only infants ages 12 months and older detected the violation in the covering condition (Wang et al., in press). In yet other experiments, 7.5-month-old infants saw an object standing next to a transparent occluder (occlusion condition) or container (containment condition).

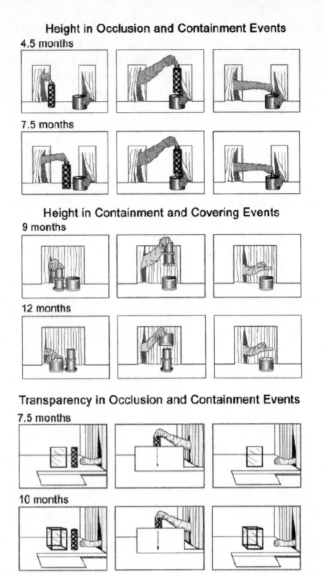

Fig. 2. Examples of lags in infants' reasoning about the same variable in different event categories. The top two rows illustrate the lag in infants' identification of the height variable in containment as opposed to occlusion events. Although 4.5-month-old infants detect the violation in the occlusion event, it is not until infants are about 7.5 months old that they detect the violation in the containment event (Hespos & Baillargeon, 2001a). The middle two rows illustrate the lag in infants' identification of the height variable in covering as opposed to containment events: Although 9-month-old infants detect the violation in the containment event, it is not until infants are about 12 months old that they detect the violation in the covering event (Wang, Baillargeon, & Paterson, in press). The bottom two rows illustrate the lag in infants' identification of the transparency variable in containment as opposed to occlusion events: Although 7.5-month-old infants detect the violation in the occlusion event, it is not until infants are about 10 months old that they detect the violation in the containment event (Luo & Baillargeon, 2004).

Next, a large screen hid the occluder or container, and then an experimenter lifted the object and lowered it behind the occluder or inside the container. Finally, the screen was lowered to reveal only the transparent occluder or container. The infants detected the violation in the occlusion but not the containment condition; only infants ages 10 months and older detected the violation in the containment condition (Luo & Baillargeon, 2004).

These results indicate that infants do not generalize variables from occlusion to containment or covering events, but learn separately about each event category. Thus, the height variable is identified at about 3.5 months in occlusion events, but only at about 7.5 months in containment events and 12 months in covering events. Similarly, the transparency variable is identified at about 7.5 months in occlusion events, but only at about 10 months in containment events.

A NEW ACCOUNT OF INFANTS' PHYSICAL REASONING

Discrepancies

The developmental evidence I have just discussed suggests that the expectations infants acquire about events are not event-general expectations that are applied broadly to all relevant events, but rather event-specific expectations. Infants do not acquire general principles of height or transparency: They identify these variables separately in each event category. But if infants are capable of acquiring only event-specific expectations, how could they possess event-general principles of continuity and solidity, and as early as 2.5 months of age? One possibility is that infants' learning mechanism is initially geared toward acquiring event-general expectations, but soon evolves into a different mechanism capable of acquiring only event-specific expectations. Another possibility, which I think more likely, is that infants' general principles of continuity and solidity are innate (Spelke, 1994).

Whichever possibility one chooses, difficulties remain. If infants interpret events in accord with general continuity and solidity principles (whether learned or innate), one might expect them to detect all salient violations of these principles. However, we saw that although some continuity and solidity violations are detected as early as 2.5 months, others are not detected until much later: Recall, for example, that infants younger than 7.5 months do not respond with increased attention when a tall object becomes hidden inside a short container, and that infants younger than 12 months do not respond with increased attention when a tall object becomes hidden under a short cover.

A New Account

A new account of physical reasoning (see Fig. 3) attempts to make sense of infants' early successes and late failures at detecting continuity and solidity violations (Baillargeon, 2002; Wang et al., in press). This account rests on four assumptions. First, when watching a physical event, infants build a specialized physical representation of the event that is used to predict and interpret its outcome. Second, all of the information, but only the information, included in the physical representation becomes subject to infants' general principles. Third, in

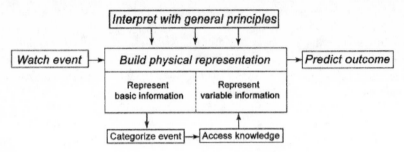

Fig. 3. A new account of physical reasoning in infancy (Baillargeon, 2002; Wang, Baillargeon, & Paterson, in press).

the first weeks of life, infants' physical representations are rather impoverished: When representing an event, infants typically include only basic spatial and temporal information about it. For example, when watching a containment event, infants represent that an object is being lowered inside a container. This information captures the essence of the event, but leaves out most of its details: whether the container is taller or wider than the object, whether it is transparent or opaque, and so on.

Fourth, as infants form event categories and learn what variables to consider in each category, they include information about these variables in their physical representations. When watching an event, infants represent the basic information about the event and use this information to categorize it. They then access their knowledge of the event category selected; this knowledge specifies the variables that have been identified as relevant to the category and hence that should be included in the physical representation. Going back to our example, infants who have identified height as a containment variable would include information about the relative heights of the object and container in their representation of the event; this information would then become subject to their general principles, enabling them to detect violations involving tall objects and short containers.

Thus, according to this reasoning account, even very young infants should detect continuity and solidity violations that involve only the basic information they can represent; and much older infants should fail to detect continuity and solidity violations that involve information about variables they do not yet include in their physical representations.

TESTS OF THE ACCOUNT

Change-Blindness Effects

According to the reasoning account, infants who have not yet identified a variable as relevant to an event category, and hence do not include information about this variable when representing events from the category, should be unable to detect surreptitious changes involving the variable; in other words, they should be blind to these changes. An experiment with 11- and 12-month-old infants tested this prediction; this experiment built on the findings that height is identified at about 3.5 months as an occlusion variable but only at about 12 months as a covering variable. The infants watched an experimenter lower a tall cover in front of (occlusion condition) or over (covering condition) a short object; next, the cover was removed to reveal an object as tall as the cover. Both the 11- and the 12-month-olds detected the change in the occlusion condition, but only the 12-month-olds detected the change in the covering condition. As predicted by the reasoning account, the 11-month-olds in the covering condition were blind to the surreptitious change in the height of the object (Wang & Baillargeon, 2004a).

Teaching Effects

Another prediction from the reasoning account concerns teaching effects. If infants could be taught a new variable in an event category, then they would include information about this variable when representing novel events from the category, enabling them to detect violations involving the variable earlier than they would otherwise. Wang and I recently attempted to teach 9.5-month-old infants the height variable in covering events (Wang & Baillargeon, 2004b).

What might be the key ingredients in a successful teaching experiment? The process by which infants typically identify a new variable in an event category is assumed to be one of explanation-based learning and to involve three main steps (e.g., Baillargeon, 2002). First, infants notice contrastive outcomes for the variable (e.g., they notice that when a cover is placed over an object, the object is sometimes fully and sometimes only partly hidden). Second, infants search for the conditions that relate to these outcomes (e.g., they detect that the object becomes fully hidden when it is shorter than the cover, and becomes partly hidden when it is taller than the cover). Finally, infants build an explanation for these condition-outcome data using their prior knowledge (e.g., infants' continuity and solidity principles specify that a tall object can extend to its full height inside a tall but not a short cover).

In line with this analysis, the infants in our experiment received three pairs of teaching trials. Each pair consisted of a tall- and a short-cover event. In each event, an experimenter rotated the cover forward to show its hollow interior, placed the cover next to a tall object (to facilitate height comparisons), and then lifted and lowered the cover over the object. The object became fully hidden in the tall-cover event, and partly hidden in the short-cover event. Different covers were used in the three pairs of trials. The infants next saw test events in which a novel tall (expected event) or short (unexpected event) cover was lowered over a novel tall object until it became fully hidden. The infants detected the violation in the short-cover event, suggesting that they were able to identify the height variable in covering events during the teaching trials. Positive results were also obtained when a 24-hr delay separated the teaching and test trials.

Subsequent experiments examined some of the assumptions behind our teaching trials. As expected, infants showed no evidence of learning when the teaching trials were modified so that they provided either no contrastive outcomes (the object was shorter and became fully hidden under the tall and short covers), no condition information (the cover was never placed next to the tall object on the apparatus floor, making it difficult for infants to compare their heights), or no explanation (false bottoms inside the covers—revealed when the covers were rotated forward—rendered them all equally shallow). The infants tested with the shallow covers were exposed to the same condition-outcome data as in our original teaching experiment, but could not make sense of the fact that the tall object became fully hidden under the tall but shallow covers.

FUTURE DIRECTIONS

I have focused on a small portion of infants' physical world: their knowledge of occlusion, containment, and covering events. Similar analyses can be offered for infants' knowledge of other event categories, such as support and collision events (e.g., Baillargeon, 2002). Together, this evidence provides strong support for the account of infants' physical reasoning presented here, and more generally for the notion that both event-general and event-specific expectations contribute to infants' responses to physical events.

In future research, my collaborators and I plan to expand our reasoning account in several directions. Infants recognize that events involving inert and self-moving objects may have different outcomes, so a complete account should explain infants' reasoning about both event and object categories. Furthermore, to make sense of events as they unfold, infants must not only represent individual events but also integrate successive events, so a complete account should specify how infants link successive physical representations.

We are also beginning to explore possible connections between infants' physical reasoning system and other cognitive systems. For example, infants can at first include in their physical representations only objects they directly see or have seen; only after some time are they able to infer the presence of additional objects, perhaps when connections are forged with a separate problem-solving system. Similarly, infants are at first limited to reasoning qualitatively about continuous variables (e.g., height or width); only after some time do they become able to engage in quantitative reasoning about these variables, perhaps when connections are formed with a system for representing absolute spatial information. Finally, infants may not reveal some of their physical knowledge in action (as opposed to violation-of-expectation) tasks until suitable connections are established with the system responsible for planning and executing actions (Berthier et al., 2001).

As researchers continue to make progress in understanding how infants attain and use their physical knowledge, we come closer to unveiling the complex architecture that makes it possible for them to learn, so very rapidly, about the world around them.

Recommended Reading

Baillargeon, R. (2002). (See References)
Leslie, A.M. (1994). ToMM, ToBY, and agency: Core architecture and domain specificity. In L.A. Hirschfeld & S.A. Gelman (Eds.), *Mapping the mind* (pp. 119–148). Cambridge, England: Cambridge University Press.
Spelke, E.S. (1994). (See References)

Acknowledgments—This research was supported by the National Institute of Child Health and Human Development (Grant HD-21104).

References

Aguiar, A., & Baillargeon, R. (1999). 2.5-month-old infants' reasoning about when objects should and should not be occluded. *Cognitive Psychology, 39,* 116–157.

Baillargeon, R. (2002). The acquisition of physical knowledge in infancy: A summary in eight lessons. In U. Goswami (Ed.), *Handbook of childhood cognitive development* (pp. 47–83). Oxford, England: Blackwell.

Baillargeon, R., & DeVos, J. (1991). Object permanence in 3.5- and 4.5-month old infants: Further evidence. *Child Development, 62,* 1227–1246.

Baillargeon, R., & Wang, S. (2002). Event categorization in infancy. *Trends in Cognitive Sciences, 6,* 85–93.

Berthier, N.E., Bertenthal, B.I., Seaks, J.D., Sylvia, M.R., Johnson, R.L., & Clifton, R.K. (2001). Using object knowledge in visual tracking and reaching. *Infancy, 2,* 257–284.

Hespos, S.J., & Baillargeon, R. (2001a). Infants' knowledge about occlusion and containment events: A surprising discrepancy. *Psychological Science, 12,* 140–147.

Hespos, S.J., & Baillargeon, R. (2001b). Knowledge about containment events in very young infants. *Cognition, 78,* 204–245.

Luo, Y., & Baillargeon, R. (2004). *Infants' reasoning about occlusion and containment events: Further evidence of décalages.* Unpublished manuscript, University of Illinois, Urbana-Champaign.

Luo, Y., & Baillargeon, R. (in press). When the ordinary seems unexpected: Evidence for rule-based physical reasoning in young infants. *Cognition.*

Spelke, E.S. (1994). Initial knowledge: Six suggestions. *Cognition, 50,* 431–445.

Spelke, E.S., Breinlinger, K., Macomber, J., & Jacobson, K. (1992). Origins of knowledge. *Psychological Review, 99,* 605–632.

Wang, S., & Baillargeon, R. (2004a). *Change blindness in infants: Event category effects.* Unpublished manuscript, University of California, Santa Cruz.

Wang, S., & Baillargeon, R. (2004b). *Teaching infants the variable height in covering events.* Unpublished manuscript, University of California, Santa Cruz.

Wang, S., Baillargeon, R., & Paterson, S. (in press). Detecting continuity violations in infancy: A new account and new evidence from covering and tube events. *Cognition.*

Wilcox, T., Nadel, L., & Rosser, R. (1996). Location memory in healthy preterm and full-term infants. *Infant Behavior and Development, 19,* 309–323.

Critical Thinking Questions

1. What are occlusion, containment, and covering, and how do they inform us about how infants understand physical events?

2. What is the violation-of-expectation method and why is it used in research with infants? Why would this same method not be used in studies with adults?

3. What does change blindness tell us about an infant's expectation for an event?

Gender and Group Process:
A Developmental Perspective

Eleanor E. Maccoby[1]

Department of Psychology, Stanford University, Stanford, California

Abstract

Until recently, the study of gender development has focused mainly on sex typing as an attribute of the individual. Although this perspective continues to be enlightening, recent work has focused increasingly on children's tendency to congregate in same-sex groups. This self-segregation of the two sexes implies that much of childhood gender enactment occurs in the context of same-sex dyads or larger groups. There are emergent properties of such groups, so that certain sex-distinctive qualities occur at the level of the group rather than at the level of the individual. There is increasing research interest in the distinctive nature of the group structures, activities, and interactions that typify all-male as compared with all-female groups, and in the socialization that occurs within these groups. Next steps in research will surely call for the integration of the individual and group perspectives.

Keywords

sex; gender; groups; socialization

Among researchers who study the psychology of gender, a central viewpoint has always been that individuals progressively acquire a set of behaviors, interests, personality traits, and cognitive biases that are more typical of their own sex than of the other sex. And the individual's sense of being either a male or a female person (*gender identity*) is thought to be a core element in the developing sense of self. The acquisition of these sex-distinctive characteristics has been called *sex typing*, and much research has focused on how and why the processes of sex typing occur. A favorite strategy has been to examine differences among individuals in how sex typed they are at a given age, searching for factors associated with a person's becoming more or less "masculine" or more or less "feminine" than other individuals. In early work, there was a heavy emphasis on the family as the major context in which sex typing was believed to take place. Socialization pressures from parents were thought to shape the child toward "sex-appropriate" behaviors, personality, and interests and a firm gender identity.

On the whole, the efforts to understand gender development by studying individual differences in rate or degree of sex typing, and the connections of these differences to presumed antecedent factors, have not been very successful. The various manifestations of sex typing in childhood—toy and activity preferences, knowledge of gender stereotypes, personality traits—do not cohere together to form a cluster that clearly represents a degree of sex typing in a given child. And whether or not a given child behaves in a gender-typical way seems to vary greatly from one situation to another, depending on the social context and other conditions that make an individual's gender salient at a given moment. Only weak and inconsistent connections have been found between within-family socialization practices and children's sex-typed behavior (Ruble & Martin, 1998). And so far, the study of individual variations in sex typing has not helped us to understand the most robust manifestation of gender during childhood: namely, children's strong tendency to segregate themselves into same-sex social groups. Although work on gender development in individual children continues and shows renewed vigor, a relatively new direction of interest is in children's groups. This current research and theorizing considers how gender is implicated in the formation, interaction processes, and socialization functions of childhood social groupings.

In some of this work, the dyad or larger group, rather than the individual child, is taken as the unit of analysis. Through the history of theoretical writings by sociologists and social psychologists, there have been claims that groups have emergent properties, and that their functioning cannot be understood in terms of the characteristics of their individual members (Levine & Moreland, 1998). Accumulating evidence from recent work suggests that in certain gender configurations, pairs or groups of children elicit certain behaviors from each other that are not characteristic of either of the participants when alone or in other social contexts (Martin & Fabes, 2001). Another possibility is that the group context amplifies what are only weak tendencies in the individual participants. For example, in their article "It Takes Two to Fight," Coie and his colleagues (1999) found that the probability of a fight occurring depended not only on the aggressive predispositions of the two individual boys involved, but also on the unique properties of the dyad itself. Other phenomena, such as social approach to another child, depend on the sex of the approacher and the approachee taken jointly, not on the sex of either child, when children's sociability is analyzed at the level of the individual (summarized in Maccoby, 1998). It is important, then, to describe and analyze children's dyads or larger groups as such, to see how gender is implicated in their characteristics and functioning.

GENDER COMPOSITION OF CHILDREN'S GROUPS

Beginning at about age 3, children increasingly choose same-sex playmates when in settings where their social groupings are not managed by adults. In preschools, children may play in loose configurations of several children, and reciprocated affiliation between same-sex pairs of children is common while such reciprocation between pairs of opposite sex is rare (Strayer, 1980; Vaughan, Colvin, Azria, Caya, & Krzysik, 2001). On school playgrounds, children sometimes play in mixed-sex groups, but increasingly, as they move from age 4 to about age 12, they spend a large majority of their free play time exclusively with others of their own sex, rarely playing in a mixed-sex dyad or in a larger group in which no other child of their own sex is involved. Best friendships in middle childhood and well into adolescence are very heavily weighted toward same-sex choices. These strong tendencies toward same-sex social preferences are seen in the other cultures around the world where gender composition of children's groups has been studied, and are also found among young nonhuman primates (reviewed in Maccoby, 1998).

GROUP SIZE

Naturally occurring face-to-face groups whose members interact with one another continuously over time tend to be small—typically having only two or three members, and seldom having more than five or six members. Some gender effects on group size can be seen. Both boys and girls commonly form same-sex dyadic friendships, and sometimes triadic ones as well. But from about the age of 5 onward, boys more often associate together in larger clusters. Boys are more often involved in organized group games, and in their groups, occupy more space on school playgrounds. In an experimental situation in which same-sex groups of six children were allowed to utilize play and construction materials in any way they wished, girls tended to split into dyads or triads, whereas boys not only interacted in larger groups but were much more likely to undertake some kind of joint project, and organize and carry out coordinated activities aimed at achieving a group goal (Benenson, Apostolaris, & Parnass, 1997). Of course, children's small groups—whether dyads or clusters of four, five, or six children—are nested within still larger group structures, such as cliques or "crowds."

Group size matters. Recent studies indicate that the interactions in groups of four or more are different from what typically occurs in dyads. In larger groups, there is more conflict and more competition, particularly in all-male groups; in dyads, individuals of both sexes are more responsive to their partners, and a partner's needs and perspectives are more often taken into account than when individuals interact with several others at once (Benenson, Nicholson, Waite, Roy, & Simpson, 2001; Levine & Moreland, 1998). The question of course arises: To what extent are certain "male" characteristics, such as greater competitiveness, a function of the fact that boys typically interact in larger groups than girls do? At present, this question is one of active debate and study. So far, there are indications that group size does indeed mediate sex differences to some degree, but not entirely nor consistently.

INTERACTION IN SAME-SEX GROUPS

From about age 3 to age 8 or 9, when children congregate together in activities not structured by adults, they are mostly engaged in some form of play. Playtime interactions among boys, more often than among girls, involve rough-and-tumble play, competition, conflict, ego displays, risk taking, and striving to achieve or maintain dominance, with occasional (but actually quite rare) displays of direct aggression. Girls, by contrast, are more often engaged in what is called collaborative discourse, in which they talk and act reciprocally, each responding to what the other has just said or done, while at the same time trying to get her own initiatives across. This does not imply that girls' interactions are conflict free, but rather that girls pursue their individual goals in the context of also striving to maintain group harmony (summary in Maccoby, 1998).

The themes that appear in boys' fantasies, the stories they invent, the scenarios they enact when playing with other boys, and the fictional fare they prefer (books, television) involve danger, conflict, destruction, heroic actions by male heroes, and trials of physical strength, considerably more often than is the case for girls. Girls' fantasies and play themes tend to be oriented around domestic or romantic scripts, portraying characters who are involved in social relationships and depicting the maintenance or restoration of order and safety.

Girls' and boys' close friendships are qualitatively different in some respects. Girls' friendships are more intimate, in the sense that girl friends share information about the details of their lives and concerns. Boys typically know less about their friends' lives, and base their friendship on shared activities.

Boys' groups larger than dyads are in some respects more cohesive than girls' groups. Boys in groups seek and achieve more autonomy from adults than girls do, and explicitly exclude girls from their activities more commonly than girls exclude boys. Boys more often engage in joint risky activities, and close ranks to protect a group member from adult detection and censure. And friendships among boys are more interconnected; that is, friends of a given boy are more likely to be friends with each other than is the case for several girls who are all friends of a given girl (Markovitz, Benenson, & Dolenszky, 2001). The fact that boys' friendships are more interconnected does not mean that they are closer in the sense of intimacy. Rather, it may imply that male friends are more accustomed to functioning as a unit, perhaps having a clearer group identity.

HOW SEX-DISTINCTIVE SUBCULTURES ARE FORMED

In a few instances, researchers have observed the process of group formation from the first meeting of a group over several subsequent meetings. An up-close view of the formation of gendered subcultures among young children has been provided by Nicolopoulou (1994). She followed classrooms of preschool children through a school year, beginning at the time they first entered the school. Every day, any child could tell a story to a teacher, who recorded the story as the child told it. At the end of the day, the teacher read aloud to the class the stories that were recorded that day, and the child author of each story was invited to act it out with the help of other children whom the child selected to act out different parts. At the beginning of the year, stories could be quite rudimentary (e.g., "There was a boy. And a girl. And a wedding."). By the end of the year, stories became greatly elaborated, and different members of the class produced stories related to themes previously introduced by others. In other words, a corpus of shared knowledge, meanings, and scripts grew up, unique to the children in a given classroom and reflecting their shared experiences.

More important for our present purposes, there was a progressive divergence between the stories told by girls and those told by boys. Gender differences were present initially, and the thematic content differed more and more sharply as time went on, with boys increasingly focusing on themes of conflict, danger, heroism, and "winning," while girls' stories increasingly depicted family, nonviolent themes. At the beginning of the year, children might call upon others of both sexes to act in their stories, but by the end of the year, they almost exclusively called upon children of their own sex to enact the roles in their stories. Thus, although all the children in the class were exposed to the stories told by both sexes, the girls picked up on one set of themes and the boys on another, and two distinct subcultures emerged.

Can this scenario serve as a prototype for the formation of distinctive male and female "subcultures" among children? Yes, in the sense that the essence of these cultures is a set of socially shared cognitions, including common knowledge and mutually congruent expectations, and common interests in specific themes and scripts that distinguish the two sexes. These communalities can be augmented in a set of children coming together for the first time, since by age 5 or 6, most will already have participated in several same-sex groups, or observed them in operation on TV, so they are primed for building gender-distinct subcultures in any new group of children they enter. Were we to ask, "Is gender socially constructed?" the answer would surely be "yes." At the same time, there may well be a biological contribution to the nature of the subculture each sex chooses to construct.

SOCIALIZATION WITHIN SAME-SEX GROUPS

There has long been evidence that pairs of friends—mostly same-sex friends—influence one another (see Dishion, Spracklen, & Patterson, 1996, for a recent example). However, only recently has research focused on the effects of the amount of time young children spend playing with other children of their own sex. Martin and Fabes (2001) observed a group of preschoolers over a 6-month period, to obtain stable scores for how much time they spent with same-sex playmates (as distinct from their time spent in mixed-sex or other-sex play). They examined the changes that occurred, over the 6 months of observation, in the degree of sex typing in children's play activities. Martin and Fabes reported that the more time boys spent playing with other boys, the greater the increases in their activity level, rough-and-tumble play, and sex-typed choices of toys and games, and the less time they spent near adults. For girls, by contrast, large amounts of time spent with other girls was associated with increasing time spent near adults, and with decreasing aggression, decreasing activity level, and increasing choices of girl-type play materials and activities. This new work points to a powerful role for same-sex peers in shaping one another's sex-typed behavior, values, and interests.

WHAT COMES NEXT?

The recent focus on children's same-sex groups has revitalized developmental social psychology, and promising avenues for the next phases of research on gender development have appeared. What now needs to be done?

1. Investigators need to study both the variations and the similarities among same-sex groups in their agendas and interactive processes. The extent of generality across groups remains largely unexplored. The way gender is enacted in groups undoubtedly changes with age. And observations in other cultures indicate that play in same-sex children's groups reflects what different cultures offer in the way of materials, play contexts, and belief systems. Still, it seems likely that there are certain sex-distinctive themes that appear in a variety of cultural contexts.
2. Studies of individual differences need to be integrated with the studies of group process. Within each sex, some children are only marginally involved in same-sex groups or dyads, whereas others are involved during much of their free time. And same-sex groups are internally differentiated, so that some children are popular or dominant while others consistently occupy subordinate roles or may even be frequently harassed by others. We need to know more about the individual characteristics that underlie these variations, and about their consequences.
3. Children spend a great deal of their free time in activities that are not gender differentiated at all. We need to understand more fully the con-

ditions under which gender is salient in group process and the conditions under which it is not.

Recommended Reading

Benenson, J.F., Apostolaris, N.H., & Parnass, J. (1997). (See References)
Maccoby, E.E. (1998). (See References)
Martin, C.L., & Fabes, R.A. (2001). (See References)

Note

1. Address correspondence to Eleanor E. Maccoby, Department of Psychology, Stanford University, Stanford, CA 94305-2130.

References

Benenson, J.F., Apostolaris, N.H., & Parnass, J. (1997). Age and sex differences in dyadic and group interaction. *Developmental Psychology, 33*, 538–543.
Benenson, J.F., Nicholson, C., Waite, A., Roy, R., & Simpson, A. (2001). The influence of group size on children's competitive behavior. *Child Development, 72*, 921–928.
Cole, J.D., Dodge, K.A., Schwartz, D., Cillessen, A.H.N., Hubbard, J.A., & Lemerise, E.A. (1999), It takes two to fight: A test of relational factors, and a method for assessing aggressive dyads. *Developmental Psychology, 36*, 1179–1188.
Dishion, T.J., Spracklen, K.M., & Patterson, G.R. (1996). Deviancy training in male adolescent friendships. *Behavior Therapy, 27*, 373–390.
Levine, J.M., & Moreland, R.L. (1998). Small groups. In D.T. Gilbert, S.T. Fiske, & G. Lindzey (Eds.), *Handbook of social psychology* (Vol. 2, pp. 415–469). Boston: McGraw-Hill.
Maccoby, E.E. (1998). *The two sexes: Growing up apart, coming together.* Cambridge, MA: Harvard University Press.
Markovitz, H., Benenson, J.F., & Dolenszky, E. (2001). Evidence that children and adolescents have internal models of peer interaction that are gender differentiated. *Child Development, 72*, 879–886.
Martin, C.L., & Fabes, R.A. (2001). The stability and consequences of young children's same-sex peer interactions. *Developmental Psychology, 37*, 431–446.
Nicolopoulou, A. (1997). Worldmaking and identity formation in children's narrative play-acting. In B. Cox & C. Lightfoot (Eds.), *Sociogenic perspectives in internalization* (pp. 157–187). Hillsdale, NJ: Erlbaum.
Ruble, D.N., & Martin, C.L. (1998). Gender development. In W. Damon & N. Eisenberg (Eds.), *Handbook of child psychology* (5th ed., Vol. 3, pp. 933–1016). New York: John Wiley & Sons.
Strayer, F.F. (1980). Social ecology of the preschool peer group. In W.A. Collins (Ed.), *Minnesota Symposium on Child Psychology: Vol. 13. Development of cognitions, affect and social relations* (pp. 165–196). Hillsdale, NJ: Erlbaum.
Vaughn, B.E., Colvin, T.N., Azria, M.R., Caya, L., & Krzysik, L. (2001). Dyadic analyses of friendship in a sample of preschool-aged children attending Headstart. *Child Development, 72*, 862–878.

Critical Thinking Questions

1. In what ways do same-sex social groups reflect both sides of the nature-nurture debate?

2. How do naturally occurring social groups of boys and girls differ in size and in their interactions?

3. Explain how distinctive male and female "subcultures" form among children.

The Emerging Field of Adolescent Romantic Relationships

Wyndol Furman[1]

Department of Psychology, University of Denver, Denver, Colorado

Abstract

Romantic relationships are central in adolescents' lives. They have the potential to affect development positively, but also place adolescents at risk for problems. Romantic experiences change substantially over the course of adolescence; the peer context plays a critical role as heterosexual adolescents initially interact with the other sex in a group context, then begin group dating, and finally have dyadic romantic relationships. Adolescents' expectations and experiences in romantic relationships are related to their relationships with their peers as well as their parents. Although research on adolescents' romantic relationships has blossomed in the past decade, further work is needed to identify the causes and consequences of romantic experiences, examine the diversity of romantic experiences, and integrate the field with work on sexuality and adult romantic relationships.

Keywords

romantic relationships; attachment; love; friendships; adolescent adjustment

A review of the literature on adolescent romantic relationships a decade ago would have uncovered little empirical research. The work that had been conducted consisted primarily of descriptive studies on the frequency of dating other romantic behaviors. A substantial amount of work on sexual behavior had been conducted, but much of that was descriptive as well, and did not say much about the relational context in which the sexual behavior occurred. In other words, the literature contained a lot of information about the proportions of adolescents of different ages or backgrounds who were sexually active, but much less about who their partners were and what their relationships with them were like.

Happily, the field has changed substantially in the past decade. A cadre of social scientists have been studying adolescents' romantic relationships, and the number of articles and conference presentations seems to increase each year. The fields of adolescent romantic relationships and sexual behavior are still not well integrated, but the connections between them are increasing. Most of the work has been done on heterosexual relationships, but research on lesbian, gay, and bisexual relationships is beginning as well.

The increasing interest in adolescents' romantic relationships may partially stem from a recognition that these relationships are not simply trivial flings. As young people move from preadolescence through late adolescence, their romantic relationships become increasingly central in their social world. Preadolescents spend an hour or less a week interacting with the other sex. By the 12th grade, boys spend an average of 5 hr a week with the other sex, and girls spend an average of 10 hr a week. Furthermore, 12th-grade boys and girls spend an additional 5 to 8 hr a week thinking about members of the other sex when not with them (Richards, Crowe, Larson, & Swarr, 1998). Romantic partners are also a major source of support for many adolescents. Among 10th graders, only close friends provide more support. During the college years, romantic relationships are the most supportive relationships for males, and among the most supportive relationships for females (Furman & Buhrmester, 1992).

Romantic relationships may also affect other aspects of adolescents' development. For example, they have been hypothesized to contribute to the development of an identity, the transformation of family relationships, the development of close relationships with peers, the development of sexuality, and scholastic achievement and career planning (Furman & Shaffer, in press). One particularly interesting question is whether adolescent romantic experiences influence subsequent romantic relationships, including marriages. Unfortunately, there is limited empirical data on these possible impacts.

Adolescent romantic relationships are not, however, simple "beds of roses." One fifth of adolescent women are victims of physical or sexual abuse by a dating partner (Silverman, Raj, Mucci, & Hathaway, 2001). Breakups are one of the strongest predictors of depression (Monroe, Rhode, Seeley, & Lewinsohn, 1999). Sexually transmitted diseases and teenage pregnancy are also major risks.

Of course, the benefits and risks of particular romantic experiences vary. Having romantic experience at an early age and having a high number of partners are associated with problems in adjustment (see Zimmer-Gembeck, Siebenbruner, & Collins, 2001), although researchers do not know yet the direction of the influence. That is, the romantic experiences may lead to the difficulties, but it is also possible that adolescents who are not well adjusted are more likely than their better adjusted peers to become prematurely or overly involved in romantic relationships. Moreover, little is known about how the length or qualities of romantic relationships may be linked to adjustment.

DEVELOPMENTAL COURSE

Adolescents vary widely in when they become interested in romantic relationships, and the experiences they have once they begin dating. Accordingly, there is not one normative pattern of development. Some commonalities in the nature and sequence of heterosexual experiences can be seen, however. Prior to adolescence, boys and girls primarily interact with same-sex peers. In early adolescence, they begin to think more about members of the other sex, and then eventually to interact more with them (Richards et al., 1998). Initial interactions typically occur in mixed boy-girl groups; then group dating begins, with several pairs engaging in some activity together; finally, dyadic romantic relationships begin to form (Connolly, Goldberg, & Pepler, 2002). Having a large network of other-sex friends increases the likelihood of developing a romantic relationship with someone (Connolly, Furman, & Konarski, 2000).

The developmental course of romantic experiences for gay, lesbian, and bisexual youths is less charted, but is likely to be somewhat different. Most have some same-sex sexual experience, but relatively few have same-sex romantic relationships because of both the limited opportunities to do so and the social disapproval such relationships may generate from families or heterosexual peers

(Diamond, Savin-Williams, & Dubé, 1999). Many sexual-minority youths date other-sex peers; such experiences can help them clarify their sexual orientation or disguise it from others.

The nature of heterosexual or homosexual romantic relationships changes developmentally. Early relationships do not fulfill many of the functions that adult romantic relationships often do. Early adolescents do not commonly turn to a partner for support or provide such caregiving for a partner. In fact, what may be important is simply having such a relationship, especially if the partner is a popular or desired one.

Eventually, adolescents develop some comfort in these interactions and begin to turn to their partners for specific social and emotional needs. Wehner and I proposed that romantic relationships become important in the functioning of four behavioral systems—affiliation, sex-reproduction, attachment, and caregiving (Furman & Wehner, 1994). The affiliative and sexual-reproductive systems are the first to become salient, as young adolescents spend time with their partners and explore their sexual feelings. The attachment and caretaking systems become more important during late adolescence and early adulthood, as relationships become more long term. Several findings are consistent with our proposal. When asked to describe their romantic relationships, adolescents mention affiliative features more often than attachment or caregiving features (Feiring, 1996). Similarly, in another study, young adults retrospectively described their romances in adolescence in terms of companionship and affiliation, and described their relationships in young adulthood in terms of trust and support (Shulman & Kipnis, 2001).

The work on the developmental course of romantic experiences illustrates several important points. First, these relationships do not occur in isolation. Relationships with peers typically serve as a social context for the emergence of heterosexual relationships, and often are a deterrent for gay and lesbian relationships. Second, adolescents' romantic relationships are more than simple sexual encounters; at the same time, one could not characterize most of them as the full-blown attachment relationships that committed adult relationships become (Shaver & Hazan, 1988). Affiliation, companionship, and friendship seem to be particularly important aspects of most of these relationships. Finally, the developmental changes in these relationships are striking. Although at first they are based on simple interest, in the course of a decade, adolescents go from simply being interested in boys or girls to having significant relationships that are beginning to be characterized by attachment and caregiving. Because the changes are qualitative as well as quantitative, they present challenges for investigators trying to describe them or to compare the experiences of different adolescents. Wehner and I (Furman & Wehner, 1994) have tried to provide a common framework for research by examining adolescents' expectations for and beliefs about these relationships, a point I discuss more extensively in the next section.

LINKS WITH OTHER RELATIONSHIPS

Much of the current research on adult romantic relationships has been guided by attachment theory. More than a decade ago, Shaver and Hazan (1988) proposed that committed romantic relationships could be characterized as attachments, just as relationships between parent and child were. Moreover, they suggested that experiences with parents affect individuals' expectations of romantic relationships. Individuals who had secure relationships with parents would be likely to have secure expectations of romantic relationships and, in fact, would be likely to develop secure romantic attachments, whereas those who had adverse experiences with parents would be expected to develop insecure expectations of romantic relationships.

Although researchers generally emphasized the links between relationships with parents and romantic relationships, Wehner and I suggested that friendships would be related to romantic relationships as well (Furman & Wehner, 1994). Friendships and romantic relationships are both egalitarian relationships characterized by features of affiliation, such as companionship and mutual intimacy. Accordingly, we proposed that adolescents' experiences with friends and expectations concerning these relationships influence their expectations of romantic relationships. Subsequently, several studies using multiple methods of assessment demonstrated links between adolescents' expectations of friendships and romantic relationships (see Furman, Simon, Shaffer, & Bouchey, 2002). In fact, these links were more consistent than those between parent-child relationships and romantic relationships. Interestingly, the latter links were found to strengthen over the course of adolescence. Such a developmental shift may occur as the attachment and caregiving features of romantic relationships become increasingly salient.

These studies were cross-sectional, and thus cannot support inferences about causality. However, the findings again underscore the importance of recognizing that romantic relationships are peer relationships and thus, links with friendships are likely as well.

At the same time, various types of relationships have only moderate effects on one another. Experiences in other relationships may influence romantic relationships, but romantic relationships also present new challenges, and thus past experiences are not likely to be simply replicated. What influence do past romantic relationships have on future romantic relationships? Individuals' perceptions of support and negative interaction in their romantic relationships have been found to be stable over the span of a year, even across different relationships (Connolly et al., 2000), but otherwise researchers know little about what does and does not carry over from one romantic relationship to the next.

CURRENT AND FUTURE DIRECTIONS

The existing literature on romantic relationships has many of the characteristics of initial research on a topic. One such characteristic is the methodologies used to date: Investigators have principally relied on questionnaires, administered at one point in time. Interview and observational studies are now beginning to appear, though, and investigators conducting longitudinal studies have begun to report their results concerning adolescent romantic relationships. For example, Capaldi and Clark (1998) found that having a parent whose behavior is antisocial and who is unskilled in parenting is predictive of antisocial behavior in midadolescence, which in turn is predictive of aggression toward dating partners in late adolescence. Reports from other ongoing longitudinal studies of the childhood precursors of adolescent romantic relationships and the consequences of these relationships for subsequent development should appear shortly.

In this article, I have described some of the common developmental changes characteristic of adolescent romantic relationships and how these relationships may be influenced by relationships with friends and parents. At the same time, the diversity of romantic experiences should be underscored. The links between romantic experiences and adjustment vary as a function of the timing and degree of romantic involvement (Zimmer-Gembeck et al., 2001). Investigators are beginning to examine how romantic experiences may be associated with characteristics of the adolescent, such as antisocial or bullying behavior, health status, or sensitivity to being rejected. To date, most of the work has focused on heterosexual youths from middle-class Euro-American backgrounds, and further work with other groups is certainly needed. Additionally, almost all of the research has been conducted in Western societies, yet romantic development is likely to be quite different in other societies where contacts with the other sex are more constrained, and marriages are arranged.

Efforts to integrate the field with related ones are needed. Just as research on sexual behavior could profit from examining the nature of the relationships between sexual partners, investigators studying romantic relationships need to examine the role of sexual behavior in romantic relationships. Ironically, few investigators have done so, and instead these relationships have been treated as if they were platonic. Similarly, research on adolescent relationships could benefit from the insights of the work on adult romantic relationships, which has a rich empirical and theoretical history. At the same time, investigators studying adult relationships may want to give greater consideration to the developmental changes that occur in these relationships and to their peer context—themes that have been highlighted by adolescence researchers. In sum, research on adolescent romantic relationships has blossomed in the past decade, but a broad, integrative perspective will be needed to fully illuminate their nature.

Recommended Reading

Bouchey, H.A., & Furman, W. (in press). Dating and romantic experiences in adolescence. In G.R. Adams & M. Berzonsky (Eds.), *The Blackwell handbook of adolescence.* Oxford, England: Blackwell.

Florsheim, P. (Ed.). (in press). *Adolescent romantic relations and sexual behavior: Theory, research, and practical implications.* Mahwah, NJ: Erlbaum.

Furman, W., Brown, B.B., & Feiring, C. (Eds.). (1999). *The development of romantic relationships in adolescence.* New York: Cambridge University Press.

Shulman, S., & Collins, W. (Eds.). (1997). *Romantic relationships in adolescence: Developmental perspectives.* San Francisco: Jossey-Bass.

Shulman, S., & Seiffge-Krenke, I. (Eds.). (2001). Adolescent romance: From experiences to relationships [Special issue]. *Journal of Adolescence, 24*(3).

Acknowledgments—Preparation of this manuscript was supported by Grant 50106 from the National Institute of Mental Health.

Note

1. Address correspondence to Wyndol Furman, Department of Psychology, University of Denver, Denver, CO 80208; e-mail: wfurman@nova.psy.du.edu.

References

Capaldi, D.M., & Clark, S. (1998). Prospective family predictors of aggression toward female partners for at-risk young men. *Developmental Psychology, 34,* 1175–1188.

Connolly, J., Furman, W., & Konarski, R. (2000). The role of peers in the emergence of romantic relationships in adolescence. *Child Development, 71,* 1395–1408.

Connolly, J., Goldberg, A., & Pepler, D. (2002). *Romantic development in the peer group in early adolescence.* Manuscript submitted for publication.

Diamond, L.M., Savin-Williams, R.C., & Dubé, E.M. (1999). Sex, dating, passionate friendships, and romance: intimate peer relations among lesbian, gay, and bisexual adolescents. In W. Furman, B.B. Brown, & C. Feiring (Eds.), *The development of romantic relationships in adolescence* (pp. 175–210). New York: Cambridge University Press.

Feiring, C. (1996). Concepts of romance in 15-year-old adolescents. *Journal of Research on Adolescence, 6,* 181–200.

Furman, W., & Buhrmester, D. (1992). Age and sex differences in perceptions of networks of personal relationships. *Child Development, 63,* 103–115.

Furman, W., & Shaffer, L. (in press). The role of romantic relationships in adolescent development. In P. Florsheim (Ed.), *Adolescent romantic relations and sexual behavior: Theory, research, and practical implications.* Mahwah, NJ: Erlbaum.

Furman, W., Simon, V.A., Shaffer, L., & Bouchey, H.A. (2002). Adolescents' working models and styles for relationships with parents, friends, and romantic partners. *Child Development, 73,* 241–255.

Furman, W., & Wehner, E.A. (1994). Romantic views: Toward a theory of adolescent romantic relationships. In R. Montemayor, G.R. Adams, & G.P. Gullota (Eds.), *Advances in adolescent development: Vol. 6. Relationships during adolescence* (pp. 168–175). Thousand Oaks, CA: Sage.

Monroe, S.M., Rhode, P., Seeley, J.R., & Lewinsohn, P.M. (1999). Life events and depression in adolescence: Relationship loss a a prospective risk factor for first onset of major depressive disorder. *Journal of Abnormal Psychology, 108,* 606–614.

Richards, M.H., Crowe, P.A., Larson, R., & Swarr, A. (1998). Developmental patterns and gender differences in the experience of peer companionship during adolescence. *Child Development, 69,* 154–163.

Shaver, P., & Hazan, C. (1988). A biased overview of the study of love. *Journal of Social and Personal Relationships, 5,* 473–501.

Shulman, S., & Kipnis, O. (2001). Adolescent romantic relationships: A look from the future. *Journal of Adolescence, 24,* 337–351.

Silverman, J.G., Raj, A., Mucci, L.A., & Hathaway, J.E. (2001). Dating violence against adolescent girls and associated substance use, unhealthy weight control, sexual risk behavior, pregnancy, and suicidality. *Journal of the American Medical Association, 285,* 572–579.

Zimmer-Gembeck, M.J., Siebenbruner, J., & Collins, W.A. (2001). Diverse aspects of dating: Associations with psychosocial functioning from early to middle adolescence. *Journal of Adolescence, 24,* 313–336.

Critical Thinking Questions

1. What happens to romantic relationships from preadolescence through late adolescence?

2. Why are adolescent romantic relationships important?

3. In what ways are adolescents' romantic relationships linked to their existing relations with parents and friends?

Enhancing the Cognitive Vitality of Older Adults

Arthur F. Kramer[1] and Sherry L. Willis

Beckman Institute, University of Illinois, Urbana, Illinois (A.F.K.), and Department of Human Development and Family Studies, Pennsylvania State University, University Park, Pennsylvania (S.L.W.)

Abstract

Aging is associated with decline in a multitude of cognitive processes and brain functions. However, a growing body of literature suggests that age-related decline in cognition can sometimes be reduced through experience, cognitive training, and other interventions such as fitness training. Research on cognitive training and expertise has suggested that age-related cognitive sparing is often quite narrow, being observed only on tasks and skills similar to those on which individuals have been trained. Furthermore, training and expertise benefits are often realized only after extensive practice with specific training strategies. Like cognitive training, fitness training has narrow effects on cognitive processes, but in the case of fitness training, the most substantial effects are observed for executive-control processes.

Keywords

aging; plasticity; cognitive enhancement

One of the most ubiquitous findings in research on cognition and aging is that a wide variety of cognitive abilities show an increasing decline across the life span. Declines in cognitive function over the adult life span have been found in both cross-sectional and longitudinal studies for a variety of tasks, abilities, and processes. Cross-sectional studies, which compare the performance of one age group with that of another, have found linear decreases in a number of measures of cognition over the adult life span (Salthouse, 1996). Longitudinal studies, which range in length from a few years to more than 40 years, have found that the rate and onset of decline is variable, depending on the ability, and that accelerated decline occurs in the late 70s (Schaie, 2000). Although there are a number of factors that may be responsible for the different results obtained in the cross-sectional and longitudinal studies (e.g., differential attrition, non-age-related differences between age groups in cross-sectional studies, effects of practice, and study length in longitudinal studies), the important common observation is a reduction in cognitive efficiency with age.

Although age-related cognitive decline is quite broad, there are some notable exceptions. It has generally been observed that knowledge-based abilities (also called crystallized abilities) such as verbal knowledge and comprehension continue to be maintained or improve over the life span. In contrast, process-based abilities (also called fluid abilities) display age-related declines.

An important current issue concerns the source (or sources) of age-related declines in process-based abilities. A large number of mostly cross-sectional studies have found that age-related influences on different skills are highly related, prompting the suggestion that a common factor may be responsible for age-related declines (Salthouse, 1996). Many proposals concerning the source or mechanism responsible for this general decline have been advanced. For example, reduced processing speed, decreased attentional resources, sensory deficits, reduced working memory[2] capacity, impaired frontal lobe function, and impaired neurotransmitter function have all been cited as possible mechanisms of age-related cognitive decline.

Contrary to the general-decline proposals, a growing body of literature has pointed out a number of situations in which age-related differences remain after a general age-related factor has been statistically or methodologically controlled for (Verhaeghen, Khegl, & Mayr, 1997). Such data suggest that a variety of different mechanisms may be responsible for age-related declines in information processing and that these mechanisms may be differentially sensitive to age.

DOES EXPERIENCE MODULATE AGE-RELATED COGNITIVE DECLINE?

Over the past several decades, researchers have examined whether previous experience in content areas (domains) such as driving, flying, and music serves to (a) reduce age-related decline in basic abilities, (b) aid in the development of domain-specific strategies that can compensate for the effects of aging on basic abilities, or (c) both reduce decline and help develop compensating strategies. In general, these studies have found that well- learned skills can be maintained at relatively high levels of proficiency, well into the 70s. However, these same studies have found that general perceptual, cognitive, and motor processes are not preserved in these highly skilled individuals. Thus, preservation of cognitive abilities for highly skilled individuals appears to be domain-specific and compensatory in nature. For example, Salthouse (1984) examined the performance of young and old adult typists and found a significant age-related decline in the performance of general psychomotor tasks, but no age-related deficit in measures of typing proficiency. Furthermore, the older typists were better able than the young typists to use preview of the text to decease their interkeystroke times, thereby enhancing their typing. Thus, the older typists were able to employ their accrued knowledge of the task domain to implement a strategy that compensated for declines in processing speed.

Krampe and Ericsson (1996) examined how amateur and expert pianists' expertise influenced their general processing speed, as well as performance on music-related tasks (i.e., single-hand and bimanual finger coordination). The general processing-speed measures showed an age-related decrement, regardless of the level of the individuals' music expertise. However, in the case of the music-related tasks, age-related effects were abolished for the expert pianists, although not for the amateur pianists. Furthermore, among the experts, high levels of deliberate practice over the past 10 years were found to be associated with decreases in age-related differences in music-related performance.

Despite the impressive cognitive sparing observed in the studies just discussed, as well as other studies, a variety of studies have failed to demonstrate an effect of expertise on age-related decline. The variability of the findings could be the result of several factors, including (a) the recency and amount of deliberate practice, (b) the degree to which the criterion tasks were specific to the domain of expertise, and (c) the age and health of the study participants.

In summary, the answer to the question of whether experience can reduce age-related cognitive decline is affirmative. However, this answer must be qualified. Sparing seems to be domain-specific, rather than general, and appears to depend on deliberate practice of the relevant skills and possibly also development of compensatory strategies.

CAN LABORATORY-BASED TRAINING REDUCE COGNITIVE DECLINE?

In this section, we discuss the results of laboratory-based practice and training studies on development and improvement of cognitive skills. We also address the specificity of these skills. We begin with a discussion of cross- sectional studies of the effects of training and conclude with an examination of longitudinal studies, in which specific individuals served as their own controls.

Cross-Sectional Training Studies

In general, old and young adults have been found to learn new tasks and skills at approximately the same rate and to show the same magnitude of benefit from training. Such data clearly suggest that older adults can learn new skills. However, given that older adults' baseline performance on most tasks is lower than that of younger adults, these data also suggest that age-related differences in level of performance will be maintained after training.

There have, however, been some interesting exceptions to these general observations. For example, Baron and Mattila (1989) examined the influence of training on the speed and accuracy with which young and older adults performed a memory search task; that is, the subjects memorized a set of items and then compared a newly presented item to the items in memory, to decide whether the new item was a member of the original memory set or not. Subjects were trained for 44 hr with a deadline procedure in which they were required to constantly increase the speed with which they performed the task. Prior to training, young and older adults performed the task with comparable accuracy, but the older adults were substantially slower. During training with the deadline procedure, both young and older adults performed more quickly, but with a substantially elevated error rate. Interestingly, when the deadline procedure was relaxed, the young and older adults performed with equivalent accuracies, and the speed differences between the groups were substantially reduced. Thus, these data suggest that the older adults improved their speed of responding more than the younger adults did.

A similar pattern of results was obtained in a study of training effects on dual-task performance (Kramer, Larish, Weber, & Bardell, 1999). Young and old adults were trained to concurrently perform two tasks, a pattern-learning task and a tracking task (i.e., a task that involved using a joystick to control the position of an object so that it constantly matched the position of a computer-controlled object), with either of two training strategies. In the fixed-priority training condition, subjects were asked to treat the two tasks as equal in importance. In the variable-priority training condition, subjects were required to constantly vary their priorities between the two tasks. In both training conditions, subjects received continuing feedback on their performance.

Several interesting results were obtained. First, as in previous studies, young and old adults improved their dual-task performance at the same rate when using the fixed-priority training strategy. Second, variable-priority training led to faster learning of the tasks, a higher level of mastery, superior transfer of learning to new tasks, and better retention than did fixed-priority training. Finally, age-related differences in the efficiency of dual-task performance were substantially reduced for individuals trained in the variable-priority condition.

Although these studies and several others found that training decreased age-related performance differences, other studies have failed to demonstrate such training effects. What is the reason for these seemingly contradictory results? Although there is quite likely not a single answer to this question, one possibility centers on the nature of the training procedures. The training strategies in the two studies we just summarized explicitly focused on aspects of performance on which young and older adults showed large differences. For example, the deadline strategy employed by Baron and Mattila encourages individuals to emphasize speed rather than accuracy, something older adults are hesitant to do. Similarly, older adults have been observed to have difficulty in flexibly setting and modifying processing priorities among concurrently performed tasks. The variable-priority training strategy explicitly targets this skill. Thus, although additional research is clearly needed to further examine the situations in which the age gap in performance can be reduced, one potentially fruitful area of inquiry concerns targeting training strategies to specific difficulties encountered by older adults.

Longitudinal Studies of Practice and Training

A central focus of longitudinal studies has been to examine the extent to which training remediates or improves elders' performance on tasks for which there is long-term data. Given the wide individual differences in timing of age-related ability decline, two questions arise: First, is training effective in remediating decline for elders who have shown loss in a specific ability? Second, can training enhance the performance of elders showing no decline in a specific ability?

Data from the Seattle Longitudinal Study provide some initial answers to these questions. In this study, elders were classified as to whether they had shown reliable decline over a 14-year interval on two fluid abilities known to show early age-related decline-inductive reasoning and spatial orientation (Schaie & Willis, 1986). These individuals then received 5 hr of training on either inductive reasoning or spatial orientation. More than two thirds of elders who received training on each ability showed reliable improvement on that ability. Of those who had declined on the ability trained, 40% showed remediation, such that their performance was at or above their level of performance 14 years prior to the training. Elders who had not declined also showed reliable improvement. Moreover, the effects of training on inductive reasoning lasted up to 7 years after training (Saczynski & Willis, 2001).

Summary

Cross-sectional training research suggests that both young and old adults profit from training, but that strategies targeted at skills known to decline with age are particularly effective in training of elders. Longitudinal studies make it possible to identify abilities that have declined for a given individual and to assess whether the individual can benefit from training targeted at his or her specific deficits. Using the longitudinal approach, researchers can examine the range of plasticity (i.e., the extent to which an individual can benefit from training) over time within the same individual, rather than comparing the magnitude of training effects for different age groups. Both types of training research support the position that even individuals of advanced age have considerable plasticity in their cognitive functioning. The training findings also support the descriptive experiential studies of cognitive decline in showing that effects are specific to the particular domain that was practiced or trained.

FITNESS AND COGNITIVE SPARING?

The relationship between fitness and mental function has been a topic of interest to researchers for the past several decades. Their research has been predicated on the assumption that improvements in aerobic fitness translate into increased brain blood flow, which in turn supports more efficient brain function, particularly in older adults for whom such function is often compromised. Indeed, research with older nonhuman animals has found that aerobic fitness promotes beneficial changes in both the structure and the function of the brain (Churchill et al., in press).

However the results from human studies that have examined the influence of aerobic fitness training on cognition have been mixed. Some studies have demonstrated fitness-related improvements for older adults, but others have failed to show such improvements. Clearly, there are a number of potential theoretical and methodological reasons for this ambiguity. For example, studies have differed in the length and the nature of the fitness interventions, the health and age of the study populations, and the aspects of cognition that have been examined.

A recent analysis statistically combining the results of fitness intervention studies that have been conducted since the late 1960s (Colcombe & Kramer, in press) lends support to the idea that fitness training can improve cognitive functioning. Perhaps the most important finding obtained in this analysis was that the effects of fitness were selective rather than general. That is, aerobic fitness training had a substantially larger positive impact on performance of tasks with large executive-control components (i.e., tasks that required planning, scheduling, working memory, resistance to distraction, or multitask processing) than on performance of tasks without such components. Interestingly, substantial age-related deficits have been reported for executive-control tasks and the brain regions that support them. Thus, it appears that executive-control processes can benefit through either training or improved fitness. An important question for future research is whether such benefits are mediated by the same underlying mechanisms.

CONCLUSIONS AND FUTURE DIRECTIONS

The research we have reviewed clearly suggests that the cognitive vitality of older adults can be enhanced through cognitive training, in the form of domain-relevant expertise or laboratory training, and improved fitness. However, it is important to note that these benefits are often quite specific and have not been observed in all published studies (Salthouse, 1990). Therefore, one important goal for future research is to determine when these benefits are and are not produced. Clearly, there are some obvious candidate factors that should be examined in more detail. These include age, health conditions, medication use, gender, education, lifestyle choices, genetic profile, and family and social support.

The nature and length of training, whether cognitive or fitness training, bears further study. It is important to note that many of the previous studies of "training" have examined unsupervised practice rather than specific training procedures that might be well suited to the capabilities of older adults, The development of new methods, such as the testing-the-limits approach[3] (Kliegl, Smith, & Baltes, 1989), will clearly also be important in future studies of training and other interventions.

At present, psychologists have little understanding of the mechanisms that subserve age-related enhancements in cognitive efficiency. Possibilities include improvements in basic cognitive abilities, the development of compensatory strategies, and automatization of selective aspects of a skill or task (Baltes, Staudinger, & Lindenberger, 1999). Thus, the nature of cognitive and brain processes that support improvements in cognitive efficiency is an important topic for future research.

Finally, we would like to emphasize the importance of theory-guided research in the study of interventions targeted to enhancing the cognitive function of older adults. Theories of life-span change, such as the theory of selective optimization with compensation[4] (Baltes et al., 1999), offer great promise in this endeavor.

Recommended Reading

Charness, N. (1999). Can acquired knowledge compensate for age-related declines in cognitive efficiency? In S.H. Qualls & N. Ables (Eds.), *Psychology and the aging revolution: How we adapt to longer life* (pp. 99–117). Washington, DC: American Psychological Association.

Morrow, D.G., Menard, W.E., Stine Morrow, E.A.L,, Teller, T., & Bryant, D. (2001). The influence of expertise and task factors on age differences in pilot communication. *Psychology and Aging, 16,* 31–46.

Salthouse, T.A. (1990). (See References)

Notes

1. Address correspondence to Arthur Kramer, Beckman Institute, University of Illinois, Urbana, IL 61801; e-mail: akramer@s.psych.uiuc.edu.

2. Working memory refers to processes needed to both store and retrieve information over brief periods, as well as processes necessary to manipulate the stored information (e.g., remembering a few weight measurements in pounds and converting them to kilograms).

3. Testing-the-limits examines the range and limits of cognitive reserve capacity as an approach to understanding age differences in cognitive processes.

4. This theory suggests that during aging, individuals maintain skill by focusing on selective aspects of broader skills, practicing these subskills often, and sometimes shifting strategies (e.g., shifting from speed to accuracy) to maintain performance.

References

Baltes, P.B., Staudinger, U.M., & Lindenberger, U. (1999). Lifespan psychology: Theory and application to intellectual functioning. *Annual Review of Psychology, 50,* 471–507.

Baron, A., & Mattila, W.R. (1989). Response slowing of older adults: Effects of time-contingencies on single and dual-task performances. *Psychology and Aging, 4,* 66–72.

Churchill, J.D., Galvez, R., Colcombe, S., Swain, R.A., Kramer, A.F., & Greenough, W.T. (in press). Exercise, experience and the aging brain. *Neurobiology of Aging.*

Colcombe, S., & Kramer, A.F. (in press). Fitness effects on the cognitive function of older adults: A meta-analytic study. *Psychological Science.*

Kliegl, R., Smith, J., & Baltes, P.B. (1989). Testing-the-limits and the study of adult age difference in cognitive plasticity of a mnemonic skill. *Developmental Psychology, 2,* 247–256.

Kramer, A.F., Larish, J., Weber, T., & Bardell, L. (1999). Training for executive control: Task coordination strategies and aging. In D. Gopher & A. Koriat (Eds.), *Attention and performance XVII* (pp. 617–652). Cambridge, MA: MIT Press.

Krampe, R.T., & Ericsson, K.A. (1996). Maintaining excellence: Deliberate practice and elite performance in young and older pianists. *Journal of Experimental Psychology: General, 125,* 331–359.

Saczynski, J., & Willis, S.L. (2001). *Cognitive training and maintenance of intervention effects in the elderly.* Manuscript submitted for publication.

Salthouse, T.A. (1984). Effects of age and skill in typing. *Journal of Experimental Psychology. General, 213,* 345–371.

Salthouse, T.A. (1990). Influence of experience on age difference in cognitive functioning. *Human Factors, 32,* 551–569.

Salthouse, T.A. (1996). Processing-speed theory of adult age differences in cognition. *Psychological Review, 103,* 403–428.

Schaie, K.W. (2000). The impact of longitudinal studies on understanding development from young adulthood to old age. *International Journal of Behavioral Development, 24,* 257–266.

Schaie, K.W., & Willis, S.L. (1986). Can decline in adult intellectual functioning be reversed? *Developmental Psychology, 22,* 223–232.

Verhaeghen, P., Kliegl, R., & Mayr, U. (1997). Sequential and coordinative complexity in time-accuracy functions for mental arithmetic. *Psychology and Aging, 12,* 555–564.

Critical Thinking Questions

1. How would you describe the decline in cognitive functions over the adult life span? Specifically, what declines and when?

2. Can certain life experiences slow age-related declines in performance? Explain.

3. Can laboratory-based training reduce declines in performance? What effects are revealed in cross-sectional and longitudinal research?

4. What is basis for the hypothesis that aerobic fitness can improve cognitive functions, and what does human research show?

Social and Cultural Psychology

Do you ever behave in ways that are profoundly "out of character" just to suit the situation you're in? Drawn together by the theme that people are gregarious by nature and that situations have the power to overwhelm even the best of us, social psychologists study the ways in which we influence and are influenced by one another. By observing people in carefully staged social settings, researchers in this area study a range of social behaviors—such as attraction and the development of relationships, conformity, altruism, aggression, persuasion, and group dynamics. They also study the role of culture and the problems that arise when individuals harbor stereotypes and prejudices about others who are different.

Hillary Elfenbein and Nalini Ambady (2003) open the section with an article on the recognition of emotion. These researchers report that while facial expressions of emotions are universally recognized, people are more accurate at judging members of their own cultural groups. Studying the self-esteem, Michael Ross and Anne Wilson (2003) report on studies showing that people unwittingly rewrite their autobiographical memories in a way that enable them to see current selves as improved over distant past selves. Interested in the interface of social psychology and the law, John Darley (2001) discusses people's commonsense notions of crime, punishment, and justice and how they may influence legal decision-making, as on juries. Based on the fact that people tend to conform to perceived social norms, Robert Cialdini (2003) presents research-based persuasion strategy that public service communicators can use to get people to behave in environmentally responsible ways. Finally, John Dovidio and Samuel Gaertner (1999) distinguish overt and covert forms of prejudice and describe research-based ways to combat prejudice among individuals and groups.

Universals and Cultural Differences in Recognizing Emotions

Hilary Anger Elfenbein[1] and Nalini Ambady
Department of Organizational Behavior and Industrial Relations, University of California, Berkeley, California (H.A.E.), and Department of Psychology, Harvard University, Cambridge, Massachusetts (N.A.)

Abstract

Moving beyond the earlier nature-versus-nurture debate, modern work on the communication of emotion has incorporated both universals and cultural differences. Classic research demonstrated that the intended emotions in posed expressions were recognized by members of many different cultural groups at rates better than predicted by random guessing. However, recent research has also documented evidence for an in-group advantage, meaning that people are generally more accurate at judging emotions when the emotions are expressed by members of their own cultural group rather than by members of a different cultural group. These new findings provide initial support for a dialect theory of emotion that has the potential to integrate both classic and recent findings. Further research in this area has the potential to improve cross-cultural communication.

Keywords

emotion; universality; cross-cultural differences

The scientific study of how people express emotion has been intertwined with the question of whether or not emotions are universal across cultures and species. Many psychology textbooks describe classic research from the 1960s demonstrating that participants around the world could judge the intended basic emotional states portrayed in posed photographs at rates better than would be expected from random guessing (Ekman, 1972; Izard, 1971). On the basis of these and related studies, many psychologists concluded that the recognition of emotion is largely universal, with the implication that this skill is not learned, but rather has an evolutionary and thus biological basis.

More recently, researchers have attempted to move beyond an either-or approach to the nature-versus-nurture debate, in order to explore how differences across cultures may affect the universal processes involved in expressing and understanding emotions. In this article, we contrast the ability of two theories to account for recent research findings.

EVIDENCE FOR BOTH UNIVERSALS AND CULTURAL DIFFERENCES IN COMMUNICATING EMOTION

The communication of emotion has a strong universal component. For example, people of different cultures can watch foreign films and understand much of their original feeling. Likewise, people can develop strong bonds with pets while communicating largely through nonverbal displays of emotion. Thus, messages on an emotional level can cross the barrier of a cultural or species difference.

Still, although much of an emotional message is retained across these barriers, some of the message gets lost along the way. For example, when traveling or living abroad, or when working in multinational environments, many people develop an intuition that their basic communication signals tend to be misinterpreted more frequently when they interact with individuals from cultures foreign to them than when they interact with compatriots. Therefore, it is not a contradiction to say that the expression of emotion is largely universal but there are subtle differences across cultures that can create a challenge for effective communication.

New Interpretations of Classic Research

The early researchers who studied how people communicate emotion across cultures focused their efforts on establishing universality, and therefore did not pay as much attention to the cultural differences as to the cross-cultural similarities in their data (Matsumoto & Assar, 1992). For example, Table 1 lists the results from Ekman's (1972) five-culture study. Participants viewed photographs and for each one selected an emotion label from six possible choices, so that guessing entirely at random would yield one correct answer out of six, or 16.7% accuracy. Because all cultural groups' performance for all six emotional expressions was much higher than 16.7%, Ekman and his colleagues concluded that there is a *universal affect program*, a biologically programmed guide that governs the communication of emotion.

However, other researchers have noticed different patterns in these same data. For example, Matsumoto (1989) noted that U.S. participants outperformed the Japanese in the study. He argued that some cultures, such as Japanese culture, encourage the use of decoding rules (Buck, 1984), social norms that inhibit the understanding of emotion in cases when understanding may be disruptive to social harmony. Further, he argued that some languages, such as English, are superior to others in their emotion vocabulary (Matsumoto & Assar, 1992). Thus, he argued that Americans are generally more effective than most other cultural groups at understanding emotion.

Table 1 Accuracy at recognizing American facial expressions (Ekman's 1972 five-culture study)

	Participant group				
Expression	United States	Chile	Brazil	Argentina	Japan
Happiness	97	90	92	94	87
Fear	88	78	77	68	71
Disgust	84	85	86	79	82
Anger	68	76	82	72	63
Surprise	91	88	81	93	87
Sadness	87	91	82	88	80
Average	86	85	83	82	78

Note. All values listed are the percentage of participants who correctly judged the emotional epxression indicated.

We noticed yet a different pattern in the data in Table 1: The group with the highest performance is also the same group from which the experimental stimuli originated (Elfenbein & Ambady, 2002b). All participants in the study viewed photographs of American facial expressions, so Americans were the only participants to view members of their own cultural group, or in-group. Everyone else in the study judged expressions from a foreign group, or out-group. We found it interesting that the South American participants were only slightly less accurate than U.S. participants, whereas the difference in performance was larger for the Japanese, who were the most culturally distant.

New Findings on In-Group Advantage

In explaining these cultural differences, earlier researchers tended to focus either on the attributes of the group expressing the emotions or on the attributes of the group perceiving the emotions. In contrast, we tried to think about both groups at the same time, in terms of the match between them. In other words, we considered whether observers were judging emotional expressions made by members of their own cultural in-group or made by members of a cultural out-group. In a meta-analysis (a statistical analysis that combines the results of multiple studies), we assembled the results of 97 studies, which involved 182 different samples representing more than 22,000 total participants (Elfenbein & Ambady, 2002a). These studies included the classic research of Ekman (1972) and Izard (1971), more recent work on the understanding of emotions across cultures, and unintentionally cross-cultural studies in which researchers borrowed testing materials that portrayed people who were not from the geographic location where they were conducting their research.

Our results strongly replicated the earlier finding that people can understand the intended emotional state in posed expressions from other cultures with accuracy greater than predicted by chance guessing. However, this observation alone does not necessarily mean that emotion recognition is governed entirely by universals (Russell, 1994). We also found evidence for an *in-group advantage* in the understanding of emotion: Participants were generally more accurate in recognizing emotions expressed by members of their own culture than in recognizing emotions expressed by members of a different cultural group. The in-group advantage was replicated across a range of experimental methods, positive and negative emotions, and different nonverbal channels of communicating emotion, such as facial expressions, tone of voice, and body language.

Even when the cultural differences in understanding emotion are small, they can still have important real-world consequences. If cross-cultural interactions are slightly less smooth than same-culture interactions, then misunderstandings can accumulate over time and make interpersonal relationships less satisfying. However, the findings of this and our other studies also provide a hopeful message regarding cross-cultural communication: The in-group advantage is lower when groups are nearer geographically or have greater cross-cultural contact with each other, and over time participants appeared to learn how to understand the emotions of people from foreign cultures (Elfenbein & Ambady, 2002b, 2003a, 2003b).

The idea of an in-group advantage has been controversial (Elfenbein & Ambady, 2002a, Matsumoto, 2002), largely because of a theoretical disagreement about whether it is necessary to force members of different cultures to express their emotions using exactly the same style. Researchers are divided as to whether the studies that have not done this are a valid test of the in-group advantage. Understanding this controversy requires first understanding some theoretical perspectives on the communication of emotion.

A PRELIMINARY DIALECT THEORY

Researchers have attempted to weave together diverse strands of evidence to develop theory about how biology and culture influence the communication of emotion.

Ekman's Neurocultural Theory

The neurocultural theory of emotion (Ekman, 1972), based on Tomkins's earlier work (Tomkins & McCarter, 1964), posits the existence of a universal *facial affect program* that provides a one-to-one map between the emotion a person feels and the facial expression the person displays. According to this theory, the facial affect program is the same for all people in all cultures, and therefore everyone expresses emotion in the same manner in nonsocial settings. However, in social settings, people use conscious "management techniques" (Ekman, 1972, p. 225) called *display rules* to control and override the operation of the universal facial affect program. These display rules can vary across cultures, and they are norms that serve to intensify, diminish, neutralize, or mask emotional displays that would otherwise be produced automatically. Extending neurocultural theory from the expression to the perception of emotion, Matsumoto (1989) argued that all people in all cultures perceive emotional expressions in the same manner, but that there are culturally specific norms (i.e., decoding rules) about whether or not to acknowledge that one has understood.

Developing a Dialect Theory

Tomkins and McCarter (1964) articulated the metaphor that cultural differences in emotional expression are like "dialects" of the "more universal grammar of emotion" (p. 127): Just as dialects of a language (e.g., American vs. British English) can differ in accent, grammar, and vocabulary, the universal language of emotion may also have dialects that differ subtly from each other.

Expanding on these ideas, we developed the new dialect theory of emotion to account for the empirical evidence of an in-group advantage in understanding emotion. Earlier researchers who had noticed this effect referred to it as *bias* and argued that participants were more motivated and perhaps paid closer attention when judging in-group members than when judging out-group members. However, our evidence did not support this interpretation, because in many of the studies reviewed in our meta-analysis, participants could not have known that the emotional expressions were from a foreign culture (this was the case, e.g., in studies in which Caucasians judged facial expressions of Caucasians from other cultures and in studies in which filtered vocal tones served as stimuli). Translation difficulties (i.e., mismatches between the emotion words participants used to judge stimuli and experimenters used to instruct the posers who generated the stimuli) could have contributed to the in-group effect but could not fully explain it, given that the in-group advantage also existed across cultural groups speaking the same language. Thus, we had to find another explanation for the in-group advantage.

Two central observations inspired the dialect theory. The first observation was that any explanation of the in-group advantage must consider the cultural match between the expresser and the perceiver of an emotional display, rather than considering either group independently. This was a logical point because the definition of the in-group advantage is that perceivers' emotion judgments are more accurate with culturally matched than culturally mismatched materials. The second observation was that the cultural differences that cause the in-group advantage must be contained within the appearance of the emotional expressions themselves, because the in-group advantage was found when participants did not have any other cues about the cultural identity of the expresser. For example, Americans could have outperformed other Caucasian cultural groups when judging American facial expressions only if there was something particularly American about the expressions.

The dialect theory arose from these two observations. It begins with a universal affect program, [2] a guide for expressing emotions that is the same for all cultural groups. Because a person can express any single emotion in multiple ways, this program is not necessarily the one-to-one map of neurocultural theory.[3] Additionally, each cultural group has a *specific affect program* that incorporates some adjustments to the universal program. Acquired through social learning, these adjustments create subtle differences in the appearance of emotional expression across cultures. These stylistic differences do not necessarily have a specific purpose or meaning; thus, they differ from display and decoding rules, which are conscious management techniques for the benefit of social harmony. Figure 1 illustrates the relation between the universal affect program and specific affect programs from different cultures.

Figure 2 illustrates the dialect theory of how emotion is communicated and perceived. A key distinction between dialect theory and neurocultural theory is

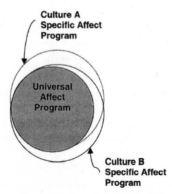

Fig. 1. Illustration of the relation between the universal affect program and the specific affect programs for two cultures. Copyright 2003 by Hillary Anger Elfenbein. Reprinted with permission of the author.

that dialect theory suggests that cultural differences in emotional expression can arise from two sources—the specific affect program and display rules—rather than from display rules alone. Similarly, dialect theory posits two different sources of cultural differences in perceiving emotion—the specific affect program and decoding rules—rather than decoding rules alone.

A second key distinction from neurocultural theory is that dialect theory suggests there is a direct link between the cultural differences that arise in the expression and perception of emotion. This link is the specific affect program, which governs the two complementary processes. After all, people tend to interpret another person's behavior in terms of what they would have intended if they had used the same expression. In contrast, neurocultural theory posits that cultural differences in emotional expression and perception emerge from two separate processes: display rules and decoding rules. Because these two sets of rules are not explicitly linked to each other, neurocultural theory does not account for the empirical evidence of the in-group advantage. This is because, as we have noted, any explanation of the in-group advantage must consider the cultural match between the expresser and the perceiver of an emotional display, rather than either group independently.

Evidence for the In-Group Advantage

This background assists in clarifying the disagreement regarding whether the evidence supports the existence of an in-group advantage in emotion. Matsumoto (2002) argued that an in-group advantage in perceiving emotion should result only from differences across perceivers. This is because his theoretical perspective treats cultural differences in expressing and perceiving emotion as two unlinked processes, and he argued that they should be examined separately.

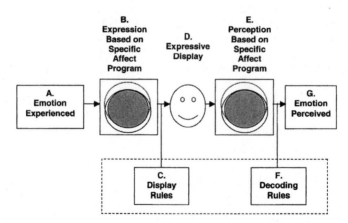

Fig. 2. Representation of a dialect theory of emotion. This theory incorporates processes described by Brunswick (1955), Buck (1984), and Ekman (1972). The universal affect program is represented by the gray circles, and specific affect programs of two different cultures are represented by the partially overlapping white circles (see Fig. 1). The dashed box shows the only sources of cultural differences in the communication of emotion according to Ekman (1972) and Matsumoto (1989). Copyright 2003 by Hillary Anger Elfenbein. Reprinted with permission of the author.

Thus, he argued that a valid test of the in-group advantage in emotion recognition should remove all cultural differences in the appearance of emotional expressions in order to achieve "stimulus equivalence" (Matsumoto, 2002, p. 236). However, according to dialect theory, there are cultural differences in the appearance of emotional expressions resulting from the specific affect program. Therefore, forcibly eliminating all cultural differences in the appearance of facial expressions also would eliminate one of the two matched processes responsible for the in-group advantage, cultural differences in expression and perception that arise from the specific affect program. Thus, failures to demonstrate an in-group advantage under stimulus equivalence fit rather than disconfirm the predictions of dialect theory. Further, not only is eliminating cultural differences in the appearance of emotional expression an undesirable step for researchers according to dialect theory, but recent empirical evidence demonstrates that in practice it can be nearly impossible to do so—such differences are so robust that they can leak through processes designed specifically to neutralize them (Marsh, Elfenbein, & Ambady, 2003).

FUTURE DIRECTIONS

Universals and cultural differences in the communication of emotion have been hotly debated and will likely continue to be. Research studies that can help to tease apart the competing perspectives—while acknowledging the complex roles of both nature and nurture—would greatly benefit the field.

The dialect theory of emotion is still speculative and being developed primarily on the basis of recent empirical data. The theory requires direct testing. The most authoritative studies would uncover the particular aspects of emotional expression that vary across cultures—such as specific facial muscle movements, features of vocal tones, or body movements—and would map the use of these cues directly to cross-cultural differences in perceiving emotion. It is important to do this research in a context that limits alternative explanations for the in-group advantage, such as language differences and bias. Further research could determine how these cues are learned.

Although differences in emotion across cultures can create a barrier to effective communication, it is heartening to know that people can overcome these barriers. Further work in this field has the potential to help bridge intergroup differences by contributing to training and intervention programs that can help to improve cross-cultural communication.

Recommended Reading

Darwin, C. (1998) *The expression of the emotions in man and animals* (3rd ed.). New York: Oxford University Press. (Original work published 1872)
Ekman, P. (1993) Facial expression and emotion. *American Psychologist, 48,* 384-392.
Elfenbein, H.A., & Ambady, N. (2002b). (See References)
Russell, J.A. (1994). (See References)

Acknowledgements—We thank James Russell, Anita Williams Woolley, and Kevyn Yong for their helpful comments on the manuscript.

Notes

1. Address correspondence to Hillary Anger Elfenbein, Department of Organizational Behavior and Industrial Relations, Haas School of Business, University of California, Berkeley, CA 94720-1900; e-mail:hillary@post.Harvard.edu.

2. We do not refer to the universal affect program as a facial affect program in order to emphasize that it includes additional nonverbal channels of communication, such as vocal tone and body movements.

3. We thank James Russell for this observation.

References

Brunswick, E. (1955). Representative design and probabilistic theory in a functional psychology. *Psychology Review, 62,* 193-217

Buck, R. (1984). *The communication of emotion.* New York: Guilford Press

Ekman, P. (1972). Universals and cultural differences in facial expressions of emotion. In J. Cole (Ed.), *Nebraska Symposium on Motivation, 1971* (Vol. 19, pp. 207-282). Lincoln: University of Nebraska Press.

Elfenbein, H.A., & Ambady, N. (2002a). Is there an in-group advantage in emotion? *Psychological Bulletin, 128,* 243-239.

Elfenbein, H.A., & Ambady, N. (2002b). On the universality and cultural specificity of emotion recognition: A meta-analysis. *Psychological Bulletin, 128,* 203-235.

Elfenbein, H.A., & Ambady, N. (2003a). Cultural similarity's consequences: A distance perspective on cross-cultural differences in emotion recognition. *Journal of Cross-Cultural Psychology, 34,* 92-110.

Elfenbein, H.A., & Ambady, N. (2003b). When familiarity breeds accuracy: Cultural exposure and facial emotion recognition. *Journal of Personality and Social Psychology, 85,* 276–290.

Izard, C.E. (1971). *The face of emotion.* New York: Appleton-Century-Crofts.

Marsh, A., Elfenbein, H.A., & Ambady, N. (2003). Nonverbal "accents": Cultural differences in facial expressions of emotion. *Psychological Science, 14,* 373-376.

Matsumoto, D. (1989). Cultural influences on the perception of emotion. *Journal of Cross-Cultural Psychology, 20,* 92-105.

Matsumoto, D. (2002). Methodological requirements to test a possible in-group advantage in judging emotions across cultures: Comments on Elfenbein and Ambady and evidence. *Psychological Bulletin, 128,* 236-242.

Matsumoto, D., & Assar, M. (1992). The effects of language on judgments of universal facial expressions of emotion. *Journal of Nonverbal Behavior, 16,* 85-99.

Russell, J.A. (1994). Is there universal recognition of emotion from facial expression? A review of the cross-cultural studies. *Psychological Bulletin, 115,* 102-141.

Tomkins, S.S., & McCarter, R. (1964). What and where are the primary affects: Some evidence for a theory. *Perceptual and Motor Skills, 18,* 119-158.

Critical Thinking Questions

1. What evidence supports a universal basis for the communication of emotions?

2. Describe evidence of a cultural "in-group advantage" in the communication of emotions.

3. Compare and contrast the two main theories of emotion recognition.

4. Speculate on the kinds of research that may tease apart the universals and cultural differences in the facial expression of emotion.

Autobiographical Memory and Conceptions of Self: Getting Better All the Time

Michael Ross[1] and Anne E. Wilson

Psychology Department, University of Waterloo, Waterloo, Ontario, Canada (M.R.), and Psychology Department, Wilfrid Laurier University, Waterloo, Ontario, Canada (A.E.W.)

Abstract

We examine links between self-assessment and autobiographical memory. People generally view themselves as improving over time, relative to their peers. We suggest that this sense of improvement is sometimes illusory, and motivated by the desire to enhance the current self. Our research focuses on people's subjective feeling of temporal distance between an earlier period and the present, a feeling that is only modestly associated with actual time. Research participants praise or criticize the same former self, depending on how far away it feels. An equally distant episode feels close or remote, depending on whether it has favorable or damaging implications for evaluations of the current self. The identical achievement boosts evaluations of the current self or has little impact, depending on how far away it feels. The same failure does or does not harm appraisals of the current self, depending on how far away it feels.

Keywords

subjective time; self-assessment; temporal self-appraisal

At the age of 60, actor Mary Tyler Moore offered the following evaluation of the stages in her life: "Of all the lives that I have lived, I would have to say that this one is my favorite. I am proud that I have developed into a kinder person than I ever thought I would be" (Gerosa, 1997, p. 83). We have found a similar tendency to praise current selves and belittle past selves in autobiographies. In his memoirs, Koestler (1952) observed that people ridicule former selves:

> The gauche adolescent, the foolish young man that one has been, appears so grotesque in retrospect and so detached from one's own identity that one automatically treats him with amused derision. It is a callous betrayal, yet one cannot help being a traitor to one's past. (p. 96)

This observation is intriguing, because today becomes yesterday. The current exemplary self seems less praiseworthy in retrospect.

TEMPORAL SELF-APPRAISAL THEORY

When we began to study people's evaluations of their current and former selves, there was plenty of psychological research showing that individuals are typically impressed with their present selves (Baumeister, 1998), but little research on people's evaluations of what they were like in the past. There were at least two psychological reasons to suppose that most people would also be delighted with their former selves. If, as social psychologists often assume, individuals are motivated to think highly of themselves, why would they criticize a former self? It might be even easier for people to imagine perfection in the past than in the present, because there is less evidence to challenge their claims. Also, psychologists have argued that to maintain a coherent self-view, people make their recollections of themselves consistent with their current self-view (Albert, 1977). Both theory and research implied that people who see themselves as exemplary now should recall themselves as always having been outstanding.

Yet we kept noticing that people seemed rather unimpressed with their past selves. Why and when do people criticize earlier selves? Although Koestler considered his self-criticism to be a betrayal, Orwell (1946) regarded a harsh retrospective evaluation as a realistic appraisal: "Autobiography is only to be trusted when it reveals something disgraceful. A man who gives a good account of himself is probably lying, since any life when viewed from the inside is simply a series of defeats" (p. 170). Do people remove their rose-colored glasses when they glance backward in time, appraising former selves and deeds impartially?

We were intrigued by the possibility that individuals who are supposedly motivated to think highly of themselves disparage former selves. How common is such criticism? Does it occur only when merited or accurate? How are people's current self-views affected by their criticism of past selves? We have tried to answer these questions in our theory of temporal self-appraisal and associated research.

A couple of terms are central to our analyses. First, consider the demarcation between present and past selves. The tiny point in time that is actually "right now" is not what people mean when they refer to the present. People create a more extended present by assimilating earlier instances into it. Philosophers label this contracting of successive events into a single instant the *specious present* (James, 1890/1950, p. 609). Extending the breadth of the specious present to suit their purposes, people speak of the present minute, week, year, and so forth. In our studies, we typically assess the present self by asking people to describe what they are like currently and over the past couple of weeks. Although 2 weeks is clearly an arbitrary division, it is an interlude that our participants comfortably incorporate into the present. We also ask participants what they were like in the more distant past, months and years earlier. Although we consider the targets of these retrospective assessments to be former selves of the participants, the identification of former selves is also complicated. People can think of a former self as extended in time (their teenage self) or more limited (their 18-year-old self or their self last New Year's Eve). In our experiments, we ask people to evaluate themselves at a specific time in the past.

We use the label *subjective temporal distance* to refer to how far away people feel from past selves. People's reactions to former selves are strongly affected by how far away they feel from those selves (Ross & Wilson, 2000; Wilson & Ross, in press). People feel remote and detached from some former selves and close and connected to other past selves. We suppose that subjective temporal distance and actual time are correlated. In general, events that happened 1 year ago feel closer than episodes that occurred 10 years ago. Along with many psychologists including William James, we also suggest that the relation between subjective and actual time is imperfect. People can feel close to past selves (and associated events) from 10 years ago (e.g., their wedding day) and far from past selves (and associated episodes) from 1 year ago (e.g., their last birthday).

We propose that people are motivated to evaluate their past selves in a way that makes them feel good about themselves now. Typically, people are motivated to evaluate subjectively recent past selves favorably, especially when considering important attributes. People can continue to take credit for achievements of past selves that feel close. By praising past selves to whom they feel connected, they also compliment their current self. They cannot continue forever to bask in the glory of their earlier triumphs, however. As specific achievements (and associated selves) feel farther and farther away, the attainments shine less brightly on the current self. Subjectively distant successes feel as if they belong almost exclusively to earlier selves. Similarly, as failures or transgressions feel farther and farther away, individuals might view their current self as less blameworthy.

EVALUATING PRESENT AND PAST SELVES

In our research, we examined various groups of people, including Canadian and Japanese university students, middle-aged Canadians, and celebrities interviewed in magazines, to better understand people's evaluations of current and past selves. In each sample, people evaluated their present self as superior to their former selves (e.g., Wilson & Ross, 2001). Japanese students were less enamored with themselves than were their Canadian counterparts, but both groups evaluated their current self more favorably than earlier selves. Similarly, middle-aged participants' ratings of their social skills, common sense, and self-confidence indicated that they viewed themselves as improving steadily with age.

Participants in our studies considered their own self-improvement to be greater than that of their peers. At age 50, middle-aged participants regarded themselves as even better than their peers than they were at age 20. Similarly, university students described themselves as more superior to their peers currently than they had been at age 16 (Wilson & Ross, 2001).

Perhaps most people do learn from experience and get better with age— even if they cannot all improve more than their peers. We suspected, however, that the derogation of former selves is not fully explained by actual improvement or even the wisdom of hindsight. When we studied a group of participants over time, we found that they perceived personal improvement where none had actually occurred (Wilson & Ross, 2001). To explain this illusory improvement, we focused on the concept of subjective temporal distance. The theory of temporal self-appraisal suggests that evaluations of former selves should become increasingly unfavorable as those selves feel farther away, even if actual temporal distance does not change. In one experiment, we altered participants' subjective experience of temporal distance by describing the same point in time as either recent or fairly distant. As anticipated, participants were more critical of their former self when it felt farther away. According to the theory of temporal self-appraisal, people are especially motivated to perceive improvement on important attributes, because these attributes have a particularly great impact on self-eval-

162

uation. As expected, we found that criticism of "distant" past selves was more pronounced on important characteristics than on less important characteristics.

Simple hindsight or actual improvement cannot explain these findings. Participants in the "near" and "far" conditions evaluated the very same past self. The difference in evaluation due to variations in subjective time cannot be warranted on objective grounds. Also, the finding for important versus unimportant characteristics seems counterintuitive. People were most critical of subjectively distant past selves on the very traits that they cared most about. Our explanation is that such criticism of past selves allows people to feel better about their current performance on important dimensions.

To show that people regard criticism of past selves as benefiting the current self, we asked participants to write either accurate or flattering self-descriptions. Participants writing flattering descriptions were more likely than those who wrote accurate descriptions to include an inferior past self in their self-descriptions (Wilson & Ross, 2000). Apparently, people suppose that contrasting their present self to a lesser earlier self enhances how the present self looks.

If people are motivated to self-enhance, why do they not inflate their assessment of their current self rather than derogate subjectively distant former selves? People do boost their present self, but there are psychological advantages to downgrading the past rather than dramatically inflating the present. When people artificially enhance their current self, their self-evaluation may become implausibly inconsistent with objective standards. Retrospective criticism allows individuals to be relatively satisfied with even a mediocre present evaluation. A man may regard himself as too shy, but much more outgoing than he used to be.

SUBJECTIVE DISTANCE FROM PAST EVENTS

So far, we have described how variations in actual and subjective temporal distance affect people's evaluations of a past self. We also theorize that feelings of subjective distance help people to maintain favorable current self-views. Individuals should be motivated to feel farther from past failings than from equally distant achievements. A student who performed poorly on an exam 2 weeks ago should feel more distant from the exam than a student who performed well on the same test. Both students might be fully aware of the date of their exam, but their experience of subjective distance should differ. By attributing a subjectively distant failure to an inferior, former self (the "old me"), individuals can shield their current self from blame. In contrast, people can continue to claim credit for former accomplishments by feeling close to such episodes. Subjectively recent accomplishments "belong" to the present self almost as much as to an earlier self.

In our research, we have examined feelings of subjective distance from past episodes that could have negative or positive implications for the current self. In one study (Ross & Wilson, 2002), we randomly assigned participants to remember the course in which they received either their best or their worst grade the previous term. After reporting their grade, participants indicated how distant they felt from the target course on a scale with endpoints labeled "feels like yesterday" and "feels far away." Participants who obtained a relatively low grade felt farther from the course than did those who received a high grade, even though the actual passage of time was the same in the two conditions. Across a number of studies, subjective distance was only modestly related to actual temporal distance from positive and negative personal experiences.

SUBJECTIVE DISTANCE OF PAST OUTCOMES AND EVALUATION OF THE CURRENT SELF

We assume that the subjective distance of past outcomes affects evaluations of the current self. For example, people should evaluate their current self more favorably if an achievement such as an academic award feels close, rather than far away. To examine whether subjective distance has this effect on self-evaluation, we experimentally varied people's feelings of distance from past outcomes (Wilson, 2000; Wilson & Ross, in press). We altered feelings of subjective distance by changing representations of the spatial distance between two points on a time line. University students were presented with a time line that spanned either many years (e.g., birth to today) or only the fairly recent past (e.g., age 16 to today) and were instructed to locate and mark a target event on the time line. As Figure 1 illustrates, they tended to place an event (in this case, their last semester of high school) much closer to "today" when the time line spanned many rather than a few years. Most important, we found that the students felt subjectively closer to events the nearer they placed those events to the present on the time line.

Using the time line as a tool, we encouraged some participants to feel subjectively close to a failure (by having them locate the episode on a time line spanning many years) and other participants to feel far away from the failure (by having them place the episode on a time line spanning only a few years). As anticipated, respondents who felt close to former failures evaluated their current self less favorably than did those who were persuaded to feel distant from

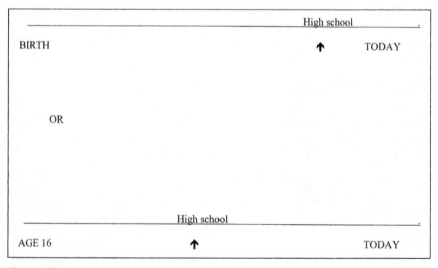

Fig. 1. Time-line manipulation of spatial distance. The birth-to-today time line makes high school seem subjectively more recent than does the age-16-to-today time line.

the very same failures. Similarly, participants who felt close to earlier successes evaluated their current self more favorably than did those who were led to regard the same accomplishments as more remote. The identical event has a different impact depending on whether people remember it as near or far away in time.

CONCLUSIONS

Our research suggests that people's views of their personal histories are remarkably dependent on feelings of subjective temporal distance. They praise or criticize the same former self, depending on how distant it feels. An equally distant event feels close or remote, depending on whether it has favorable or damaging implications for evaluations of the current self. The identical achievement boosts evaluations of the current self or has little impact, depending on how far away it feels. The same failure does or does not harm appraisals of the current self, depending on how far away it feels.

In everyday life, people are unlikely to come across time lines, but they do encounter events that can affect the subjective distance of past selves and episodes. Transitions such as marriage or changing religions, jobs, cities, or romantic partners might cause the pretransition self to seem remote. Even physical or material changes (e.g., getting a new haircut or car) might represent transitions to some individuals and serve to distance earlier selves. Personal experiences can also cause the past to feel close rather than distant. Visiting the neighborhood where one lived as a child or attending a school reunion may pull ancient history back into the subjective present.

In the future, we intend to extend our research in several directions. We will study people in late adulthood to examine how they protect their current self in the face of age-related declines in important attributes. We will also study whether subjective temporal distance plays an important role in judgments of other people and, perhaps more interesting, of historical events. Over time, all societies are forced to consider what aspects of historical experience are best forgotten, as well as what episodes should be preserved and carried forward into the future. We will examine whether the principles governing individual memory also help explain when societies distance and memorialize historical events.

Recommended Reading

James, W. (1950). (See References)
Wilson, A.E., & Ross, M. (2001). (See References)
Wilson, A.E., & Ross, M. (in press). (See References)

Note

1. Address correspondence to Michael Ross, Psychology Department, University of Waterloo, Waterloo, Ontario, Canada N2L 3G1; e-mail: mross@uwaterloo.ca.

References

Albert, S. (1977). Temporal comparison theory. *Psychological Review, 84,* 485–503.
Baumeister, R.F. (1998). The self. In D.T. Gilbert, S.T. Fiske, & G. Lindzey (Eds.), *Handbook of social psychology* (4th ed., pp. 680–740). New York: McGraw Hill.

Gerosa, M. (1997, Fall). Moore than ever. *More*, pp. 79–83.

James, W. (1950). *Principles of psychology.* New York: Dover. (Original work published 1890)

Koestler, A. (1952). *Arrow in the blue, an autobiography.* New York: Macmillan.

Orwell, G. (1946). Benefit of clergy: Some notes on Salvador Dali. In G. Orwell (Ed.), *Dickens, Dali & others: Studies in popular culture* (pp. 170–184). Cornwall, NY: Cornwall Press.

Ross, M., & Wilson, A.E. (2000). Constructing and appraising past selves. In D.L. Schacter & E. Scarry (Eds.), *Memory, brain, and belief* (pp. 231–258). Cambridge, MA: Harvard University Press.

Ross, M., & Wilson, A.E. (2002). It feels like yesterday: Self-esteem, valence of personal past experiences, and judgments of subjective distance. *Journal of Personality and Social Psychology, 82,* 792–803.

Wilson, A.E. (2000). *How do people's perceptions of their former selves affect their current self-appraisals?* Unpublished doctoral dissertation, University of Waterloo, Waterloo, Ontario, Canada.

Wilson, A.E., & Ross, M. (2000). The frequency of temporal-self and social comparisons in people's personal appraisals. *Journal of Personality and Social Psychology, 78,* 928–942.

Wilson, A.E., & Ross, M. (2001). From chump to champ: People's appraisals of their earlier and current selves. *Journal of Personality and Social Psychology, 80,* 572–584.

Wilson, A.E., & Ross, M. (in press). Autobiographical memory and self-identity. *Memory.*

Critical Thinking Questions

1. Psychologists have long known that memories shape our self-concept. How does this article suggest the reverse proposition, that the self-concept shapes our memories?

2. What is temporal self-appraisal theory and what does it predict about people's view of their past selves?

3. Under what conditions, and why, might people recall their past selves in less-than-glowing terms?

Citizens' Sense of Justice and the Legal System

John M. Darley[1]
Psychology Department, Princeton University, Princeton, New Jersey

Abstract

When an actor commits a wrong action, citizens have perceptions of the kind of responsibility the actor incurs, the degree to which the act was mitigated or justified, and the appropriate punishment for the actor. The legislatively mandated law of criminal courts, statutes, and criminal codes deals with the same issues. Experimental evidence shows that there are important discrepancies between the principles that people and legal codes use to assign responsibility. That is, the moral retributive-justice principles that people use are sometimes in conflict with the directions in which modern code drafters are taking criminal law. These discrepancies may cause citizens to feel alienated from authority, and to reduce their voluntary compliance with legal codes.

Keywords

justice; morality; criminal responsibility; legal decisions

There are many contributions that psychology can make to the criminal justice system. For instance, psychological studies and theories are relevant to the distortions that can affect eyewitness testimony, or whether an individual is competent to stand trial. Other possible contributions are more controversial, in that they might require some considerable rethinking of significant aspects of the legal system. One such area centers around citizens' perceptions of justice, and the relation between those notions of justice and the rules of justice written into the various legal codes.

Why should we care about "commonsense justice?"[2] The reason is that if a legal system's rules for assigning blame and punishment diverge in important ways from the principles that the citizens believe in, then those citizens may lose respect for the legal system. They may continue to obey the rules that the "justice" system imposes, but will do so largely to avoid punishment. No society can continue to exist if its citizens take that attitude toward its legal system.

Does the system of justice in the United States have this problem? Are there important discrepancies between the laws and the citizens' sense of justice?

MAPPING THE CONTOURS OF THE CITIZENS' SENSE OF JUSTICE

A number of investigations have elucidated the outlines of U.S. citizens' sense of just procedures. A landmark series of studies (Thibaut & Walker, 1975) demonstrated Americans' preference for procedures that give all participants repeated opportunities to express "their side" of the case, rather than more court-guided inquisitorial procedures. Continuing this tradition, Tyler (1990) studied persons who had gone through court proceedings. If they felt the proceedings were fair and impartial, and that they had been treated with respect, they were willing to accept the verdict even when it went against them.

There is less research on citizens' sense of retributive justice, punishments for acts of wrongdoing, but researchers recently have been turning to this area as well. The criminal code in force is decided in the United States on a state-by-state basis, but a large majority of states have based their criminal code on the Model Penal Code (MPC; American Law Institute, 1962), which was drafted by the American Law Institute in the 1950s. It is useful to contrast citizens' intuitions with this code both because it is likely to be the code in force in most jurisdictions and because the code set forth general principles of justice. We can therefore ask whether those principles, thought by the code drafters to be modern and rational, accord with the citizens' sense of just principles.

Attempted Crimes

In one such study (Darley, Sanderson, & LaMantha, 1996), my colleagues and I examined the MPC treatment of the concept of criminal attempt. The question at issue was this: When has a person come close enough toward committing a crime that he or she has committed a criminal action, and what should the penalty for that action be? The MPC holds that a person deserves punishment when he or she has "formed a settled intent" to commit a crime; this is a subjectivist standard that focuses on the person's criminal intent. In keeping with the view that intent is what matters, the MPC assigns the same penalty to attempt as it does to the completed offense. The MPC, in other words, criminalizes taking the early steps leading up to committing a crime and punishes taking those steps as severely as it punishes the completed crime. The older common-law standard was vastly different: It did not criminalize attempt until the actor was in what was called "dangerous proximity" to the crime (e.g., the would-be burglar had broken into the store), and it punished attempt to a lesser degree than the completed offense.

How do ordinary people think about attempt? Do they follow the subjectivist stance of the MPC, or do they hold the older commonlaw view? Pause for a moment and think about how to research this. One could ask people whether they agree with a series of statements, such as "A person's intent to commit a crime is what should determine his or her punishment." The problem with doing this is that the researcher is likely to find general agreement with a number of potentially contradictory principles. For this reason, researchers generally use what is called a policycapturing approach, in which respondents are asked to judge a set of cases that differ along dimensions suggested by the competing theories being tested.

That is how my colleagues and I examined the competing principles that determine how attempts should be punished: We asked respondents to assign punishment after reading short scenarios involving agents who had taken one or more steps toward committing either robbery or murder. The pattern of results corresponded far more closely with the older common-law formulation than with the MPC. For the cases in which the agent had taken action preliminary to the crime (e.g., examining the premises that he planned to burgle), most respondents judged the person not guilty of any offense, and a few assigned a mild penalty.

The punishments showed a sharp increase in severity when the person reached the point of dangerous proximity to the crime, and even then they were only half as severe as the penalties assigned to the completed offense. The results of this and other studies (Robinson & Darley, 1998) indicate that people do not share the subjectivist perspective that forming the intent to take an action is the moral equivalent of taking the action.

Rape and Sexual Intercourse

In other studies, we have found other areas in which the code and the community disagree in important ways. In some cases, it seems intuitively plausible that the code-community differences might be due to a change in community standards over the years (although we do not think this is the cause of the differences regarding attempted crimes). For example, the MPC, drafted during the 1950s, assigns a very serious punishment to consensual intercourse with an underage partner, but our respondents saw this offense as much less serious (Robinson & Darley, 1995). However, the code mitigates the sentence if the underage partner has a history of promiscuity, and our respondents did not. The code also mitigates the penalty for forcible rape if a previous relationship existed between the rapist and the victim, or if the victim was a voluntary social companion of the rapist at the time of the rape. Our respondents, questioned in the 1990s, focused on whether the victim was the nonconsenting victim of sexual assault; if she was, then they did not care whether a previous sexual relationship existed or the victim had been on a date with the rapist (many state codes have moved in this direction; Robinson & Darley, 1995, p. 204).

Omissions: Failing to Help

In Anglo-American law, no penalty is imposed for failing to help a stranger, even if that stranger's life is at risk and the help could be given at no risk to the helper. Macauley (1837), busily drafting the penal code for India, remarked, "It is evident that to attempt to punish men by law for not rendering to others all the service which is their [moral] duty to render to others would be preposterous" (note M, pp. 53–54). But why would this be preposterous? Macauley was making a disguised appeal to what people think. Do people think there should be no criminal liability assigned to a person who fails to rescue? Certainly, the MPC imposes no punishment for failure to rescue, even when the rescue could be accomplished without much inconvenience to the rescuer.

To test people's thoughts about failure to help, we presented subjects with a scenario in which a person was pushed into the deep water off a pier and called out that he was drowning (Robinson & Darley, 1995). A person who witnessed this could not swim, but saw that there was a life-saving flotation device that he could throw to the drowning man. He did not throw it, and the man died. Later, he reported that he did not want the man to drown, but "just didn't want to get too involved."

Respondents assigned an average punishment of about 2 months in jail to this person. When we varied how inconvenient it was for the person to intervene, respondents still gave about the same level of punishment. Only by creating a danger for a person who intervened did we begin to cancel the liability assigned to the nonhelper. Thus, people expect strangers to intervene to help when a person's life is in danger, and think that failure to do so is criminal and deserves a penalty.

THE POSSIBLE CONSEQUENCES OF CITIZEN-CODE DISAGREEMENTS

Why should anyone care about discrepancies between legal codes and the community's commonsense notions of justice? One reason is that the people of the state are citizens, who have some right to have their voices heard when important moral issues are being turned into laws. A second reason concerns what happens to the community's respect for the legal system if the code violates citizens' consensus. Examples such as prohibition suggest that in such cases, the community moves toward contempt for the legal system. Initial contempt for the specific laws in question soon spreads to the criminal justice system enforcing those laws, the police force and the judges, and finally the legal code in general. When this happens, the law loses its most powerful force for keeping order: the citizens' belief that the laws are to be obeyed because they represent the moral consensus of the community, and therefore the moral views that all citizens should hold.

This is not only a conclusion of psychologists. Legal theorists have argued the same point. Lately, disturbingly, Congress has "criminalized" many actions that do not fit Americans' prototype of a wrongful action, intentionally committed. A number of these prototypically innocent or thoughtless actions are now treated as crimes that require the heavy punishments available within the criminal justice system. Coffee (1991), a leading legal commentator, commented that "this blurring . . . will weaken the efficacy of the criminal law as an instrument of social control" because "the criminal law is obeyed not simply because there is a legal threat underlying it, but because the public perceives its norms to be legitimate and deserving of compliance" (pp. 193–194). That is, people think of criminal conduct as immoral conduct, so if the law criminalizes actions that people do not think of as immoral, it loses credibility. Such a law is obeyed, *if* it is obeyed, only to avoid jail.

Other legal scholars agree. Pound (1907) remarked that in "all cases of divergence between the standard of the common law and the standard of the public, it goes without saying that the latter will prevail in the end" (p. 615). Holmes (1881) wrote that the "first requirement of a sound body of law is, that it should correspond with the actual feelings and demands of the community" (pp. 41–42).

CONCLUSIONS

The psychological study of citizens' perceptions of what counts as wrongdoing and the appropriate punishments for wrongdoing is quite a recent activity. Still, two sorts of discoveries have been made. The first are procedural. Studies have shown that a useful technique is to ask people to assign innocence or guilt and punishment to agents in a set of vignettes that differ in ways that correspond to legal distinctions. Using this technique has enabled researchers to trace the chains of reasoning that respondents follow to judge blame and responsibility.

Other discoveries have been substantive: First, the community does have coherent and consistent views of what counts as criminal behavior. Second, there are important differences between legal codes and citizens' intuitions about just punishments. For example, the MPC adopts a subjectivist definition of the essence of a crime, and Americans do not. This finding suggests that it may be useful to investigate whether there are other doctrines incorporated in the MPC that violate the modal citizen's perceptions of justice.

I have argued that contradictions between criminal codes and the moral views of the community put people's respect for the legal system at risk. But this speculation requires research, and if it is found to be valid, additional work will be needed to uncover the processes by which these divergences affect citizens' perceptions of the justness of the legal system and willingness to voluntarily make the code's standards their own. What are the psychological processes of alienation involved? Because it is inevitable that occasionally, for policy reasons, legal codes will deviate from the moral intuitions of the citizens, it is imperative to discover how this alienation and disobedience can be avoided.

Fundamental questions often emerge as a research project progresses, and this happened in our work on the citizen's sense of justice. Why is it, when an actor knowingly commits an offense, that an observer feels that punishment is objectively required? What is the justification for punishment? Psychologists have been quite silent about this, although philosophers have suggested answers: deterrence for Bentham, "just desserts" for Kant. But what does the ordinary citizen take to be the justification for punishment of wrongdoing? This is perhaps the most intriguing remaining question about retributive justice.

Recommended Reading

Finkel, N. (1997). *Common sense justice: Jurors' notions of the law.* Cambridge, MA: Harvard University Press.
Finkel, N., & Sales, B. (Eds.). (1997). Common sense justice [Special issue]. *Psychology, Public Policy, and Law, 3*(2/3).
Hamilton, V.L., & Sanders, J. (1992). *Everyday justice: Responsibility and the individual in Japan and the United States.* New Haven, CT: Yale University Press.
Robinson, P.H., & Darley, J.M. (1995). (See References)
Robinson, P.H., & Darley, J.M. (1997). The utility of desert. *Northwestern University Law Review, 91,* 453–499.

Notes

1. Address correspondence to John Darley, Psychology Department, Princeton University, Princeton, NJ 08544; e-mail: jdarley@princeton.edu.

2. "Common sense justice" is Norman Finkel's term for ordinary people's perceptions of just rules for determining such matters as a perpetrator's degree of responsibility for a harm. Finkel has been one of the leaders in discovering these naive psychological rules. Lee Hamilton, often working with Joseph Sanders, has been another. Volume 3, number 2/3, of *Psychology, Public Policy, and Law* (1997) is entirely on aspects of commonsense justice.

References

American Law Institute. (1962). *Model Penal Code official draft, 1962*. Philadelphia: Author. Coffee, J.D. (1991). Does 'unlawful' mean 'criminal'? Reflections on the disappearing tort/crime distinction in American law. *Boston University Law Review, 71*, 193–246.

Darley, J., Sanderson, C., & LaMantha, P. (1996). Community standards for defining attempt: Inconsistencies with the Model Penal Code. *American Behavioral Scientist, 39*, 405–420.

Holmes, O.W., Jr. (1881). *The common law.* Boston: Little, Brown.

Macauley, T. (1837). *A penal code prepared by the Indian law commissioners.* Calcutta, India: Bengal Military Orphans Press.

Pound, R. (1907). The need of a sociological juris prudence. *Green Bag, 19*, 607–615.

Robinson, P.H., & Darley, J.M. (1995). *Justice, liability, and blame: Community views and criminal laws.* Boulder, CO: Westview Press.

Robinson, P.H., & Darley, J.M. (1998). Objective vs. subjectivist views of criminality: A study in the role of social science in criminal law theory. *Oxford Journal of Legal Studies, 18*, 409–447.

Thibaut, J., & Walker, L. (1975). *Procedural justice: A psychological analysis.* Mahwah, NJ: Erlbaum.

Tyler, T. (1990). *Why people obey the law.* New Haven, CT: Yale University Press.

Critical Thinking Questions

1. The author talks about "common sense justice." But why is it important for citizens' sense of justice to match legal codes?

2. What is an area of law in which citizens and the criminal code disagree?

3. How does the author use historical quotes to support the idea that consistency between common sense justice and the law is important? Can you think of other examples?

Crafting Normative Messages to Protect the Environment

Robert B. Cialdini[1]

Department of Psychology, Arizona State University, Tempe, Arizona

Abstract

It is widely recognized that communications that activate social norms can be effective in producing societally beneficial conduct. Not so well recognized are the circumstances under which normative information can backfire to produce the opposite of what a communicator intends. There is an understandable, but misguided, tendency to try to mobilize action against a problem by depicting it as regrettably frequent. Information campaigns emphasize that alcohol and drug use is intolerably high, that adolescent suicide rates are alarming, and—most relevant to this article— that rampant polluters are spoiling the environment. Although these claims may be both true and well intentioned, the campaigns' creators have missed something critically important: Within the statement "Many people are doing this *undesirable* thing" lurks the powerful and undercutting normative message "Many people *are* doing this." Only by aligning descriptive norms (what people typically do) with injunctive norms (what people typically approve or disapprove) can one optimize the power of normative appeals. Communicators who fail to recognize the distinction between these two types of norms imperil their persuasive efforts.

Keywords

norms; environment; public service announcements

It is rare when a public service announcement (PSA) is believed to have the sort of effectiveness achieved by the most successful mass media commercial messages, which typically benefit from much larger production budgets and broadcast frequencies. Yet there is one PSA that is regularly credited as having such status. Called the "Iron Eyes Cody spot" (after the Native American actor who starred in it), it begins with a shot of a stately, buckskin-clad American Indian paddling his canoe up a river that carries various forms of industrial and individual pollution. After coming ashore near the littered side of a highway, the Indian watches as a bag of garbage is thrown, splattering and spreading along the road, from the window of a passing car. From the refuse at his feet, the camera pans up slowly to the Indian's face, where a tear is shown tracking down his cheek, and the slogan appears: "People Start Pollution, People Can Stop It."

Broadcast for many years in the 1970s and 1980s, the spot won numerous awards and millions upon millions of dollars of donated airtime. Indeed, it has even been named the 16th best television commercial of all time by *TV Guide* magazine ("The Fifty Greatest," 1999). However, despite the fame of this touching piece of public service advertising, research suggests that it contains features that may be less than optimal, and perhaps even negative, in their impact on the littering actions of those who see it. In addition to the laudable message in the ad urging viewers to stop littering, there is the underlying message, as well, that a lot of people *do* litter: Debris floats on the river, litter lies at the roadside, trash is tossed from an automobile.

DESCRIPTIVE VERSUS INJUNCTIVE NORMS

Thus, the creators of the Iron Eyes Cody spot may well have pitted two kinds of norms against one another, *injunctive norms* (involving perceptions of which behaviors are typically approved or disapproved) and *descriptive norms* (involving perceptions of which behaviors are typically performed). Much research indicates that both kinds of norms motivate human action; people tend to do what is socially approved as well as what is popular. The wisdom of setting these two kinds of motivations in line with (rather than in opposition to) one another within a communication has direct implications for the development of proenvironmental messages. Experiences that focus individuals on the all-too-frequent occurrence of an offense against the environment have the potential to increase the occurrence of that offense.

An Initial Experiment

To explore this possibility as it applies to individuals' decisions to despoil the environment, my colleagues and I have conducted a variety of studies over the past several years. In one investigation (Cialdini, Reno, & Kallgren, 1990, Experiment 1), participants were given the opportunity to litter (a handbill they found on their car windshields) into either a previously clean or a fully littered environment after first witnessing a confederate who either dropped trash into the environment or simply walked through it. By varying the state of the environment (clean vs. littered), we sought to manipulate the perceived descriptive norm for littering in the situation. By manipulating whether the confederate dropped trash into the environment, we sought to differentially focus participants' attention on the state of the environment and, consequently, to manipulate the salience of the perceived descriptive norm there (i.e., what most people did).

We had three main predictions. First, we expected that participants would be more likely to litter into an already littered environment than into a clean one. Second, we expected that participants who saw the confederate drop trash into a fully littered environment would be most likely to litter there themselves, because they would have had their attention drawn to evidence of a pro-littering descriptive norm—that is, to the fact that people typically litter in that setting. Conversely, we anticipated that participants who saw the confederate drop trash into a clean environment would be least likely to litter there, because they would have had their attention drawn to evidence of an anti-littering descriptive norm—that is, to the fact that (except for the confederate) people typically do not litter in that setting. This last expectation distinguished our normative account from explanations based on simple modeling processes in that we were predicting decreased littering after participants witnessed a model litter.

As can be seen in Figure 1, the data supported our experimental hypotheses. Overall, there was more littering in the littered environment than in the clean environment. In addition, the most littering occurred when participants saw a

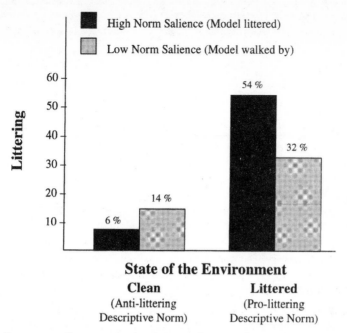

High Norm Salience (Model littered)

Low Norm Salience (Model walked by)

State of the Environment

Clean
(Anti-littering
Descriptive Norm)

Littered
(Pro-littering
Descriptive Norm)

Fig. 1. Percentage of participants littering as a function of the salience of the descriptive norm and the state of the environment.

model drop trash into a littered environment; and, most tellingly, the least littering occurred when participants saw a model drop trash into a clean environment.

Rethinking the Iron Eyes Cody PSA

At this point, it is appropriate to look back at the Iron Eyes Cody PSA, as the findings of our study point to reasons for concern about the effectiveness of that ad. Recall that it depicts a character who sheds a tear after encountering an array of litter. No doubt the tear is a powerful reminder of the injunctive norm against littering in U.S. culture. But accompanying the beneficial reminder is the potentially damaging message that many people *do* litter. Thus, the resultant impact of the injunctive norm against littering may be undermined by the unintended presentation of a descriptive norm for littering. Moreover, that presentation occurs in a way that, according to the results of our study, may be especially damaging. That is, the creators of the ad seem to have been correct in their decision to show a dismaying instance of someone (the passing motorist) actively littering the environment; but they may have been mistaken in their decision to use an already-littered environment, as the observation of another person littering into a littered environment produced the greatest littering in our study. In contrast, the combination of a (single) litterer and an otherwise clean environment generated the least littering from our participants.

Were we to suggest a revision of the Iron Eyes Cody PSA, then, it would be to make the procedurally small but conceptually meaningful modification of

175

changing the depicted environment from trashed to clean—and thereby changing the perceived descriptive norm regarding littering. Then, when the disapproving tear appeared, viewers would be exposed to injunctive and descriptive norms guiding behavior in the same direction.

ENVIRONMENTAL THEFT

In situations already characterized by high levels of socially censured conduct, the distinction between descriptive and injunctive norms offers a clear implication: It is a serious error to focus an audience on the descriptive norm (i.e., what is done in those situations); instead, public service messages should focus the audience on the injunctive norm (i.e., what is approved or disapproved in those situations). Take, for instance, the case of Arizona's Petrified Forest National Park, which suffers from the estimated theft of more than a ton of wood per month by visitors. New arrivals quickly learn of the past thievery from prominently placed signage: "Your heritage is being vandalized every day by theft losses of petrified wood of 14 tons a year, mostly a small piece at a time."

Although it is understandable that park officials would want to instigate corrective action by describing the dismaying size of the problem, such a message ought to be far from optimal. According to an informed normative account, it would be better to design park signage to focus visitors on the social disapproval (rather than the harmful prevalence) of environmental theft. Recently, my colleagues and I sought to examine this hypothesis—that in a situation characterized by unfortunate levels of socially disapproved conduct, a message that focuses recipients on the injunctive norm will be superior to messages that focus recipients on the descriptive norm (Cialdini et al., 2003).

To test our expectation, we gained permission from Petrified Forest National Park officials to place secretly marked pieces of petrified wood along visitor pathways. During five consecutive weekends, at the entrance to each path, we displayed signage that emphasized either descriptive or injunctive norms regarding the theft of petrified wood from the park. The descriptive-norm sign stated, "Many past visitors have removed petrified wood from the Park, changing the natural state of the Petrified Forest." This wording was accompanied by pictures of three visitors taking wood. In contrast, the injunctive-norm sign stated, "Please don't remove the petrified wood from the Park, in order to preserve the natural state of the Petrified Forest." This wording was accompanied by a picture of a lone visitor stealing a piece of wood, with a red circle-and-bar symbol superimposed over his hand. Our measure of message effectiveness was the percentage of marked pieces of wood stolen over the 5-week duration of the study. As predicted, the descriptive-norm message resulted in significantly more theft than the injunctive-norm message (7.92% vs. 1.67%).[2]

RECYCLING

Should one conclude from these results that highlighting descriptive norms is always likely to be a counterproductive tactic in environmental information campaigns? No. Although highlighting descriptive norms is detrimental when environmentally harmful behavior is prevalent, this approach should be effective when the prevalent behavior is environmentally beneficial. For example, if the majority of citizens conserve energy at home, campaign developers would be well advised to include such descriptive normative information in their presentations intended to increase residential energy conservation. Of course, if the majority of citizens also approve of such efforts, the campaign developers would be wise to incorporate this injunctive normative information as well.

Thus, the most effective norm-based persuasive approach under these circumstances would be one that enlists the conjoint influence of descriptive and injunctive norms. To examine the impact of an information campaign that combined the influence of injunctive and descriptive norms, my colleagues and I created three PSAs designed to increase recycling, an activity that was both performed and approved by the majority of local residents in our study area. Each PSA portrayed a scene in which the majority of depicted individuals engaged in recycling, spoke approvingly of it, and spoke disparagingly of a single individual in the scene who failed to recycle. When, in a field test, these PSAs were played on the local TV and radio stations of four Arizona communities, a 25.35% net advantage in recycling tonnage was recorded over a pair of control communities not exposed to the PSAs.

Although a 25% recycling advantage is impressive from a practical standpoint, that study did not allow for confident theoretical conclusions about the causes of the advantage. For instance, it was not possible to determine the extent to which our PSAs may have been effective because of their normative elements. After all, it is conceivable that the PSAs were successful because they included humorous and informational components unrelated to norms. In order to assess whether and to what degree descriptive and injunctive norms—separately and in combination—contributed to the messages' effectiveness, additional evidence was necessary. To that end, we conducted a study in which college students viewed our three recycling PSAs and rated their impact along several relevant dimensions (Cialdini et al., 2003).

That study was designed to determine whether our PSAs had the intended effect of conveying to viewers that recycling was prevalent (descriptive norm) and approved (injunctive norm), whether these perceived norms influenced viewers' intentions to recycle, and whether the two types of norms operated similarly or differently to affect recycling intentions. A statistical analysis of the results indicated that both normative and nonnormative factors influenced the intent to recycle (see Fig. 2). Of course, the finding that nonnormative factors (prior attitude, new information, humor) had causal impact is not incompatible with our theoretical position, as we certainly would not claim that normative factors are the only motivators of human responding.

At the same time, it is encouraging from our theoretical perspective that both injunctive and descriptive normative information significantly influenced recycling intentions. That is, as a result of viewing the ads, the more participants came to believe that recycling was (a) approved and (b) prevalent, the more they planned to recycle in the future. It is noteworthy that, despite a strong correlation ($r = .79$) between participants' perceptions of the existing prevalence and approval of recycling, these two sources of motivation had independent effects

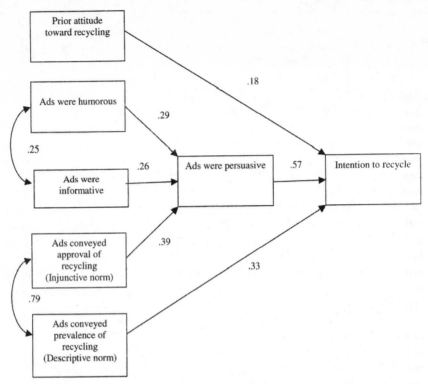

Fig. 2. Impact of public service announcements intended to promote recycling. The arrows in the diagram depict the pathways through which viewers' attitudes and perceptions affected their intentions to recycle. Alongside each arrow is the corresponding path coefficient, a measure of causal impact; all the path coefficients shown are significant at $p = .05$.

on recycling intentions. Such results affirm the theoretical distinction between descriptive and injunctive norms.

CONCLUSION

Public service communicators should avoid the tendency to send the normatively muddled message that a targeted activity is socially disapproved but widespread. Norm-based persuasive communications are likely to have their best effects when communicators align descriptive and injunctive normative messages to work in tandem rather than in competition with one another. Such a line of attack unites the power of two independent sources of normative motivation and can provide a highly successful approach to social influence.

At the same time, certain issues remain to be clarified if communicators are to optimize the impact of norm-based messages. The first concerns the nature of the psychological mechanisms that underlie descriptive and injunctive norms. The results of our last study suggest an intriguing difference between them. Information about social approval or disapproval affected recycling intentions by influencing assessments of the ads' persuasiveness (see Fig. 2). Information about relative prevalence, in contrast, influenced intentions directly, without affecting the perceived persuasiveness of the ads. Why should that be the case? One possibility is that because descriptive norms are based in the raw behavior of other individuals, it is relatively easy to accommodate to such norms without much cognitive analysis. Indeed, organisms with little cognitive capacity do so: Birds flock, fish school, and social insects swarm. Injunctive norms, however, are based in an understanding of the moral rules of the society (i.e., what other people are likely to approve), and should therefore require more cognitive analysis to operate successfully. Hence, one might expect that the impact of injunctive (but not descriptive) normative information would be mediated through cognitive assessments of the quality or persuasiveness of the normative information. Additional work is necessary to test this possibility.

A second important research issue concerns the problem of diminished salience of the normative message at the time when a targeted behavior is likely to be performed. Often, the message is no longer present when the desired behavior must take place. For example, PSAs are typically radio, television, and print communications that are encountered at times far removed from the opportunities to perform the socially desirable actions that the PSAs promote. A crucial question to be answered by future investigation is how communicators can structure their messages to maximize the likelihood that the motivational components of those messages will be salient at the time for action. Research that identifies persuasive or mnemonic devices for achieving this goal will be of immense benefit to public service communication efforts.

Recommended Reading

Bator, R.J., & Cialdini, R.B. (2000). The application of persuasion theory to the development of effective pro-environmental public service announcements. *Journal of Social Issues, 56*, 527–541.

Kallgren, C.A., Reno, R.R., & Cialdini, R.B. (2000). A focus theory of normative conduct: When norms do and do not affect behavior. *Personality and Social Psychology Bulletin, 26*, 1002–1012.

Schultz, P.W. (1999). Changing behavior with normative feedback interventions: A field experiment on curbside recycling. *Basic and Applied Social Psychology, 21*, 25–38.

Notes

1. Address correspondence to Robert B. Cialdini, Department of Psychology, Arizona State University, Tempe, AZ 85287-1104; e-mail: robert.cialdini@asu.edu.

2. These data are best understood in the context of previous research indicating that the ratio of thefts to park visitors falls just under 3%.

References

Cialdini, R.B., Barrett, D.W., Bator, R., Demaine, L.J., Sagarin, B.J., Rhoads, K.v.L., & Winter, P.L. (2003). *Activating and aligning social norms for persuasive impact.* Manuscript submitted for publication.

Cialdini, R.B, Reno, R.R., & Kallgren, C.A. (1990). A focus theory of normative conduct: Recycling the concept of norms to reduce littering in public places. *Journal of Personality and Social Psychology, 58*, 1015–1026.

The fifty greatest TV commercials of all time. (1999, July 3–9). *TV Guide*, pp. 2–34.

Critical Thinking Questions

1. What is the "Iron Eyes Cody spot," why is this public service announcement considered so powerful, and why might it be less effective than realized?

2. How do descriptive and injunctive norms differ, and why is this distinction important?

3. To reduce littering, should you expose people to a model that drops trash into a clean or dirty environment? Why?

Reducing Prejudice: Combating Intergroup Biases

John F. Dovidio[1] and Samuel L. Gaertner

Department of Psychology, Colgate University, Hamilton, New York (J.F.D.), and Department of Psychology, University of Delaware, Newark, Delaware (S.L.G.)

Abstract

Strategies for reducing prejudice may be directed at the traditional, intentional form of prejudice or at more subtle and perhaps less conscious contemporary forms. Whereas the traditional form of prejudice may be reduced by direct educational and attitude-change techniques, contemporary forms may require alternative strategies oriented toward the individual or involving intergroup contact. Individual-oriented techniques can involve leading people who possess contemporary prejudices to discover inconsistencies among their self-images, values, and behaviors; such inconsistencies can arouse negative emotional states (e.g., guilt), which motivate the development of more favorable attitudes. Intergroup strategies can involve structuring intergroup contact to produce more individualized perceptions of the members of the other group, foster personalized interactions between members of the different groups, or redefine group boundaries to create more inclusive, superordinate representations of the groups. Understanding the nature and bases of prejudice can thus guide, theoretically and pragmatically, interventions that can effectively reduce both traditional and contemporary forms of prejudice.

Keywords

attitude change; intergroup contact; prejudice; racism; social categorization

Prejudice is commonly defined as an unfair negative attitude toward a social group or a member of that group. Stereotypes, which are overgeneralizations about a group or its members that are factually incorrect and inordinately rigid, are a set of beliefs that can accompany the negative feelings associated with prejudice. Traditional approaches consider prejudice, like other attitudes, to be acquired through socialization and supported by the beliefs, attitudes, and values of friends and peer groups (see Jones, 1997). We consider the nature of traditional and contemporary forms of prejudice, particularly racial prejudice, and review a range of techniques that have been demonstrated empirically to reduce prejudice and other forms of intergroup bias. Bias can occur in many forms, and thus it has been assessed by a range of measures. These measures include standardized tests of prejudice toward another social group, stereotypes, evaluations of and feelings about specific group members and about the group in general, support for policies and individual actions benefiting the other group, and interaction and friendship patterns.

In part because of changing norms and the Civil Rights Act and other legislative interventions that made discrimination not simply immoral but also illegal, overt expressions of prejudice have declined significantly over the past 35 years. Contemporary forms of prejudice, however, continue to exist and affect the lives of people in subtle but significant ways (Dovidio & Gaertner, 1998;

Gaertner & Dovidio, 1986). The negative feelings and beliefs that underlie contemporary forms of prejudice may be rooted in either individual processes (such as cognitive and motivational biases and socialization) or intergroup processes (such as realistic group conflict or biases associated with the mere categorization of people into in-groups and out-groups). These negative biases may occur spontaneously, automatically, and without full awareness.

Many contemporary approaches to prejudice based on race, ethnicity, or sex acknowledge the persistence of overt, intentional forms of prejudice but also consider the role of these automatic or unconscious processes[2] and the consequent indirect expressions of bias. With respect to the racial prejudice of white Americans toward blacks, for example, in contrast to "old-fashioned" racism, which is blatant, aversive racism represents a subtle, often unintentional, form of bias that characterizes many white Americans who possess strong egalitarian values and who believe that they are nonprejudiced. Aversive racists also possess negative racial feelings and beliefs (which develop through normal socialization or reflect social-categorization biases) that they are unaware of or that they try to dissociate from their non-prejudiced self-images. Because aversive racists consciously endorse egalitarian values, they will not discriminate directly and openly in ways that can be attributed to racism; however, because of their negative feelings, they will discriminate, often unintentionally, when their behavior can be justified on the basis of some factor other than race (e.g., questionable qualifications for a position). Thus, aversive racists may regularly engage in discrimination while they maintain self-images of being non-prejudiced. According to symbolic racism theory, a related perspective that has emphasized the role of politically conservative rather than liberal ideology (Sears, 1988), negative feelings toward blacks that whites acquire early in life persist into adulthood but are expressed indirectly and symbolically, in terms of opposition to busing or resistance to preferential treatment, rather than directly or overtly, as in support for segregation.

Contemporary expressions of bias may also reflect a dissociation between cultural stereotypes, which develop through common socialization experiences and because of repeated exposure generally become automatically activated, and individual differences in prejudicial motivations. Although whites both high and low in prejudice may be equally aware of cultural stereotypes and show similar levels of automatic activation, only those low in prejudice make a conscious attempt to prevent those negative stereotypes from influencing their behavior (Devine & Monteith, 1993).

INDIVIDUAL PROCESSES AND PREJUDICE REDUCTION

Attempts to reduce the direct, traditional form of racial prejudice typically involve educational strategies to enhance knowledge and appreciation of other groups (e.g., multicultural education programs), emphasize norms that prejudice is wrong, and involve direct persuasive strategies (e.g., mass media appeals) or indirect attitude-change techniques that make people aware of inconsistencies in their attitudes and behaviors (Stephan & Stephan, 1984). Other techniques are aimed at changing or diluting stereotypes by presenting counter-stereotypic or non-stereotypic information about group members. Providing stereotype-disconfirming information is more effective when the information concerns a broad range of group members who are otherwise typical of their group rather than when the information concerns a single person who is not a prototypical representative of the group. In the latter case, people are likely to maintain their overall stereotype of the group while subtyping, with another stereotype, group members who disconfirm the general group stereotype (e.g., black athletes; Hewstone, 1996). The effectiveness of multicultural education programs is supported by the results of controlled intervention programs in the real world; evidence of the effectiveness of attitude- and stereotype-change approaches, and the hypothesized underlying processes, comes largely (but not exclusively) from experimental laboratory research.

Approaches for dealing with the traditional form of prejudice are generally less effective for combating the contemporary forms. With respect to contemporary racism, for example, whites already consciously endorse egalitarian, non-prejudiced views and disavow traditional stereotypes. Instead, indirect strategies that benefit from people's genuine motivation to be non-prejudiced may be more effective for reducing contemporary forms of prejudice. For example, techniques that lead people who possess contemporary prejudices to discover inconsistencies among their self-images, values, and behaviors may arouse feelings of guilt, tension about the inconsistencies, or other negative emotional states that can motivate the development of more favorable racial attitudes and produce more favorable intergroup behaviors (even nonverbal behaviors) several months later. Also, people who consciously endorse non-prejudiced attitudes, but whose behaviors may reflect racial bias, commonly experience feelings of guilt and compunction when they become aware of discrepancies between their potential behavior toward minorities (i.e., what they *would* do) and their personal standards (i.e., what they *should* do) during laboratory interventions. These emotional reactions, in turn, can motivate people to control subsequent spontaneous stereotypical responses and behave more favorably in the future (Devine & Monteith, 1993). People's conscious efforts to suppress stereotypically biased reactions can inhibit even the immediate activation of normally automatic associations, and with sufficient practice, these efforts can eliminate automatic stereotype activation over the long term.

Approaches oriented toward the individual, however, are not the only way to combat contemporary forms of prejudice. Strategies that emphasize intergroup processes, such as intergroup contact and social categorization and identity, are alternative, complementary approaches.

INTERGROUP CONTACT

Real-world interventions, laboratory studies, and survey studies have demonstrated that intergroup contact under specified conditions (including equal status between the groups, cooperative intergroup interactions, opportunities for personal acquaintance, and supportive egalitarian norms) is a powerful technique for reducing intergroup bias and conflict (Pettigrew, 1998). Drawing on these principles, cooperative learning and "jigsaw" classroom interventions (Aronson

& Patnoe, 1997) are designed to increase interdependence between members of different groups working on a designated problem-solving task and to enhance appreciation for the resources they bring to the task. Cooperation is effective for reducing subsequent intergroup bias when the task is completed successfully, group contributions to solving the problem are seen as different or complementary, and the interaction among participants during the task is friendly, personal, and supportive.

Recent research has attempted to elucidate how the different factors of intergroup contact (e.g., cooperation, personal interaction) operate to reduce bias. Engaging in activities to achieve common, superordinate goals, for instance, changes the functional relations between groups from actual or symbolic competition to cooperation. Through psychological processes to restore cognitive balance or reduce inconsistency between actions and attitudes, attitudes toward members of the other group and toward the group as a whole may improve to be consistent with the positive nature of the interaction. Also, the rewarding properties of achieving success may become associated with members of other groups, thereby increasing attraction.

SOCIAL CATEGORIZATION AND IDENTITY

Factors of intergroup contact, such as cooperation, may also reduce bias through reducing the salience of the intergroup boundaries, that is, through *decategorization*. According to this perspective, interaction during intergroup contact can individuate members of the out-group by revealing variability in their opinions (Wilder, 1986) or can produce interactions in which people are seen as unique individuals (personalization), with the exchange of intimate information (Brewer & Miller, 1984). Alternatively, intergroup contact may be structured to maintain but alter the nature of group boundaries, that is, to produce *recategorization*. One recategorization approach involves either creating or increasing the salience of crosscutting group memberships. Making interactants aware that members of another group are also members of one's own group when groups are defined by a different dimension can improve intergroup attitudes (Urban & Miller, 1998). Another recategorization strategy, represented by our own work on the Common In-Group Identity Model, involves interventions to change people's conceptions of groups, so that they think of membership not in terms of several different groups, but in terms of one, more inclusive group (Gaertner, Dovidio, Anastasio, Bachman, & Rust, 1993).

The Common In-Group Identity Model recognizes the central role of social categorization in reducing as well as in creating intergroup bias (Tajfel & Turner, 1979). Specifically, if members of different groups are induced to conceive of themselves more as members of a single, superordinate group rather than as members of two separate groups, attitudes toward former out-group members will become more positive through processes involving pro-in-group bias. Thus, changing the basis of categorization from race to an alternative dimension can alter who is a "we" and who is a "they," undermining a contributing force to contemporary forms of racism, such as aversive racism. The development of a superordinate identity does not always require people to abandon their previous group identities; they may possess dual identities, conceiving of themselves as belonging both to the superordinate group and to one of the original two groups included within the new, larger group. The model also recognizes that decategorization (seeing people as separate individuals) can also reduce bias. In contrast, perceptions of the groups as different entities (we/they) maintains and reinforces bias. The Common In-Group Identity Model is presented schematically in Figure 1.

In experiments in the laboratory and in the field, and in surveys in natural settings (a multi-ethnic high school, banking mergers, and blended families), we have found evidence consistent with the Common In-Group Identity Model and the hypothesis that intergroup contact can reduce prejudice. Specifically, we have found that key aspects of intergroup contact, such as cooperation, decrease intergroup bias in part through changing cognitive representations of the groups. The development of a common ingroup identity also facilitates helping behaviors and self-disclosing interactions that can produce reciprocally positive

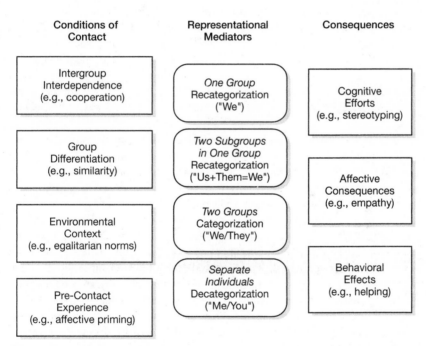

Fig. 1. The Common In-Group Identity Model. In this model, elements of an intergroup contract situation (e.g., intergroup interdependence) influence cognitive representations of the groups as one superordinate group (recategorization), as two subgroups in one group (recategorization involving a dual identity), as two groups (categorization), or as separate individuals (decategorization). Recategorization and decategorization, in turn, can both reduce cognitive, affective, and behavioral biases, but in different ways. Recategorization reduces bias by extending the benefits of in-group favoritism to former out-group members. Attitudes and behavior toward these former out-group members thus become more favorable, approaching attitudes and behaviors toward in-group members. Decategorization, in contrast, reduces favoritism toward original in-group members as they become perceived as separate individuals rather than members of one's own group.

responses and that can further reduce intergroup prejudices through other mechanisms such as personalization.

Moreover, the development of a common in-group identity does not necessarily require groups to forsake their original identities. Threats to important personal identities or the "positive distinctiveness" of one's group can, in fact, exacerbate intergroup prejudices. The development of a dual identity (two subgroups in one group; see Fig. 1), in which original and superordinate group memberships are simultaneously salient, is explicitly considered in the model. Even when racial or ethnic identity is strong, perceptions of a superordinate connection enhance interracial trust and acceptance. Indeed, the development of a dual identity, in terms of a bicultural or multicultural identity, not only is possible but can contribute to the social adjustment, psychological adaptation, and overall well-being of minority-group members (LaFromboise, Coleman, & Gerton, 1993). Recognizing both different and common group membership, a more complex form of a common in-group identity, may also increase the generalizability of the benefits of intergroup contact for prejudice reduction. The development of a common in-group identity contributes to more positive attitudes toward members of other groups present in the contact situation, whereas recognition of the separate group memberships provides the associative link by which these more positive attitudes may generalize to other members of the groups not directly involved in the contact situation.

CONCLUSION

Prejudice can occur in its blatant, traditional form, or it may be rooted in unconscious and automatic negative feelings and beliefs that characterize contemporary forms. Whereas the traditional form of prejudice may be combated by using direct techniques involving attitude change and education, addressing contemporary forms requires alternative strategies. Individual-level strategies engage the genuine motivations of people to be non-prejudiced. Intergroup approaches focus on realistic group conflict or the psychological effects of categorizing people into in-groups and out-groups. The benefits of intergroup contact can occur through many routes, such as producing more individuated perceptions of out-group members and more personalized relationships. Intergroup contact can also produce more inclusive, superordinate representations of the groups, which can harness the psychological forces that contribute to intergroup bias and redirect them to improve attitudes toward people who would otherwise be recognized only as out-group members. Understanding the processes involved in the nature and development of prejudice can thus guide, both theoretically and pragmatically, interventions that can effectively reduce both traditional and contemporary forms of prejudice.

Recommended Reading

Brewer, M.B., & Miller, N. (1996). *Intergroup relations.* Pacific Grove, CA: Brooks/Cole.
Brown, R.J. (1995). *Prejudice.* Cambridge, MA: Blackwell.
Hawley, W.D., & Jackson, A.W. (Eds.). (1995). *Toward a common destiny: Improving race and ethnic relations in America.* San Francisco: Jossey-Bass.

Landis, D., & Bhagat, R.S. (Eds.). (1996). *Handbook of intercultural training*. Thousand Oaks, CA: Sage.
Stephan, W.G., & Stephan, C.W. (1996). *Intergroup relations*. Boulder, CO: Westview Press.

Acknowledgments—Preparation of this article was facilitated by National Institute of Mental Health Grant MH 48721.

Notes

1. Address correspondence to John F. Dovidio, Department of Psychology, Colgate University, Hamilton, NY 13346; e-mail: jdovidio@mail.colgate. edu.
2. For further information and a demonstration in which you can test the automaticity of your own racial attitudes using the Implicit Association Test, see Anthony Greenwald's World Wide Web site: http://weber.u.washington.edu/~agg/ (e-mail: agg@u.washington.edu).

References

Aronson, E., & Patnoe, S. (1997). *The jigsaw classroom*. New York: Longman.

Brewer, M.B., & Miller, N. (1984). Beyond the contact hypothesis: Theoretical perspectives on desegregation. In N. Miller & M.B. Brewer (Eds.), *Groups in contact: The psychology of desegregation* (pp. 281-302). Orlando, FL: Academic Press.

Devine, RG., & Monteith, M.J. (1993). The role of discrepancy–associated affect in prejudice reduction. In D.M. Mackie & D.L. Hamilton (Eds.), *Affect, cognition, and stereotyping: Interactive processes in intergroup perception* (pp. 317-344). Orlando, FL: Academic Press.

Dovidio, J.F., & Gaertner, S.L. (1998). On the nature of contemporary prejudice: The causes, consequences, and challenges of aversive racism. In J. Eberhardt & S.T. Fiske (Eds.), *Confronting racism: The problem and the response* (pp. 3-32). Newbury Park, CA: Sage.

Gaertner, S.L., & Dovidio, J.F. (1986). The aversive form of racism. In J.F. Dovidio & S.L. Gaertner (Eds.), *Prejudice, discrimination, and racism* (pp. 61-89). Orlando, FL: Academic Press.

Gaertner, S.L., Dovidio, J.F., Anastasio, P.A., Bachman, B.A., & Rust, M.C. (1993). The Common Ingroup Identity Model: Recategorization and the reduction of intergroup bias. In W. Stroebe & M. Hewstone (Eds.), *European review of social psychology* (Vol. 4, pp. 1-26). London: Wiley.

Hewstone, M. (1996). Contact and categorization: Social psychological interventions to change intergroup relations. In N. Macrae, M. Hewstone, & C. Stangor (Eds.), *Foundations of stereotypes and stereotyping* (pp. 323-368). New York: Guilford Press.

Jones, J.M. (1997). *Prejudice and racism* (2nd ed.). New York: McGraw-Hill.

LaFromboise, T, Coleman, H.L.K., & Gerton, J. (1993). Psychological impact of biculturalism: Evidence and theory. *Psychological Bulletin, 114,* 395-412.

Pettigrew, T.F. (1998). Intergroup Contact Theory. *Annual Review of Psychology, 49,* 65-85.

Sears, D.O. (1988). Symbolic racism. In P.A. Katz & D.A. Taylor (Eds.), *Eliminating racism: Profiles in controversy* (pp. 53-84). New York: Plenum Press.

Stephan, W.G., & Stephan, C.W (1984). The role of ignorance in intergroup relations. In N. Miller & M.B. Brewer (Eds.), *Groups in contact: The Psychology of desegregation* (pp. 229-257). Orlando, FL: Academic Press.

Tajfel, H., & Turner, J.C. (1979). An integrative theory of intergroup conflict. In W.G. Austin & S. Worchel (Eds.), *The social psychology of intergroup relations* (pp. 33-48). Monterey, CA: Brooks/Cole.

Urban, L.M., & Miller, N. (1998). A theoretical analysis of crossed categorization effects: A meta-analysis. *Journal of Personality and Social Psychology, 74,* 894-908.

Wilder, D.A. (1986). Social categorization: Implications for creation and reduction of intergroup bias. In L. Berkowitz (Ed.), *Advances in experimental social psychology* (Vol. 19, pp. 291-355). Orlando, FL: Academic Press.

Critical Thinking Questions

1. The authors distinguish between two types of prejudice. What are they?

2. Distinguish between individual-level and intergroup approaches to reducing prejudice. Is one or the other more effective?

3. What is decategorization, why is it important, and how does intergroup contact help to promote it?

Personality, Disorder, and Health

Clinical psychology is the largest and most visible branch of the discipline. In contrast to researchers who seek to understand "normal" perceptions, thoughts, feelings, and behaviors, many psychologists study people who are "abnormal." Is personality set in stone, or do we have a capacity for change? What causes some people to become anxious or depressed, to lose touch with reality, or to suffer from other psychological disorders—and what can be done about it? How does stress affect the body and how can these toxic effects be minimized? Last but not least, this section presents readings from clinical and health psychology, two prominent part of the field.

This section opens with an article by personality researchers Robert McCrae and Paul Costa, Jr. (1994), who report on longitudinal studies showing that although adults change in predictable ways as they get older, their personalities become stable over time, essentially fixed by age 30. Richard McNally (2003) searches for scientific evidence on the question of whether people can repress and later in life recover memories of sexual abuse and other traumas. Noting that women are twice as likely as men to suffer from depression, Susan Nolen-Hoeksema (2001) reviews research suggesting that women are exposed to certain stressors more often—and are also more affected by these stressors. Turning to the psychology of health and illness, Robert Ader (2001) summarizes recent advances in psychoneuroimmunology, a field he helped to create, which focuses on the seamless interplay of the mind, brain, and immune system in health and illness. Last but not least, Bert Uchino and others (1999) report on studies which show that people with strong social support networks are healthier and live longer compared to those who live more isolated lives.

The Stability of Personality: Observations and Evaluations

Robert R. McCrae and Paul T. Costa, Jr.

"There is an optical illusion about every person we meet," Ralph Waldo Emerson wrote in his essay on "Experience":

In truth, they are all creatures of given temperament, which will appear in a given character, whose boundaries they will never pass: but we look at them, they seem alive, and we presume there is impulse in them. In the moment it seems impulse; in the year, in the lifetime, it turns out to be a certain uniform tune which the revolving barrel of the music-box must play.[1]

In this brief passage, Emerson anticipated modern findings about the stability of personality and pointed out an illusion to which both laypersons and psychologists are prone. He was also perhaps the first to decry personality stability as the enemy of freedom, creativity, and growth, objecting that "temperament puts all divinity to rout." In this article, we summarize evidence in support of Emerson's observations but offer arguments against his evaluation of them.[2]

EVIDENCE FOR THE STABILITY OF ADULT PERSONALITY

Emerson used the term temperament to refer to the basic tendencies of the individual, dispositions that we call personality traits. It is these traits, measured by such instruments as the Minnesota Multiphasic Personality Inventory and the NEO Personality Inventory, that have been investigated in a score of longitudinal studies over the past 20 years. Despite a wide variety of samples, instruments, and designs, the results of these studies have been remarkably consistent, and they are easily summarized.

1. The mean levels of personality traits change with development, but reach final adult levels at about age 30. Between 20 and 30, both men and women become somewhat less emotional and thrill-seeking and somewhat more cooperative and self-disciplined—changes we might interpret as evidence of increased maturity. After age 30, there are few and subtle changes, of which the most consistent is a small decline in activity level with advancing age. Except among individuals with dementia, stereotypes that depict older people as being withdrawn, depressed, or rigid are unfounded.

Robert R. McCrae is Research Psychologist and **Paul T. Costa, Jr.**, is Chief, Laboratory of Personality and Cognition, both at the Gerontology Research Center, National Institute on Aging, National Institutes of Health. Address correspondence to Robert R. McCrae, Personality, Stress and Coping Section, Gerontology Research Center, 4940 Eastern Ave., Baltimore, MD 21224.

2. Individual differences in personality traits, which show at least some continuity from early childhood on, are also essentially fixed by age 30. Stability coefficients (test-retest correlations over substantial time intervals) are typically in the range of .60 to .80, even over intervals of as long as 30 years, although there is some decline in magnitude with increasing retest interval. Given that most personality scales have short-term retest reliabilities in the range from .70 to .90, it is clear that by far the greatest part of the reliable variance (i.e., variance not due to measurement error) in personality traits is stable.

3. Stability appears to characterize all five of the major domains of personality—neuroticism, extraversion, openness to experience, agreeableness, and conscientiousness. This finding suggests that an adult's personality profile as a whole will change little over time, and studies of the stability of configural measures of personality support that view.

4. Generalizations about stability apply to virtually everyone. Men and women, healthy and sick people, blacks and whites all show the same pattern. When asked, most adults will say that their personality has not changed much in adulthood, but even those who claim to have had major changes show little objective evidence of change on repeated administrations of personality questionnaires. Important exceptions to this generalization include people suffering from dementia and certain categories of psychiatric patients who respond to therapy, but no moderators of stability among healthy adults have yet been identified.[3]

When researchers first began to publish these conclusions, they were greeted with considerable skepticism—"I distrust the facts and the inferences" Emerson had written—and many studies were designed to test alternative hypotheses. For example, some researchers contended that consistent responses to personality questionnaires were due to memory of past responses, but retrospective studies showed that people could not accurately recall how they had previously responded even when instructed to do so. Other researchers argued that temporal consistency in self-reports merely meant that individuals had a fixed idea of themselves, a crystallized self-concept that failed to keep pace with real changes in personality. But studies using spouse and peer raters showed equally high levels of stability.[4]

The general conclusion that personality traits are stable is now widely accepted. Some researchers continue to look for change in special circumstances and populations; some attempt to account for stability by examining genetic and environmental influences on personality. Finally, others take the view that there is much more to personality than traits, and seek to trace the adult developmental course of personality perceptions or identity formation or life narratives.

These latter studies are worthwhile, because people undoubtedly do change across the life span. Marriages end in divorce, professional careers are started in mid-life, fashions and attitudes change with the times. Yet often the same traits can be seen in new guises: Intellectual curiosity merely shifts from one field to another, avid gardening replaces avid tennis, one abusive relationship is followed by another. Many of these changes are best regarded as variations on the "uniform tune" played by individuals' enduring dispositions.

ILLUSORY ATTRIBUTIONS IN TEMPORAL PERSPECTIVE

Social and personality psychologists have debated for some time the accuracy of attributions of the causes of behavior to persons or situations. The "optical illusion" in person perception that Emerson pointed to was somewhat different. He felt that people attribute behavior to the live and spontaneous person who freely creates responses to the situation, when in fact behavior reveals only the mechanical operation of lifeless and static temperament. We may (and we will!) take exception to this disparaging, if common, view of traits, but we must first concur with the basic observation that personality processes often appear different when viewed in longitudinal perspective: "The years teach much which the days never know."

Consider happiness. If one asks individuals why they are happy or unhappy, they are almost certain to point to environmental circumstances of the moment: a rewarding job, a difficult relationship, a threat to health, a new car. It would seem that levels of happiness ought to mirror quality of life, and that changes in circumstances would result in changes in subjective well-being. It would be easy to demonstrate this pattern in a controlled laboratory experiment: Give subjects $1,000 each and ask how they feel!

But survey researchers who have measured the objective quality of life by such indicators as wealth, education, and health find precious little association with subjective well-being, and longitudinal researchers have found surprising stability in individual differences in happiness, even among people whose life circumstances have changed markedly. The explanation is simple: People adapt to their circumstances rapidly, getting used to the bad and taking for granted the good. In the long run, happiness is largely a matter of enduring personality traits:[5] "Temper prevails over everything of time, place, and condition, and . . . fix[es] the measure of activity and of enjoyment."

A few years ago, William Swann and Craig Hill provided an ingenious demonstration of the errors to which too narrow a temporal perspective can lead. A number of experiments had shown that it was relatively easy to induce changes in the self-concept by providing self-discrepant feedback. Introverts told that they were really extraverts rated themselves higher in extraversion than they had before. Such studies supported the view that the self-concept is highly malleable, a mirror of the evaluation of the immediate environment.

Swann and Hill replicated this finding, but extended it by inviting subjects back a few days later. By that time, the effects of the manipulation had disappeared, and subjects had returned to their initial self-concepts. The implication is that any one-shot experiment may give a seriously misleading view of personality processes.[6]

The relations between coping and adaptation provide a final example. Cross-sectional studies show that individuals who use such coping mechanisms as self-blame, wishful thinking, and hostile reactions toward other people score lower on measures of well-being than people who do not use these mechanisms. It would be easy to infer that these coping mechanisms detract from adaptation, and in fact the very people who use them admit that they are ineffective. But the correlations vanish when the effects of prior neuroticism scores are removed;

192

an alternative interpretation of the data is thus that individuals who score high on this personality factor use poor coping strategies and also have low well-being: The association between coping and well-being may be entirely attributable to this third variable.[7]

Psychologists have long been aware of the problems of inferring causes from correlational data, but they have not recognized the pervasiveness of the bias that Emerson warned about. People tend to understand behavior and experience as the result of the immediate context, whether intrapsychic or environmental. Only by looking over time can one see the persistent effects of personality traits.

THE EVALUATION OF STABILITY

If few findings in psychology are more robust than the stability of personality, even fewer are more unpopular. Gerontologists often see stability as an affront to their commitment to continuing adult development; psychotherapists sometimes view it as an alarming challenge to their ability to help patients;[8] humanistic psychologists and transcendental philosophers think it degrades human nature. A popular account in *The Idaho Statesman* ran under the disheartening headline "Your Personality—You're Stuck With It."

In our view, these evaluations are based on misunderstandings: At worst, stability is a mixed blessing. Those individuals who are anxious, quarrelsome, and lazy might be understandably distressed to think that they are likely to stay that way, but surely those who are imaginative, affectionate, and carefree at age 30 should be glad to hear that they will probably be imaginative, affectionate, and carefree at age 90.

Because personality is stable, life is to some extent predictable. People can make vocational and retirement choices with some confidence that their current interests and enthusiasms will not desert them. They can choose friends and mates with whom they are likely to remain compatible. They can vote on the basis of candidates' records, with some assurance that future policies will resemble past ones. They can learn which co-workers they can depend on, and which they cannot. The personal and social utility of personality stability is enormous.

But it is precisely this predictability that so offends many critics. ("I had fancied that the value of life lay in its inscrutable possibilities," Emerson complained.) These critics view traits as mechanical and static habits and believe that the stability of personality traits dooms human beings to lifeless monotony as puppets controlled by inexorable forces. This is a misunderstanding on several levels.

First, personality traits are not repetitive habits, but inherently dynamic dispositions that interact with the opportunities and challenges of the moment.[9] Antagonistic people do not yell at everyone; some people they flatter, some they scorn, some they threaten, just as the same intelligence is applied to a lifetime of changing problems, so the same personality traits can be expressed in an infinite variety of ways, each suited to the situation.

Second, there are such things as spontaneity and impulse in human life, but they are stable traits. Individuals who are open to experience actively seek out new places to go, provocative ideas to ponder, and exotic sights, sounds, and tastes to experience. Extraverts show a different kind of spontaneity, making friends, seeking thrills, and jumping at every chance to have a good time, People who are introverted and closed to experience have more measured and monotonous lives, but this is the kind of life they choose.

Finally, personality traits are not inexorable forces that control our fate, nor are they, in psychodynamic language, ego alien. Our traits characterize us; they are our very selves;[10] we act most freely when we express our enduring dispositions. Individuals sometimes fight against their own tendencies, trying perhaps to overcome shyness or curb a bad temper. But most people acknowledge even these failings as their own, and it is well that they do. A person's recognition of the inevitability of his or her one and only personality is a large part of what Erik Erikson called ego integrity, the culminating wisdom of a lifetime.

Notes

1. All quotations are from "Experience," in *Essays: First and Second Series*, R.W. Emerson (Vintage, New York, 1990) (original work published 1844).

2. For recent and sometimes divergent treatments of this topic, see R. R. McCrae and P.T. Costa, Jr., *Personality in Adulthood* (Guilford, New York. 1990); D.C. Funder, R.D. Parke, C. Tomlinson-Keasey, and K. Widaman, Eds, *Studying Lives Through Time—Personality and Development* (American Psychological Association, Washington, DC, 1993); T. Heatherton and J. Weinberger, *Can Personality Change?* (American Psychological Association, Washington, DC, 1994).

3. I.C. Siegler, K.A. Welsh, D.V. Dawson, G.G. Fillenbaum, N.L. Earl, E.B. Kaplan, and C.M. Clark, Ratings of personality change in patients being evaluated for memory disorders, *Alzheimer Disease and Associated Disorders*, 5, 240–250 (1991); R.M.A. Hirschfeld, C.L. Klerman, P. Clayton, M.B. Keller, P. McDonald-Scott, and B. Larkin, Assessing personality: Effects of depressive state on trait measurement, *American Journal of Psychiatry*, 140, 695–699 (1983): R.R. McCrae, Moderated analyses of longitudinal personality stability, *Journal of Personality and Social Psychology*, 65, 577–585 (1993).

4. D. Woodruff, The role of memory in personality continuity: A 25 year follow-up, *Experimental Aging Research*, 9, 31–34 (1983); P.T. Costa, Jr., and R.R. McCrae, Trait psychology comes of age, in *Nebraska Symposium on Motivation: Psychology and Aging*, T.B. Sonderegger. Ed. (University of Nebraska Press, Lincoln. 1992).

5. P. T. Costa, Jr., and R. R. McCrae, Influence of extraversion and neuroticism on subjective well-being: Happy and unhappy people, *Journal of Personality and Social Psychology*, 38, 668–678 (1980).

6. The study is summarized in W.B. Swann, Jr., and C.A. Hill, When our identities are mistaken: Reaffirming self-conceptions through social interactions, *Journal of Personality and Social Psychology*, 43, 59–66 (1982). Dangers of single-occasion research are also discussed in J.R. Council, Context effects in personality research, *Current Directions in Psychological Science*, 2, 31–34 (1993).

7. R.R. McCrae and P.T. Costa, Jr., Personality coping, and coping effectiveness in an adult sample. *Journal of Personality*, 54, 385–405 (1986).

8. Observations in nonpatient samples show what happens over time under typical life circumstances; they do not rule out the possibility that psychotherapeutic interventions can change personality. Whether or not such change is possible, in practice much of psychotherapy consists of helping people learn to live with their limitations, and this may be a more realistic goal than "cure" for many patients. See P.T. Costa, Jr., and R.R. McCrae, Personality stability and its implications for clinical psychology, *Clinical Psychology Review*, 6, 407–423 (1986).

9. A. Tellegen, Personality traits: Issues of definition, evidence and assessment, in *Thinking Clearly About Psychology: Essays in Honor of Paul F. Meehl*, Vol. 2, W. Grove and D. Cicchetti, Eds. (University of Minnesota Press, Minneapolis, 1991).

10. R.R. McCrae and P.T. Costa, Jr., Age, personality, and the spontaneous self-concept, *Journals of Gerontology: Social Sciences*, *43*, S177–S185 (1988).

Critical Thinking Questions

1. What did Ralph Waldo Emerson mean when he wrote, "There is an optical illusion about every person we meet?"

2. At roughly what age is an individual's personality stabilized, consistent from that point on?

3. Why do many psychologists resist the conclusion that adult personality is stable over time, and how does this resistance stem from a misunderstanding of the data?

Recovering Memories of Trauma:
A View From the Laboratory

Richard J. McNally[1]

Department of Psychology, Harvard University, Cambridge, Massachusetts

Abstract

The controversy over the validity of repressed and recovered memories of childhood sexual abuse (CSA) has been extraordinarily bitter. Yet data on cognitive functioning in people reporting repressed and recovered memories of trauma have been strikingly scarce. Recent laboratory studies have been designed to test hypotheses about cognitive mechanisms that ought to be operative if people can repress and recover memories of trauma or if they can form false memories of trauma. Contrary to clinical lore, these studies have shown that people reporting CSA histories are not characterized by a superior ability to forget trauma-related material. Other studies have shown that individuals reporting recovered memories of either CSA or abduction by space aliens are characterized by heightened proneness to form false memories in certain laboratory tasks. Although cognitive psychology methods cannot distinguish true memories from false ones, these methods can illuminate mechanisms for remembering and forgetting among people reporting histories of trauma.

Keywords

recovered memories; trauma; repression; sexual abuse; dissociation

How victims remember trauma is among the most explosive issues facing psychology today. Most experts agree that combat, rape, and other horrific experiences are unforgettably engraved on the mind (Pope, Oliva, & Hudson, 1999). But some also believe that the mind can defend itself by banishing traumatic memories from awareness, making it difficult for victims to remember them until many years later (Brown, Scheflin, & Hammond, 1998).

This controversy has spilled out of the clinics and cognitive psychology laboratories, fracturing families, triggering legislative change, and determining outcomes in civil suits and criminal trials. Most contentious has been the claim that victims of childhood sexual abuse (CSA) often repress and then recover memories of their trauma in adulthood.[2] Some psychologists believe that at least some of these memories may be false—inadvertently created by risky therapeutic methods (e.g., hypnosis, guided imagery; Ceci & Loftus, 1994).

One striking aspect of this controversy has been the paucity of data on cognitive functioning in people reporting repressed and recovered memories of CSA. Accordingly, my colleagues and I have been conducting studies designed to test hypotheses about mechanisms that might enable people either to repress and recover memories of trauma or to develop false memories of trauma.

For several of our studies, we recruited four groups of women from the community. Subjects in the *repressed-memory group* suspected they had been sexually abused as children, but they had no explicit memories of abuse. Rather, they inferred their hidden abuse history from diverse indicators, such as depressed mood, interpersonal problems with men, dreams, and brief, recurrent visual images (e.g., of a penis), which they interpreted as "flashbacks" of early trauma. Subjects in the *recovered-memory group* reported having remembered their abuse after long periods of not having thought about it.[3] Unable to corroborate their reports, we cannot say whether the memories were true or false. Lack of corroboration, of course, does not mean that a memory is false. Subjects in the *continuous-memory group* said that they had never forgotten their abuse, and subjects in the *control group* reported never having been sexually abused.

PERSONALITY TRAITS AND PSYCHIATRIC SYMPTOMS

To characterize our subjects in terms of personality traits and psychiatric symptoms, we asked them to complete a battery of questionnaires measuring normal personality variation (e.g., differences in absorption, which includes the tendency to fantasize and to become emotionally engaged in movies and literature), depressive symptoms, posttraumatic stress disorder (PTSD) symptoms, and dissociative symptoms (alterations in consciousness, such as memory lapses, feeling disconnected with one's body, or episodes of "spacing out"; McNally, Clancy, Schacter, & Pitman, 2000b).

There were striking similarities and differences among the groups in terms of personality profiles and psychiatric symptoms. Subjects who had always remembered their abuse were indistinguishable from those who said they had never been abused on all personality measures. Moreover, the continuous-memory and control groups did not differ in their symptoms of depression, posttraumatic stress, or dissociation. However, on the measure of negative affectivity—proneness to experience sadness, anxiety, anger, and guilt—the repressed-memory group scored higher than did either the continuous-memory or the control group, whereas the recovered-memory group scored midway between the repressed-memory group on the one hand and the continuous-memory and control groups on the other.

The repressed-memory subjects reported more depressive, dissociative, and PTSD symptoms than did continuous-memory and control subjects. Repressed-memory subjects also reported more depressive and PTSD symptoms than did recovered-memory subjects, who, in turn, reported more dissociative and PTSD symptoms than did control subjects. Finally, the repressed and recovered-memory groups scored higher than the control group on the measure of fantasy proneness, and the repressed-memory group scored higher than the continuous-memory group on this measure.

This psychometric study shows that people who believe they harbor repressed memories of sexual abuse are more psychologically distressed than those who say they have never forgotten their abuse.

FORGETTING TRAUMA RELATED MATERIAL

Some clinical theorists believe that sexually molested children learn to disengage their attention during episodes of abuse and allocate it elsewhere (e.g., Terr,

1991). If CSA survivors possess a heightened ability to disengage attention from threatening cues, impairing their subsequent memory for them, then this ability ought to be evident in the laboratory. In our first experiment, we used directed-forgetting methods to test this hypothesis (McNally, Metzger, Lasko, Clancy, & Pitman, 1998). Our subjects were three groups of adult females: CSA survivors with PTSD, psychiatrically healthy CSA survivors, and nonabused control subjects. Each subject was shown, on a computer screen, a series of words that were either trauma related (e.g., *molested*), positive (e.g., *charming*), or neutral (e.g., *mailbox*). Immediately after each word was presented, the subject received instructions telling her either to remember the word or to forget it. After this encoding phase, she was asked to write down all the words she could remember, irrespective of the original instructions that followed each word.

If CSA survivors, especially those with PTSD, are characterized by heightened ability to disengage attention from threat cues, thereby attenuating memory for them, then the CSA survivors with PTSD in this experiment should have recalled few trauma words, especially those they had been told to forget. Contrary to this hypothesis, this group exhibited memory deficits for positive and neutral words they had been told to remember, while demonstrating excellent memory for trauma words, including those they had been told to forget. Healthy CSA survivors and control subjects recalled remember-words more often than forget-words regardless of the type of word. Rather than possessing a superior ability to forget trauma-related material, the most distressed survivors exhibited difficulty banishing this material from awareness.

In our next experiment, we used this directed-forgetting approach to test whether repressed- and recovered-memory subjects, relative to nonabused control subjects, would exhibit the hypothesized superior ability to forget material related to trauma (McNally, Clancy, & Schacter, 2001). If anyone possesses this ability, it ought to be such individuals. However, the memory performance of the repressed- and recovered-memory groups was entirely normal: They recalled remember-words better than forget-words, regardless of whether the words were positive, neutral, or trauma related.

INTRUSION OF TRAUMATIC MATERIAL

The hallmark of PTSD is involuntary, intrusive recollection of traumatic experiences. Clinicians have typically relied on introspective self-reports as confirming the presence of this symptom. The emotional Stroop color-naming task provides a quantitative, nonintrospective measure of intrusive cognition. In this paradigm, subjects are shown words varying in emotional significance, and are asked to name the colors the words are printed in while ignoring the meanings of the words. When the meaning of a word intrusively captures the subject's attention despite the subject's efforts to attend to its color, Stroop interference—delay in color naming—occurs. Trauma survivors with PTSD take longer to name the colors of words related to trauma than do survivors without the disorder, and also take longer to name the colors of trauma words than to name the colors of positive and neutral words or negative words unrelated to their trauma (for a review, see McNally, 1998).

Using the emotional Stroop task, we tested whether subjects reporting either continuous, repressed, or recovered memories of CSA would exhibit interference for trauma words, relative to nonabused control subjects (McNally, Clancy, Schacter, & Pitman, 2000a). If severity of trauma motivates repression of traumatic memories, then subjects who cannot recall their presumably repressed memories may nevertheless exhibit interference for trauma words. We presented a series of trauma-related, positive, and neutral words on a computer screen, and subjects named the colors of the words as quickly as possible. Unlike patients with PTSD, including children with documented abuse histories (Dubner & Motta, 1999), none of the groups exhibited delayed color naming of trauma words relative to neutral or positive ones.

MEMORY DISTORTION AND FALSE MEMORIES IN THE LABORATORY

Some psychotherapists who believe their patients suffer from repressed memories of abuse will ask them to visualize hypothetical abuse scenarios, hoping that this guided-imagery technique will unblock the presumably repressed memories. Unfortunately, this procedure may foster false memories.

Using Garry, Manning, Loftus, and Sherman's (1996) methods, we tested whether subjects who have recovered memories of abuse are more susceptible than control subjects to this kind of memory distortion (Clancy, McNally, & Schacter, 1999). During an early visit to the laboratory, subjects rated their confidence regarding whether they had experienced a series of unusual, but non-traumatic, childhood events (e.g., getting stuck in a tree). During a later visit, they performed a guided-imagery task requiring them to visualize certain of these events, but not others. They later rerated their confidence that they had experienced each of the childhood events. Nonsignificant trends revealed an inflation in confidence for imagined versus non-imagined events. But the magnitude of this memory distortion was more than twice as large in the control group as in the recovered memory group, contrary to the hypothesis that people who have recovered memories of CSA would be especially vulnerable to the memory-distorting effects of guided imagery.

To use a less-transparent paradigm for assessing proneness to develop false memories, we adapted the procedure of Roediger and McDermott (1995). During the encoding phase in this paradigm, subjects hear word lists, each consisting of semantically related items (e.g., *sour, bitter, candy,* sugar) that converge on a nonpresented word—the *false target*—that captures the gist of the list (e.g., *sweet*). On a subsequent recognition test, subjects are given a list of words and asked to indicate which ones they heard during the previous phase. The false memory effect occurs when subjects "remember" having heard the false target. We found that recovered-memory subjects exhibited greater proneness to this false memory effect than did subjects reporting either repressed memories of CSA, continuous memories of CSA, or no abuse (Clancy, Schacter, McNally, & Pitman, 2000). None of the lists was trauma related, and so we cannot say whether the effect would have been more or less pronounced for words directly related to sexual abuse.

In our next experiment, we tested people whose memories were probably false: individuals reporting having been abducted by space aliens (Clancy, McNally, Schacter, Lenzenweger, & Pitman, 2002). In addition to testing these individuals (and control subjects who denied having been abducted by aliens), we tested individuals who believed they had been abducted, but who had no memories of encountering aliens. Like the repressed-memory subjects in our previous studies, they inferred their histories of trauma from various "indicators" (e.g., a passion for reading science fiction, unexplained marks on their bodies). Like subjects with recovered memories of CSA, those reporting recovered memories of alien abduction exhibited pronounced false memory effects in the laboratory. Subjects who only believed they had been abducted likewise exhibited robust false memory effects.

CONCLUSIONS

The aforementioned experiments illustrate one way of approaching the recovered-memory controversy. Cognitive psychology methods cannot ascertain whether the memories reported by our subjects were true or false, but these methods can enable testing of hypotheses about mechanisms that ought to be operative if people can repress and recover memories of trauma or if they can develop false memories of trauma.

Pressing issues remain unresolved. For example, experimentalists assume that directed forgetting and other laboratory methods engage the same cognitive mechanisms that generate the signs and symptoms of emotional disorder in the real world. Some therapists question the validity of this assumption. Surely, they claim, remembering or forgetting the word *incest* in a laboratory task fails to capture the sensory and narrative complexity of autobiographical memories of abuse. On the one hand, the differences between remembering the word *incest* in a directed-forgetting experiment, for example, and recollecting an episode of molestation do, indeed, seem to outweigh the similarities. On the other hand, laboratory studies may underestimate clinical relevance. For example, if someone cannot expel the word *incest* from awareness during a directed-forgetting experiment, then it seems unlikely that this person would be able to banish autobiographical memories of trauma from consciousness. This intuition notwithstanding, an important empirical issue concerns whether these tasks do, indeed, engage the same mechanisms that figure in the cognitive processing of traumatic memories outside the laboratory.

A second issue concerns attempts to distinguish subjects with genuine memories of abuse from those with false memories of abuse. Our group is currently exploring whether this might be done by classifying trauma narratives in terms of how subjects describe their memory-recovery experience. For example, some of the subjects in our current research describe their recovered memories of abuse by saying, "I had forgotten about that. I hadn't thought about the abuse in years until I was reminded of it recently." The narratives of other recovered-memory subjects differ in their experiential quality. These subjects, as they describe it, suddenly realize that they are abuse survivors, sometimes attributing current life difficulties to these long-repressed memories. That is, they do not say that they have remembered forgotten events they once knew, but rather indicate that they have learned (e.g., through hypnosis) the abuse occurred. It will be important to determine whether these two groups of recovered-memory subjects differ cognitively. For example, are subjects exemplifying the second type of recovered-memory experience more prone to develop false memories in the laboratory than are subjects exemplifying the first type of experience?

Recommended Reading

Lindsay, D.S., & Read, J.D. (1994). Psychotherapy and memories of childhood sexual abuse: A cognitive perspective. *Applied Cognitive Psychology, 8*, 281–338.

McNally, R.J. (2001). The cognitive psychology of repressed and recovered memories of childhood sexual abuse: Clinical implications. *Psychiatric Annals, 31*, 509–514.

McNally, R.J. (2003). Progress and controversy in the study of posttraumatic stress disorder. *Annual Review of Psychology, 54*, 229–252.

McNally, R.J. (2003). *Remembering trauma.* Cambridge, MA: Belknap Press/Harvard University Press.

Piper, A., Jr., Pope, H.G., Jr., & Borowiecki, J.J., III. (2000). Custer's last stand: Brown, Scheflin, and Whitfield's latest attempt to salvage "dissociative amnesia." *Journal of Psychiatry and Law, 28*, 149–213.

Acknowledgments—Preparation of this article was supported in part by National Institute of Mental Health Grant MH61268.

Notes

1. Address correspondence to Richard J. McNally, Department of Psychology, Harvard University, 1230 William James Hall, 33 Kirkland St., Cambridge, MA 02138; e-mail: rjm@wjh. harvard.edu.

2. Some authors prefer the term *dissociation* (or *dissociative amnesia*) to *repression*. Although these terms signify different proposed mechanisms, for practical purposes these variations make little difference in the recovered-memory debate. Each term implies a defensive process that blocks access to disturbing memories.

3. However, not thinking about a disturbing experience for a long period of time must not be equated with an inability to remember it. Amnesia denotes an inability to recall information that has been encoded.

References

Brown, D., Scheflin, A.W., & Hammond, D.C. (1998). *Memory, trauma treatment, and the law.* New York: Norton.

Ceci, S.J., & Loftus, E.F. (1994). 'Memory work': A royal road to false memories? *Applied Cognitive Psychology, 8*, 351–364.

Clancy, S.A., McNally, R.J., & Schacter, D.L. (1999). Effects of guided imagery on memory distortion in women reporting recovered memories of childhood sexual abuse. *Journal of Traumatic Stress, 12*, 559–569.

Clancy, S.A., McNally, R.J., Schacter, D.L., Lenzenweger, M.F., & Pitman, R.K. (2002). Memory distortion in people reporting abduction by aliens. *Journal of Abnormal Psychology, 111*, 455–461.

Clancy, S.A., Schacter, D.L., McNally, R.J., & Pitman, R.K. (2000). False recognition in women reporting recovered memories of sexual abuse. *Psychological Science, 11*, 26–31.

Dubner, A.E., & Motta, R.W. (1999). Sexually and physically abused foster care children and posttraumatic stress disorder. *Journal of Consulting and Clinical Psychology, 67*, 367–373.

Garry, M., Manning, C.G., Loftus, E.F., & Sherman, S.J. (1996). Imagination inflation: Imagining a childhood event inflates confidence that it occurred. *Psychonomic Bulletin & Review, 3,* 208–214.

McNally, R.J. (1998). Experimental approaches to cognitive abnormality in posttraumatic stress disorder. *Clinical Psychology Review, 18,* 971–982.

McNally, R.J., Clancy, S.A., & Schacter, D.L. (2001). Directed forgetting of trauma cues in adults reporting repressed or recovered memories of childhood sexual abuse. *Journal of Abnormal Psychology, 110,* 151–156.

McNally, R.J., Clancy, S.A., Schacter, D.L., & Pitman, R.K. (2000a). Cognitive processing of trauma cues in adults reporting repressed, recovered, or continuous memories of childhood sexual abuse. *Journal of Abnormal Psychology, 109,* 355–359.

McNally, R.J., Clancy, S.A., Schacter, D.L., & Pitman, R.K. (2000b). Personality profiles, dissociation, and absorption in women reporting repressed, recovered, or continuous memories of childhood sexual abuse. *Journal of Consulting and Clinical Psychology, 68,* 1033–1037.

McNally, R.J., Metzger, L.J., Lasko, N.B., Clancy, S.A., & Pitman, R.K. (1998). Directed forgetting of trauma cues in adult survivors of childhood sexual abuse with and without posttraumatic stress disorder. *Journal of Abnormal Psychology, 107,* 596–601.

Pope, H.G., Jr., Oliva, P.S., & Hudson, J.I. (1999). Repressed memories: The scientific status. In D.L. Faigman, D.H. Kaye, M.J. Saks, & J. Sanders (Eds.), *Modern scientific evidence: The law and science of expert testimony* (Vol. 1, pocket part, pp. 115–155). St. Paul, MN: West Publishing.

Roediger, H.L., III, & McDermott, K.B. (1995). Creating false memories: Remembering words not presented in lists. *Journal of Experimental Psychology: Learning, Memory, and Cognition, 21,* 803–814.

Terr, L.C. (1991). Childhood traumas: An outline and overview. *American Journal of Psychiatry, 148,* 10–20.

Critical Thinking Questions

1. What are two contrasting views on whether people remember traumatic events? In what context has this controversy erupted?

2. To study repressed and recovered "memories" indirectly, the author tests four groups of people in various memory tasks. What are these groups and how is testing them relevant to the question?

Gender Differences in Depression

Susan Nolen-Hoeksema[1]

Department of Psychology, University of Michigan, Ann Arbor, Michigan

Abstract

From early adolescence through adulthood, women are twice as likely as men to experience depression. Many different explanations for this gender difference in depression have been offered, but none seems to fully explain it. Recent research has focused on gender differences in stress responses, and in exposure to certain stressors. I review this research and describe how gender differences in stress experiences and stress reactivity may interact to create women's greater vulnerability to depression.

Keywords

gender; depression; stress

Across many nations, cultures, and ethnicities, women are about twice as likely as men to develop depression (Nolen-Hoeksema, 1990; Weissman et al., 1996). This is true whether depression is indexed as a diagnosed mental disorder or as subclinical symptoms. Diagnosable depressive disorders are extraordinarily common in women, who have a lifetime prevalence for major depressive disorder of 21.3%, compared with 12.7% in men (Kessler, McGonagle, Swartz, Blazer, & Nelson, 1993).

Most explanations for the gender difference in depression have focused on individual variables, and studies have attempted to show that one variable is better than another in explaining the difference. In three decades of research, however, no one variable has single-handedly accounted for the gender difference in depression. In recent years, investigators have moved toward more integrated models, taking a transactional, developmental approach. Transactional models are appropriate because it is clear that depression impairs social and occupational functioning, and thus can have a major impact on an individual's environment. Developmental models are appropriate because age groups differ markedly in the gender difference in depression. Girls are no more likely than boys to evidence depression in childhood, but by about age 13, girls' rates of depression begin to increase sharply, whereas boys' rates of depression remain low, and may even decrease. By late adolescence, girls are twice as likely as boys to be depressed, and this gender ratio remains more or less the same throughout adulthood. The absolute rates of depression in women and men vary substantially across the life span, however.

In this review, I focus on two themes in recent research. First, because women have less power and status than men in most societies, they experience certain traumas, particularly sexual abuse, more often than men. They also experience more chronic strains, such as poverty, harassment, lack of respect, and constrained choices. Second, even when women and men experience the same stressors, women may be more likely than men to develop depression because of gender differences in biological responses to stressors, self-concepts, or coping styles.

Frequent stressful experiences and reactivity to stress are likely to have reciprocal effects on each other. Stressful experiences can sensitize both biological and psychological systems to future stress, making it more likely that individuals will react with depression. In turn, reactivity to stress is associated with impaired problem solving, and, as a result, with the accumulation or generation of new stressors, which may contribute to more depression.

STRESSFUL LIFE EVENTS

Women's lack of social power makes them more vulnerable than men to specific major traumas, particularly sexual abuse. Traumas may contribute directly to depression, by making women feel they are helpless to control their lives, and may also contribute indirectly, by increasing women's reactivity to stress. Women's social roles also carry a number of chronic strains that might contribute directly or indirectly to depression. Major changes in the frequency of traumatic events and in social roles coincide with the emergence of gender differences in depression in adolescence, and may help to explain this emergence.

Victimization

Women are the victims of sexual assault—defined as being pressured or forced into unwanted sexual contact—at least twice as often as men, and people with a history of sexual assault have increased rates of depression (see Weiss, Longhurst, & Mazure, 1999). Sexual assault during childhood has been more consistently linked with the gender difference in depression than sexual assault that first occurs during adulthood. Estimates of the prevalence of childhood sexual assault range widely. Cutler and I reviewed the most methodologically sound studies including both male and female participants and found rates of childhood sexual assault between 7 and 19% for females and between 3 and 7% for males (Cutler & Nolen-Hoeksema, 1991). We estimated that, in turn, as much as 35% of the gender difference in adult depression could be accounted for by the higher incidence of assault of girls relative to boys. A few studies have examined whether depression might be an antecedent rather than a consequence of sexual assault. Depression does appear to increase risk for sexual assault in women and men, but sexual assault significantly increases risk for first or new onsets of depression.

Childhood sexual assault may increase risk for depression throughout the life span because abuse experiences negatively alter biological and psychological responses to stress (Weiss et al., 1999). Children and adolescents who have been abused, particularly those who have been repeatedly abused over an extended period of time, tend to have poorly regulated biological response to stress. Abuse experiences can also negatively alter children's and adolescents' perspectives on themselves and others, contributing to their vulnerability to depression (Zahn-Waxler, 2000).

Chronic Strains

Women face a number of chronic burdens in everyday life as a result of their social status and roles relative to men, and these strains could contribute to their higher rates of depression (see Nolen-Hoeksema, 1990). Women make less money than men, and are much more likely than men to live in poverty. Women are more likely than men to be sexually harassed on the job. Women often have full-time paid jobs and also do nearly all the child care and domestic work of the home. In addition, women are increasingly "sandwiched" between caring for young children and caring for sick and elderly family members. This role overload is said to contribute to a sense of "burn out" and general distress, including depressive symptoms, in women.

In the context of heterosexual relationships, some women face inequities in the distribution of power over important decisions that must be made, such as the decision to move to a new city, or the decision to buy an expensive item such as a car (Nolen-Hoeksema, Larson, & Grayson, 1999). Even when they voice their opinions, women may feel these opinions are not taken seriously, or that their viewpoints on important issues are not respected and affirmed by their partners. My colleagues and I measured chronic strain by grouping inequities in workload and heterosexual relationships into a single variable, and found that this variable predicted increases in depression over time, and partially accounted for the gender difference in depression (Nolen-Hoeksema et al., 1999). Depression also contributed to increased chronic strain over time, probably because it was associated with reductions in perceptions of control and effective problem solving.

Gender Intensification in Adolescence

Social pressure to conform to gender roles is thought to increase dramatically as children move through puberty. For girls, this may mean a reduction in their opportunities and choices, either real or perceived. According to adolescents' own reports, parents restrict girls' more than boys' behaviors and have lower expectations for girls' than for boys' competencies and achievements. Girls also feel that if they pursue male-stereotyped activities and preferences, such as interests in math and science or in competitive sports, they are rejected by their peers. For many girls, especially white girls, popularity and social acceptance become narrowly oriented around appearance.

This narrowing of acceptable behavior for girls in early adolescence may contribute to the increase in depression in girls at this time, although this popular theory has been the focus of remarkably little empirical research (Nolen-Hoeksema & Girgus, 1994). There is substantial evidence that excessive concern about appearance is negatively associated with wellbeing in girls, but these findings may apply primarily to white girls. In addition, very little research has examined whether appearance concerns and gender roles are risk factors for depression or only correlates.

REACTIVITY TO STRESS

Even when women and men are confronted with similar stressors, women may be more vulnerable than men to developing depression and related anxiety disorders such as posttraumatic stress disorder (Breslau, Davis, Andreski, Peterson, & Schultz, 1997). Women's greater reactivity compared with men's has been attributed to gender differences in biological responses, self-concepts, and coping styles.

Biological Responses to Stress

For many years, the biological explanations for women's greater vulnerability to depression focused on the direct effects of the ovarian hormones (especially estrogen and progesterone) on women's moods. This literature is too large and complicated to review here (but see Nolen-Hoeksema, 1990, 1995). Simply put, despite widespread popular belief that women are more prone to depression than men because of direct negative effects of estrogen or progesterone on mood, there is little consistent scientific evidence to support this belief. Although some women do become depressed during periods of hormonal change, including puberty, the premenstrual period of the menstrual cycle, menopause, and the postpartum period, it is unclear that these depressions are due to the direct effects of hormonal changes on mood, or that depressions during these periods of women's lives account for the gender differences in rates of depression.

More recent biological research has focused not on direct effects of ovarian hormones on moods, but on the moderating effects of hormones, particularly adrenal hormones, on responses to stress. The hypothalamic-pituitary-adrenal (HPA) axis plays a major role in regulating stress responses, in part by regulating levels of a number of hormones, including cortisol, which is released by the adrenal glands in response to chemicals secreted by the brain's hypothalamus and then the pituitary. In turn, cortisol levels can affect other biochemicals known to influence moods. People with major depressive disorder often show elevated cortisol responses to stress, indicating dysregulation of the HPA response.

An intriguing hypothesis is that women are more likely than men to have a dysregulated HPA response to stress, which makes them more likely to develop depression in response to stress (Weiss et al., 1999). Women may be more likely to have a dysregulated HPA response because they are more likely to have suffered traumatic events, which are known to contribute to HPA dysregulation. In addition, ovarian hormones modulate regulation of the HPA axis (Young & Korszun, 1999). Some women may have depressions during periods of rapid change in levels of ovarian hormones (the postpartum period, premenstrual period, menopause, and puberty) because hormonal changes trigger dysregulation of the stress response, making these women more vulnerable to depression, particularly when they are confronted with stress. The causal relationship between HPA axis regulation and the gender difference in depression has not been established but is likely to be a major focus of future research.

Self-Concept

Although the idea that girls have more negative self-concepts than boys is a mainstay of the pop-psychology literature, empirical studies testing this hypothesis have produced mixed results (Nolen-Hoeksema & Girgus, 1994). Several studies have found no gender differences in self-esteem, self-concept, or dysfunctional attitudes. Those studies that do find gender differences, however, tend to show that girls have poorer self-concepts than boys. Again, negative self-concepts could contribute directly to depression, and could interact with stressors to contribute to depression. Negative self-concept has been shown to predict increases in depression in some studies of children (Nolen-Hoeksema & Girgus, 1994).

One consistent difference in males' and females' self-concepts concerns interpersonal orientation, the tendency to be concerned with the status of one's relationships and the opinions others hold of oneself. Even in childhood, girls appear more interpersonally oriented than boys, and this gender difference increases in adolescence (Zahn-Waxler, 2000). When interpersonal orientation leads girls and women to subordinate their own needs and desires completely to those of others, they become excessively dependent on the good graces of others (Cyranowski, Frank, Young, & Shear, 2000). They may then be at high risk for depression when conflicts arise in relationships, or relationships end. Several recent studies have shown that girls and women are more likely than boys and men to develop depression in response to interpersonal stressors. Because depression can also interfere with interpersonal functioning, an important topic for future research is whether the gender difference in depression is a consequence or cause of gender differences in interpersonal strain.

Coping Styles

By adolescence, girls appear to be more likely than boys to respond to stress and distress with rumination—focusing inward on feelings of distress and personal concerns rather than taking action to relieve their distress. This gender difference in rumination then is maintained throughout adulthood. Several longitudinal and experimental studies have shown that people who ruminate in response to stress are at increased risk to develop depressive symptoms and depressive disorders over time (Nolen-Hoeksema et al., 1999). In turn, the gender difference in rumination at least partially accounts for the gender difference in depression. Rumination may not only contribute directly to depression, but may also contribute indirectly by impairing problem solving, and thus preventing women from taking action to overcome the stressors they face.

AN INTEGRATIVE MODEL

Women suffer certain stressors more often than men and may be more vulnerable to develop depression in response to stress because of a number of factors. Both stress experiences and stress reactivity contribute directly to women's greater rates of depression compared with men. Stress experiences and stress reactivity also feed on each other, however. The more stress women suffer, the more hyperresponsive they may be to stress, both biologically and psychologically. This hyperresponsiveness may undermine women's ability to control their environments and overcome their stress, leading to even more stress in the future. In addition, depression contributes directly to more stressful experiences, by interfering with occupational and social functioning, and to vulnerability to stress, by inciting rumination, robbing the individual of any sense of mastery she did have, and possibly sensitizing the biological systems involved in the stress response.

Important advances will be made in explaining the gender difference in depression as we understand better the reciprocal effects of biological, social, and psychological systems on each other. Key developmental transitions, particularly the early adolescent years, are natural laboratories for observing the establishment of these processes, because so much changes during these transitions, and these transitions are times of increased risk.

Additional questions for future research include how culture and ethnicity affect the gender difference in depression. The gender difference is found across most cultures and ethnicities, but its size varies considerably, as do the absolute percentages of depressed women and men. The processes contributing to the gender difference in depression may also vary across cultures and ethnicities. Understanding the gender difference in depression is important for at least two reasons. First, women's high rates of depression exact tremendous costs in quality of life and productivity, for women themselves and their families. Second, understanding the gender difference in depression will help us to understand the causes of depression in general. In this way, gender provides a valuable lens through which to examine basic human processes in psychopathology.

Recommended Reading

Cyranowski, J.M., Frank, E., Young, E., & Shear, K. (2000). (See References)
Nolen-Hoeksema, S. (1990). (See References)
Nolen-Hoeksema, S., & Girgus, J.S. (1994). (See References)
Nolen-Hoeksema, S., Larson, J., & Grayson, C. (1999). (See References)
Young, E., & Korszun, A. (1999). (See References)

Note

1. Address correspondence to Susan Nolen-Hoeksema, Department of Psychology, University of Michigan, 525 E. University Ave., Ann Arbor, MI 48109; e-mail: nolen@umich.edu.

References

Breslau, N., Davis, G.C., Andreski, P., Peterson, E.L., & Schultz, L. (1997). Sex differences in post-traumatic stress disorder. *Archives of General Psychiatry, 54*, 1044–1048.
Cutler, S., & Nolen-Hoeksema, S. (1991). Accounting for sex differences in depression through female victimization: Childhood sexual abuse. *Sex Roles, 24*, 425–438.
Cyranowski, J.M., Frank, E., Young, E., & Shear, K. (2000). Adolescent onset of the gender difference in lifetime rates of major depression. *Archives of General Psychiatry, 57*, 21–27.
Kessler, R.C., McGonagle, K.A., Swartz, M., Blazer, D.G., & Nelson, C.B. (1993). Sex and depression in the National Comorbidity Survey I: Lifetime prevalence, chronicity, and recurrence. *Journal of Affective Disorders, 29*, 85–96.
Nolen-Hoeksema, S. (1990). *Sex differences in depression.* Stanford, CA: Stanford University Press.
Nolen-Hoeksema, S. (1995). Gender differences in coping with depression across the lifespan. *Depression, 3*, 81–90.
Nolen-Hoeksema, S., & Girgus, J.S. (1994). The emergence of gender differences in depression in adolescence. *Psychological Bulletin, 115*, 424–443.
Nolen-Hoeksema, S., Larson, J., & Grayson, C. (1999). Explaining the gender difference in depression. *Journal of Personality and Social Psychology, 77*, 1061–1072.
Weiss, E.L., Longhurst, J.G., & Mazure, C.M. (1999). Childhood sexual abuse as a risk factor for depression in women: Psychosocial and neurobiological correlates. *American Journal of Psychiatry, 156*, 816–828.

Weissman, M.M., Bland, R.C., Canino, G.J., Faravelli, C., Greenwald, S., Hwu, H.-G., Joyce, P.R., Karam, E.G., Lee, C.-K., Lellouch, J., Lepine, J.P., Newman, S.C., Rubio-Stipc, M., Wells, E., Wickramaratne, P.J., Wittchen, H.-U., & Yeh, E.-K. (1996). Cross-national epidemiology of major depression and bipolar disorder. *Journal of the American Medical Association, 276,* 293–299.

Young, E., & Korszun, A. (1999). Women, stress, and depression: Sex differences in hypothalamic-pituitary-adrenal axis regulation. In E. Leibenluft (Ed.), *Gender differences in mood and anxiety disorders: From bench to bedside* (pp. 31–52). Washington, DC: American Psychiatric Press.

Zahn-Waxler, C. (2000). The development of empathy, guilt, and internalization of distress: Implications for gender differences in internalizing and externalizing problems. In R. Davidson (Ed.), *Wisconsin Symposium on Emotion: Vol. 1. Anxiety, depression, and emotion* (pp. 222–265). Oxford, England: Oxford University Press.

Critical Thinking Questions

1. At what age does a gender difference in depression begin to emerge, and why?

2. What are two reasons that women are more vulnerable than men to depression?

3. What evidence is there that women are exposed more often than men to trauma and stressful experiences?

4. What biological and psychological evidence is there that women are more vulnerable than men to becoming depressed in response to stress?

Psychoneuroimmunology

Robert Ader[1]

Center for Psychoneuroimmunology Research, Department of Psychiatry, University of Rochester School of Medicine and Dentistry, Rochester, New York

Abstract

Psychoneuroimmunology is the study of the relationships among behavioral, neural and endocrine, and immune processes. Bidirectional pathways connect the brain and the immune system and provide the foundation for neural, endocrine, and behavioral effects on immunity. Examples of such effects are conditioned and stress-induced changes in immune function and in susceptibility to immunologically mediated diseases. These data indicate that researchers should no longer study the immune system as if it functioned independently of other systems in the body. Changes in immune function are hypothesized to mediate the effects of psychological factors on the development of some diseases, and research strategies for studying the clinical significance of behaviorally induced changes in immune function are suggested.

Keywords

conditioning; immunity; stress

Once upon a time, the immune system was considered an autonomous agency of defense. Research conducted over the past 25 years, however, has provided incontrovertible evidence that the immune system is influenced by the brain and that behavior, the nervous system, and the endocrine system are influenced by the immune system. Psychoneuroimmunology, a new hybrid subspecialty at the intersection of psychology, immunology, and the neurosciences, studies these interactions (Ader, 1981b).

The immune system's defense of the organism against foreign, "nonself" material (antigens) is carried out by white blood cells, primarily T and B lymphocytes, that respond in various ways to the presence of antigens and retain a "memory" of encounters with them. Different immune processes can be distinguished by the particular cells that mount the body's defense. Antibody-mediated immunity refers to the production of antibodies by B cells derived from bone marrow; cell-mediated immunity refers to the actions of a variety of T cells derived from the thymus gland. Typically, immune defenses involve interactions among T and B cells and other specialized white blood cells (e.g., macrophages) and substances (cytokines) secreted by activated T cells. Not all immunity is based on the body's recognition of a previously encountered antigen, however. Natural killer (NK) cells, implicated in protection against the spread of cancer cells and the recognition of and defense against viruses, are a type of lymphocyte capable of reacting against some antigens without having had prior experience with them. A readily accessible overview of immune system functions is provided at the following Web site: rex.nci.nih.gov/PATIENTS/INFO_TEACHER/bookshelf/NIH_immune.

BACKGROUND

Interactions between the brain and the immune system were first observed in the laboratory in the 1920s, when scientists found that immune reactions could be conditioned (Ader, 1981a). In the 1950s, there was a short-lived interest in the immunological effects of lesions and electrical stimulation of the brain. At the same time, research was initiated to study the effects of stressful life experiences on susceptibility to experimentally induced infectious diseases. Interest in this research was rejuvenated when, beginning in the 1970s, several independent lines of research provided verifiable evidence of interactions between the brain and the immune system.

We now know that the brain communicates with the immune system via the nervous system and neuroendocrine secretions from the pituitary. Lymphoid organs are innervated with nerve fibers that release a variety of chemical substances that influence immune responses. Lymphocytes bear receptors for a variety of hormones and are thereby responsive to these neural and endocrine signals. The best known of these signals are reflected in the anti-inflammatory and generally immunosuppressive effects of adrenocortical steroids (hormones released by the adrenal gland).

Lymphocytes activated by antigens are also capable of producing hormones and other chemical substances that the brain can detect. Thus, activation of the immune system is accompanied by changes in the nervous system and endocrine activity. Cytokines released by activated immune cells provide still another pathway through which the immune system communicates with the central nervous system (CNS). Although the precise site (or sites) at which cytokines act within the brain has not been identified, cytokines cause changes in the activity of the brain, in the endocrine system, and in behavior.

At the neural and endocrine levels, then, there is abundant evidence of interactions between the brain and the immune system. At the behavioral level, the most notable evidence of interactions between the CNS and immune system is the effects of conditioning and stressful life experiences on immune function. Another important line of research (not elaborated here) concerns the effects of immune processes on emotional states and other behaviors such as activity, sleep, and appetite.

BEHAVIORAL INFLUENCES ON IMMUNE FUNCTION

Pavlovian conditioning of alterations of immune function provides the most dramatic illustration of a functional relationship between the brain and the immune system. In a prototypical study using a paradigm referred to as taste-aversion conditioning, animals consumed a novel saccharin solution, the conditioned stimulus (CS), shortly before they were injected with an immunosuppressive drug, the unconditioned stimulus (UCS). When all animals were subsequently injected with antigen, conditioned animals that were reexposed to the CS alone showed an aversion to it and an attenuated antibody response compared with conditioned animals that were not reexposed to the CS and nonconditioned animals that were exposed to saccharin (Ader & Cohen, 1975).

Studies have since documented the acquisition and extinction of conditioned nonspecific responses such as NK cell activity and various antibody- and cell-mediated immune responses (Ader & Cohen, 2001). Conditioning is not limited to changes associated with taste-aversion learning, and there is no consistent relationship between conditioned changes in behavior and conditioned changes in immune responses. Also, conditioned immunosuppressive responses cannot be ascribed to stress-induced or conditioned elevations of adrenal hormones. More recently, the conditioned enhancement, as opposed to suppression, of immune responses has been observed using antigens rather than pharmacologic agents as UCSs.

Data on conditioning in humans are limited. The anticipatory (conditioned) nausea that frequently precedes cancer chemotherapy is associated with anticipatory suppression of the capacity of lymphocytes to respond to foreign stimuli, and multiple sclerosis patients being treated with an immunosuppressive drug show a conditioned decrease in total white blood cell count in response to a sham treatment. Healthy subjects show enhanced NK cell activity when reexposed to a distinctive flavor previously paired with injections of adrenaline. In another study, it was shown that repeated injections of saline (which do not elicit an immune response) could attenuate the response to a subsequent injection of antigen. Conversely, however, repeated injections of antigen may not precipitate a reaction to a subsequent injection of saline.

Psychosocial factors, including stressful life experiences, are capable of influencing the onset or severity of a variety of immune disorders and infectious diseases. Such factors are also capable of influencing immune function. The death of a spouse, other "losses" (e.g., divorce), and other chronic stressors (e.g., caregiving for a chronically ill person)—and even less traumatic events such as school examinations—elicit distress and associated declines in immune function, including a depressed response to a viral antigen.

Clinical depression tends to be associated with some immunologically mediated diseases, and this fact has focused attention on the immunological effects of depression. Depressed patients show a decline in several measures of immunity, elevated antibody levels to herpes viruses, and a diminished ability to mount a specific cell-mediated response to varicella zoster virus, which is responsible for shingles (Herbert & Cohen, 1993). In none of these instances, however, has it been demonstrated that changes in immune function specifically cause the health effects of depression or other affective responses to stress.

Evidence documenting stress-induced alterations in immunity comes mostly from animal research. Early life experiences such as disruption of an animal's interactions with its mother, the social environment, exposure to predators, odors emitted by stressed conspecifics, and physical restraint or other noxious conditions induce neuroendocrine changes and modulate both antibody- and cell-mediated immunity. In general, stress suppresses immune function, but the direction, magnitude, and duration of the effects depend on the antigen, the nature of the stressful experience, and the temporal relationship between the stressful experience and the encounter with antigen. The effects of stress also depend on a variety of host factors, such as species, age, and gender.

The neural and endocrine changes presumed to underlie the immunological effects of stressful life experiences have not been delineated. Any number of hormones or the patterning of hormonal responses could influence immunity. Elevated levels of adrenocortical steroids, the most common manifestation of the stress response, are generally immunosuppressive, and there are many stressor-induced changes in immune function that are mediated by adrenal hormones. However, many stress-induced changes in immunity are independent of adrenal activity.

The response to stressful life experiences involves complex interactions among behavior, the nervous system, the endocrine system, and immune response (Rabin, 1999). As a result, the literature on the immunological effects of stress has yielded some equivocal or seemingly inconsistent findings. It should not be surprising, though, that different stressors—commonly thought to elicit a common stress response—can have different effects on the same immune response. Also, one particular stressor can have different effects on different immune responses. Another source of variability may relate to the direct translation of procedures used in immunological research to behavioral studies. For example, a concentration of antigen that is optimal for the study of cellular processes or immunizations against disease may not be optimal for studies designed to investigate the psychobiological interactions that appear to influence immunoregulatory processes. Thus, for the latter purpose, we need studies in which antigen concentrations are at the lower levels to which individuals may be exposed in natural settings. Varying antigen dose would reduce the risk of masking the contribution of those biopsychosocial factors that influence health and illness in the real world.

If we are not always able to predict the direction, magnitude, or duration of the effects of stressful life experiences, it is clear nevertheless that stressful life experiences can influence immune functions; they can increase or decrease susceptibility to immunologically mediated diseases, permit an otherwise inconsequential exposure to some viruses to develop into clinical disease, or contribute to the reactivation of viral infections to which the individual was exposed in the past. Unfortunately, there are relatively few studies that have measured the relationship between susceptibility to a particular disease and those immune responses that are relevant to that disease.

BIOLOGICAL IMPACT OF BEHAVIORALLY INDUCED ALTERATIONS OF IMMUNE FUNCTION

The effects of conditioning and of stressful experiences on immune function have been referred to as "small." The changes in immune function have remained within normal limits, and it is argued, therefore, that the effects of behavior on immune function have no clinical significance. Although there may be reason to question the selective application of the criterion of effect size, a concern for the biological impact of behaviorally induced changes in immune function is quite legitimate. The association between stressful life experiences and susceptibility to disease and the association between stressful life events and changes in immune function do not establish a causal chain linking stress, immune function, and disease. Thus, a central question that remains to be addressed concerns the biological (clinical) significance of behaviorally induced changes in immunity.

There is little, if any, human research in which an altered resistance to disease has been shown to be a direct result of changes in immune function induced by stressful life experiences. Animal studies of experimentally induced or spontaneously occurring diseases, however, are being developed to address this issue. Stressful stimulation delays the production of virus-specific antibodies in mice infected with influenza and suppresses NK cell activity and the development of some T lymphocytes in animals inoculated with herpes simplex virus (HSV). Although physical restraint is ineffective in reactivating HSV infections, disruption of the social hierarchy within a colony of mice increases aggressive behavior, activates the HPA axis,[2] and results in reactivation of HSV in a significant proportion of infected animals. When the spread of a lung tumor is related to NK cell function, several different stressors can decrease NK cell activity and increase lung disease.

Inflammatory processes, an essential component in the healing of wounds, can be modulated by the sympathetic nervous system and HPA axis. It is not surprising, then, that experimentally produced wounds heal more slowly in caretakers of Alzheimer's patients than in control subjects and in students tested before an examination rather than during summer vacation. Mice restrained for several days before and after they are wounded show a diminished inflammatory response, an elevated level of adrenocortical steroids, and a dramatic delay in healing.

Additional work with animals will enable studies of the mechanisms through which stressful life experiences affect health and determine whether disease susceptibility can, as hypothesized, be influenced by behaviorally induced alterations in immune function.

The biological impact of conditioning was examined using mice that spontaneously develop a disease similar to systemic lupus erythematosus in which there is an overreactivity of the immune system. In this case, a suppression of immunological reactivity would be in the biological interests of these animals. CS presentations without active drug were provided on 50% of the pharmacotherapy trials on which animals were scheduled to receive immunosuppressive drug. By capitalizing on conditioned immunosuppressive responses, it was possible to delay the onset of lupus using a cumulative amount of drug that was not, by itself, sufficient to alter progression of the autoimmune disease. Similarly, resistance to experimentally induced arthritis was achieved by exposing animals to a CS previously paired with immunosuppressive treatments. Among mice previously conditioned by pairing a CS with an immunosuppressive drug, reexposure to the CS following transplantation of foreign tissues delayed the immunologically induced rejection of the tissues. There is one clinical case study of a child with lupus who was successfully treated using a conditioning protocol to reduce the total amount of immunosuppressive drug usually prescribed. Although the effects of conditioning have been described as small, conditioned immunological effects can have a profound biological impact on the development of disorders resulting from an overreactive immune system, some cancers, and the survival of tissue transplants.

The issue of clinical significance has occasioned a lot of misplaced breast-beating and apologias in the name of scientific conservatism. Except, perhaps, for extreme and rare circumstances, the notion that a conditioned stimulus or psychosocial conditions could, by themselves, perturb the immune system to an extent that exceeds normal boundaries and leads to overt disease is somewhat simplistic from either an immunological or a behavioral perspective. Given the complexity of the cellular interactions within the immune system and the interactions between the immune and nervous systems, a behaviorally induced deviation from baseline that did not exceed the normal boundaries would seem to be the only response that could reasonably be expected. As far as susceptibility to a particular disease is concerned, however, it would not be unreasonable to theorize that changes capable of altering immune responses relevant to disease could have clinical consequences when interacting with environmental pathogens or when superimposed upon existing pathology or an immune system compromised by host factors such as age or external influences such as immunosuppressive drugs of abuse. The potential importance of psychoneuroimmunological interactions, then, requires that we adopt research strategies that capitalize on individual differences; high-risk populations (e.g., the very young or old, people whose immune systems are compromised, those with genetic predispositions to particular diseases, those with existing disease); systematic variation of the magnitude of the antigen; and the measurement of responses that are demonstrably relevant to particular diseases.

CONCLUSIONS

Psychoneuroimmunology is an interdisciplinary field that has developed and now prospers by ignoring the arbitrary and illusory boundaries of the biomedical sciences. As a result of the integrative research conducted in recent years, a paradigm shift is occurring; researchers can no longer study immunoregulatory processes as the independent activity of an autonomous immune system. These processes take place within a neuroendocrine environment that is sensitive to the individual's perception of and adaptive responses to events occurring in the external world.

Research predicated on the hypothesis that there is a single, integrated defense system could change the way we define and study certain diseases. Theoretically, it is likely that behavioral, neural, and endocrine interventions are relevant in the treatment of some immune system-related diseases (e.g., arthritis) and that immune system activity may contribute to the understanding and treatment of behavioral, neural, and endocrine disorders (e.g., depression or even schizophrenia).

We cannot yet detail the mechanisms mediating the effects of conditioning or stressful life experiences on immune responses, and further studies are needed. However, we do know that neural and endocrine changes are associated with changes in behavior and that there is a network of connections between the brain and the immune system. The existence of these bidirectional pathways reinforces the hypothesis that changes in the immune system constitute an important mechanism through which psychosocial factors could influence health and disease.

Recommended Reading

Ader, R. (1995). Historical perspectives on psychoneuroimmunology. In H. Friedman, T.W. Klein, & A.L. Friedman (Eds.), *Psychoneuroimmunology, stress and infection* (pp. 1–21). Boca Raton, FL: CRC Press.

Ader, R., Madden, K., Felten, D., Bellinger, D.L., & Schiffer, R.B. (1996). Psychoneu-roimmunology: Interactions between the brain and the immune system. In B.S. Fogel, R.B. Schiffer, & S.M. Rao (Eds.), *Neuropsychiatry* (pp. 193– 221). Philadel-phia: Williams & Wilkins.

Glaser, R., & Kiecolt-Glaser, J.K. (Eds.). (1994). *Handbook of human stress and immu-nity.* New York: Academic Press.

Schedlowski, M., & Tewes, U. (Eds.). (1999). *Psychoneuroimmunology: An interdiscipli-nary introduction.* New York. Kluwer Academic/ Plenum.

Acknowledgments—Preparation of this article was supported by a Research Scientist Award (K05 MH06318) from the National Institute of Mental Health.

Notes

1. Address correspondence to Robert Ader, Department of Psychiatry, University of Rochester Medical Center, Rochester, NY 14642.

2. This term comes from the structures involved in the secretion of so-called stress hormones. During a stress response, the brain's hypothalamus (H) releases a chemical that affects the pituitary gland (P). The pituitary then secretes a hormone that causes the adrenal glands (A) to release corticosteriods (cortisol in humans, corticosterone in rodents) into the bloodstream.

References

Ader, R. (1981a). A historical account of conditioned immunobiologic responses. In R. Ader (Ed.), *Psychoneuroimmunology* (pp. 321–354). New York: Academic Press.

Ader, R. (Ed.). (1981b). *Psychoneuroimmunology.* New York: Academic Press.

Ader, R., & Cohen, N. (1975). Behaviorally conditioned immunosuppression. *Psychosomatic Medi-cine, 37,* 333–340.

Ader, R., & Cohen, N. (2001). Conditioning and immunity. In R. Ader, D.L. Felten, & N. Cohen (Eds.), *Psychoneuroimmunology* (3rd ed., Vol. 2, pp. 3–34). New York: Academic Press.

Herbert, T.B., & Cohen, S. (1993). Depression and immunity: A meta-analytic review. *Psychologi-cal Bulletin, 113,* 472–486.

Rabin, B.S. (1999). *Stress, immune function, and health.* New York: Wiley-Liss.

Critical Thinking Questions

1. What is psychoneuroimmunology and how does it overturn an assumption long held within the medical community?

2. Briefly describe a study in which immune system activity was classically con-ditioned.

3. What evidence is there for the correlation between stress, immune system activity, and illness? What is the clinical significance of these associations?

Social Support, Physiological Processes, and Health

Bert N. Uchino,[1] Darcy Uno, and Julianne Holt-Lunstad

Department of Psychology and Health Psychology Program, University of Utah, Salt Lake City, Utah

Abstract

Social relationships serve important functions in people's everyday lives. Epidemiological research indicates that supportive relationships may also significantly protect individuals from various causes of mortality, including cardiovascular disease. An important issue is how social support influences such long-term health outcomes. In this article, we review evidence indicating that social support may influence mortality via changes in the cardiovascular, endocrine, and immune systems. These data suggest that it may be worthwhile to incorporate social-support interventions in the prevention and treatment of physical health problems.

Keywords

social support; cardiovascular function; immune function; health

Relationships with others form a ubiquitous part of people's everyday lives. In the classic analysis by Durkheim (1897/1951), suicide rates were higher among individuals who were less socially integrated than among those who had many social ties. The loneliness and despair that characterize a lack of social connections may be responsible for such unfortunate outcomes. Less obvious, however, is the possibility that individuals with poor relationships may also be more at risk for physical illnesses, such as cardiovascular disease, cancer, or infectious diseases. Is there evidence that such an association exists? If so, how is it that social relationships influence such disease processes?

The answer to the first question is relatively well documented. A review of large prospective studies comparing groups with differing degrees of social integration found that less socially integrated individuals had higher mortality rates from all causes, including cardiovascular mortality (House, Landis, & Umberson, 1988). In fact, the evidence linking social relationships to mortality was comparable to the evidence linking standard risk factors such as smoking and physical activity to mortality. What is less known is the answer to the second question, that is, how social relationships influence such long-term health outcomes. In this article, we review the evidence linking positive aspects of social relationships (i.e., social support) to physiological processes. These associations are helping us to understand how relationships may influence physical health outcomes such as cardiovascular disease.

HOW MIGHT RELATIONSHIPS INFLUENCE PHYSICAL HEALTH OUTCOMES?

Relationships serve important functions. For instance, most people can recall times when others made a difference in their lives by giving good advice (informational support); helping them feel better about themselves (emotional support); directly providing aid, such as money (tangible support); or just "hanging out" with them (belonging support). The actual or perceived availability of these helpful behaviors by others is broadly defined as social support.

Figure 1 depicts a simplified model of how social support might influence physical health outcomes (see Cohen, 1988, for a detailed model). The major pathway depicted in the top portion of the figure suggests that social support may be beneficial because it protects individuals from the deleterious behavioral and physiological consequences of stress. In theory, social support may decrease how stressful an individual finds an event to be. For instance, a person who has supportive ties may experience less job stress because close others provide helpful information or reaffirm other aspects of that person's life (e.g., familial role). The decreased stress appraisal may in turn influence psychological processes such as negative mood states, feelings of personal control, and self-esteem. These psychological processes are thought to influence the cardiovascular, endocrine, and immune systems, with implications for relevant disease outcomes (Kiecolt-Glaser & Glaser, 1995). For instance, over the long term, alterations in cardiovascular function (e.g., heart rate) may influence cardiovascular disorders such as high blood pressure, whereas a decrease in immune function may have implications for cancer and infectious diseases. However, even when individuals are not encountering stressful life events, it is possible that social support may affect physiological processes by directly influencing the psychological processes of self-esteem, feelings of personal control, and negative mood states. For instance, simply being in the company of close friends may elevate one's mood.

An additional pathway by which social support may be linked to physical health outcomes is through the modification of health behaviors, such as smoking, exercise, and diet (Umberson, 1987), that in turn influence relevant physiological processes (e.g., exercise decreases blood pressure). There are several ways in which social support may influence health behaviors. First, higher levels of stress have been linked to poorer health behaviors (Kiecolt-Glaser & Glaser, 1995). Social support may facilitate better health behaviors because it decreases the amount of stress that an individual experiences. Second, social support may

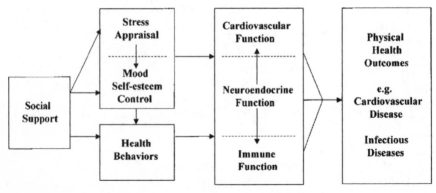

Fig. 1. Simplified model of how social support may influence physical health outcomes. Dotted lines within the boxes separate distinct pathways within the various systems.

directly motivate individuals to engage in more healthy practices. For instance, close family members may place pressures on an individual to exercise or stop smoking. It is also possible that having adequate social support communicates the fact that one is loved, and this may lead to better health behaviors by increasing the motivation to care for oneself.

IS SOCIAL SUPPORT RELATED TO PHYSIOLOGICAL PROCESSES?

The model shown in Figure 1 indicates that social support ultimately influences health outcomes via relevant biological pathways. In a recent review, we examined the evidence linking social support to physiological processes that might influence disease risk (Uchino, Cacioppo, & Kiecolt-Glaser, 1996). In particular, we focused on the cardiovascular, endocrine, and immune systems as potential pathways by which social support might influence health.

Most of the studies we examined investigated the association between social support and cardiovascular function. There were more than 50 such studies, and most focused on blood pressure. Blood pressure is an important variable because over time, elevations in blood pressure can be a risk factor for cardiovascular diseases. In fact, there is increasing concern about the potential risk of elevated blood pressure even below the range that is normally considered hypertensive (MacMahon et al., 1990). Overall, we found in our review of studies that individuals with high levels of social support had lower blood pressure than individuals with lower levels of social support.

It is noteworthy that there was also evidence linking social support to better blood pressure regulation in hypertensive patients. Most of these studies were interventions that utilized the patient's spouse as a source of support to help the patient control his or her blood pressure. These intervention studies provide direct evidence for the health relevance of social support and suggest that recruiting familial sources of support may be a particularly effective (and cost-effective) intervention strategy.

Finally, recent studies suggest that social support can reduce the magnitude of cardiovascular changes during stressful circumstances, a finding consistent with the model in Figure 1. For instance, Gerin, Pieper, Levy, and Pickering (1992) compared physiological reactivity of subjects who participated in a debate task when a supportive person (an individual who agreed with the participant) was or was not present. The presence of the supportive person was associated with lower blood pressure and heart rate changes during the task. The ability of social support to reduce cardiovascular changes during stress is important because it has been hypothesized that heightened physiological reactivity to stress may increase the risk for the development of cardiovascular disorders (Manuck, 1994). The finding of lowered cardiovascular reactivity when social support is available may also have implications for individuals who have existing cardiovascular disease, as heightened cardiovascular changes when psychological stressors are experienced can induce a temporary imbalance of oxygen supply and demand in the heart (Krantz et al., 1991). This imbalance can lead to potentially dangerous cardiac conditions in such at-risk populations.

In our review of the literature, we also examined 19 studies that tested the possibility that social support may be related to aspects of immune function. An association between social support and immunity would be important because the immune system is responsible for the body's defense against infectious and malignant (cancerous) diseases. In general, the available studies suggest that social support is related to a stronger immune response. For instance, natural killer cells are an important line of defense against virus-infected and some tumor cells. In our review, several studies found that individuals with high levels of social support had stronger natural killer cell responses (i.e., ability to kill susceptible tumor cells) than individuals with lower levels of social support.

The associations between social support and immune function are consistent with the results of a recent study by Cohen, Doyle, Skoner, Rabin, and Gwaltney (1997), who examined whether social support predicted susceptibility to the common-cold virus. In this study, consenting participants were directly exposed to common-cold viruses (i.e., via nasal drops) and quarantined for 5 days. Individuals who had more diverse social networks (i.e., relationships in a variety of domains, such as work, home, and church) were less likely to develop clinical colds than individuals with less diverse networks. The authors discussed the possibility that having a diverse social network may be particularly beneficial as support may be obtained from a variety of sources.

It is important to note that many of the studies that found an association between social support and immune function were conducted with older adult populations. Aging is associated with decreased immunity, and infectious diseases are a major source of morbidity and mortality in older adults. Thus, the lowered immune function in older individuals with low social support may be a finding with particular health relevance.

One important way in which social support may influence the immune system is via the release of endocrine hormones. Environmental factors such as stress can lead to the release of hormones (i.e., catecholamines and cortisol) that in turn influence the immune system. This is possible because many cells of the immune system have hormone receptors that can augment or inhibit the cells' function when activated by specific endocrine hormones. Unfortunately, there is not much research examining if social support is related to endocrine function. However, preliminary evidence from the MacArthur studies of successful aging suggests that higher levels of social support may be linked to lower levels of catecholamines and cortisol in men (Seeman, Berkman, Blazer, & Rowe, 1994). These data are consistent with the research linking social support to alterations in the cardiovascular system because endocrine hormones such as catecholamines directly influence cardiovascular function.

CONCLUSIONS

The available evidence is consistent with the possibility that social support may influence physical health outcomes via relevant physiological processes. What is less clear in this literature is exactly how these changes occur. As shown in Figure 1, there are a number of potential pathways, including changes in negative mood states or health behaviors, but direct evidence bearing on the validity of these pathways is presently lacking. A few studies we reviewed did look for a health-behavior pathway, along with psychological pathways involving depression and perceived stress. Although preliminary, these studies found that these factors could not account for the association between social support and physiological function. Unfortunately, many of these studies utilized cross-sectional designs that provide a less sensitive test of the pathways linking social support to physiological function than do longitudinal designs. This point underscores the importance of conducting longitudinal studies that examine how these dynamic processes involving social support, physiology, and actual health outcomes unfold over time.

An additional issue that warrants further attention is the conditions under which social relationships are most beneficial. Not all close relationships are uniformly positive (consider, e.g., marital conflict). This is an important consideration because negative interactions can interfere with effective social support. In addition, having many supportive friends and family could be beneficial, but it may also entail obligations to be a support provider. At least in some circumstances, being a support provider can be a significant source of stress (e.g., the demands of caregiving activities). These issues highlight the importance of investigating how the relative balance of positive and negative aspects of close relationships influences physiological function and subsequent health outcomes.

Overall, however, we believe that the research reviewed has significant implications for present notions of health and well-being. Would it be possible to utilize this research in combination with standard medical approaches in preventing and treating physical disease? Several interventions suggest the promise of such an approach. Spiegel, Bloom, Kraemer, and Gottheil (1989) found that breast cancer patients randomly assigned to a support group lived almost twice as long as patients simply given routine oncological care. There is also indirect evidence of beneficial effects from general psychosocial interventions that include social-support intervention (Linden, Stossel, & Maurice, 1996). For instance, Fawzy et al. (1993) evaluated the effects of a 6-week structured group intervention that provided education, problem-solving skills, stress management, and social support to cancer patients. A 6-year follow-up revealed that only 9% of individuals in the structured group intervention had died, compared with 29% of individuals in the no-intervention condition. These studies suggest the potential promise of future interventions aimed at utilizing social relationships to promote positive health outcomes.

Recommended Reading

Berkman, L.F. (1995). The role of social relations in health promotion. *Psychosomatic Medicine, 57,* 245–254.
House, J.S., Landis, K.R., & Umberson, D. (1988). (See References)
Kiecolt-Glaser, J.K., & Glaser, R. (1995). (See References)
Uchino, B.N., Cacioppo, J.T., & Kiecolt-Glaser, K.G. (1996). (See References)
Wills, T.A. (1997). Social support and health. In A. Baum, S. Newman, J. Weinman, R. West, & C. McManus (Eds.), *Cambridge handbook of psychology, health, and medicine* (pp. 168–171). New York: Cambridge University Press.

Acknowledgments—Preparation of this article was generously supported by National Institute on Aging Grant No. 1 R55 AG13968 and National Institute of Mental Health Grant No. 1 RO1MH58690. We would like to thank our supportive spouses, Heather M. Llenos, Sean Fujioka, and Nathan Lunstad, for their helpful suggestions on this manuscript. This article is dedicated to the memory of Sean K. Okumura.

Note

1. Address correspondence to Bert N. Uchino, Department of Psychology, 390 S. 1530 E., Room 502, University of Utah, Salt Lake City, UT 84112; e-mail: uchino@psych.utah.edu.

References

Cohen, S. (1988). Psychosocial models of the role of social support in the etiology of physical disease. *Health Psychology, 7*, 269–297.

Cohen, S., Doyle, W.J., Skoner, D.P., Rabin, B.S., & Gwaltney, J.M. (1997). Social ties and susceptibility to the common cold. *Journal of the American Medical Association, 277*, 1940–1944.

Durkheim, E. (1951). *Suicide* (J.A. Spaulding & G. Simpson, Trans.). New York: Free Press. (Original work published 1897)

Fawzy, F.I., Fawzy, N.W., Hyun, C.S., Gutherie, D., Fahey, J.L., & Morton, D. (1993). Malignant melanoma: Effects of an early structured psychiatric intervention, coping, and affective state on recurrence and survival six years later. *Archives of General Psychiatry, 50*, 681–689.

Gerin, W., Pieper, C., Levy, R., & Pickering, T.G. (1992). Social support in social interactions: A moderator of cardiovascular reactivity. *Psychosomatic Medicine, 54*, 324–336.

House, J.S., Landis, K.R., & Umberson, D. (1988). Social relationships and health. *Science, 241*, 540–545.

Kiecolt-Glaser, J.K., & Glaser, R. (1995). Psychoneuroimmunology and health consequences: Data and shared mechanisms. *Psychosomatic Medicine, 57*, 269–274.

Krantz, D.S., Helmers, K.F., Bairey, N., Nebel, L.E., Hedges, S.M., & Rozanski, A. (1991). Cardiovascular reactivity and mental stress-induced myocardial ischemia in patients with coronary artery disease. *Psychosomatic Medicine, 53*, 1–12.

Linden, W., Stossel, C., & Maurice, J. (1996). Psychosocial interventions for patients with coronary artery disease. *Archives of Internal Medicine, 156*, 745–752.

MacMahon, S., Peto, R., Cutler, J., Collins, R., Sorlie, P., Neaton, J., Abbott, R., Godwin, J., Dyer, A., & Stamler, J. (1990). Blood pressure, stroke, and coronary heart disease. Part 1, prolonged differences in blood pressure: Prospective observational studies corrected for the regression dilution bias. *Lancet, 335*, 765–774.

Manuck, S.B. (1994). Cardiovascular reactivity in cardiovascular disease: "Once more unto the breach." *International Journal of Behavioral Medicine, 1*, 4–31.

Seeman, T.E., Berkman, L.F., Blazer, D., & Rowe, J.W. (1994). Social ties and support and neuroendocrine function: The MacArthur studies of successful aging. *Annals of Behavioral Medicine, 16*, 95–106.

Spiegel, D., Bloom, J.R., Kraemer, H.C., & Gottheil, E. (1989). Effect of psychosocial treatment on survival of patients with metastatic breast cancer. *Lancet, 334*, 888–891.

Uchino, B.N., Cacioppo, J.T., & Kiecolt-Glaser, K.G. (1996). The relationships between social support and physiological processes: A review with emphasis on underlying mechanisms and implications for health. *Psychological Bulletin, 119*, 488–531.

Umberson, D. (1987). Family status and health behaviors: Social control as a dimension of social integration. *Journal of Health and Social Behavior, 28*, 306–319.

Critical Thinking Questions

1. Briefly describe the model presented in Figure 1. According to this model, how does social support relate to physical health?

2. What empirical evidence is there for the protective benefits of social support?

3. The authors suggest that social relationships may be more beneficial to health under some circumstances than others. What do they have in mind?